D0018625

A Feast in the Mirror
Stories by Contemporary Iranian Women

A Three Continents Book

A Feast in the Mirror
Stories by Contemporary Iranian Women

translated and edited by

Mohammad Mehdi Khorrami

Shouleh Vatanabadi

LYNNE
RIENNER
PUBLISHERS

BOULDER
LONDON

Published in the United States of America in 2000 by
Lynne Rienner Publishers, Inc.
1800 30th Street, Boulder, Colorado 80301
www.rienner.com

and in the United Kingdom by
Lynne Rienner Publishers, Inc.
3 Henrietta Street, Covent Garden, London WC2E 8LU

© 2000 by Lynne Rienner Publishers. All rights reserved

The stories in this book are works of fiction. Names, characters, places, and incidents are the products of the authors' imagination or are used fictitiously, and any resemblance to actual persons (living or dead), events, or locales is entirely coincidental.

Library of Congress Cataloging-in-Publication Data
A feast in the mirror : stories by contemporary Iranian women / edited and
translated by Mohammad Mehdi Khorrami, Shouleh Vatanabadi.
    p. cm.
    Includes bibliographical references.
    ISBN 0-89410-864-6 (hc : alk. paper)
    ISBN 0-89410-889-1 (pbk. : alk. paper)
    1. Short stories, Persian—Translations into English. 2. Persian fiction—Women
authors—Translations into English. 3. Persian fiction—20th century—Translations
into English.
PK6449.E7 F43 2000
891'.55301089287'09045—dc21

                                                                    00-032855

British Cataloguing in Publication Data
A Cataloguing in Publication record for this book
is available from the British Library.

Printed and bound in the United States of America

    The paper used in this publication meets the requirements
∞   of the American National Standard for Permanence of
    Paper for Printed Library Materials Z39.48-1984.

 5 4 3 2 1

Library
University of Texas
at San Antonio

Contents

❧ Acknowledgments

We would like to thank all the writers who submitted their stories for consideration in this anthology. We are especially grateful to Farkhondeh Hajizadeh and Mihan Bahrami, as well as to the Roshangaran Publishing Company and to the magazines *Adineh, Zanan,* and *Hoquq-e Zan,* for their help in the process of researching and collecting material in Iran. We thank Shirin Neshat for her invaluable suggestions and, above all, for her friendship. We are also grateful to members of our families, Zari, Yousef, Yasha, and, especially, Sharareh, who helped us enormously throughout this project. We are particularly grateful to our copyeditor, Patia E. M. Yasin, who went through every single page of the Persian and English texts with diligence and precision and enriched this collection with her insightful suggestions.

—*the Editors*

❧ Introduction

In the past few decades many social/intellectual movements, especially those under the heading of "postmodernism" in the United States and in many European societies, have resulted in the rejection of universalism and of any grand narrative that claimed to have the ability to explain the whole world. This development, especially in academic environments, underlined the importance of giving a voice to marginalized entities. It was in light of such approaches that many academic projects took it upon themselves to examine multiple aspects of Middle Eastern and Islamic societies. This in itself was a step in the right direction. However, it often seems that many efforts to describe and include marginalized voices have been overshadowed by persistent clichés, to the point where the main goals have been undermined. Certainly, Middle Eastern women have been among the most notable victims. In actuality, having been passed through the filter of stereotypes, many attempts, which had intended to include Middle Eastern women's voices and images, practically silenced the voices and eclipsed the images. Such studies in different forms and fields, including art and literature, resulted in artificially formed, homogenized representations.

It was within this framework that the thought of capturing multiple voices and images of Iranian women through a collection of short stories written by Iranian women was formulated.[1] To avoid falling into the trap of the recurrent stereotypes, we decided not to base our

1

process of collection on the works of only famous authors, or to emphasize specific topics or subject matter, or to limit ourselves to particular narrative tendencies. Other than the methodological flaws involved, such approaches would have ignored the emergence of a large number of women writers over the past two decades in Iran.[2] In order to represent this richness as fully as possible, we published a call for submission of work in some of the major Iranian literary and women's journals. This approach provided the writers the opportunity to send us works that had not necessarily gone through the labyrinth of limiting laws and regulations of publication in Iran. Within a very short period of time we received hundreds of manuscripts from famous, well-established, unknown, professional, and amateur writers. Our guiding principle in the selection process was to demonstrate the literary richness of the works created by Iranian women since 1980. Our contributors depict the diversity of social position and experiences of Iranian women in their stories.

Many of the stories in this collection provide a direct glimpse into women's lives and take the reader through the labyrinths of Iranian society today, while others function on a purely literary plain. There are stories that are closely intertwined with local elements, and there are those narrated in an unspecified time and place. There are stories with particular focus on particular issues in Iranian society, and there are narratives that take on more universal themes. This variety clearly defies any kind of generalization, and in fact, when reading the stories in this collection, one realizes how naive it would be to consider such a literary production as a "national allegory."

The difficulty of generalization in this case is more pronounced because through the long literary tradition in Iran, innumerable narrative experiments have developed into a variety of writing styles, such that any kind of categorization would result in reductionism. To minimize such reductionism, the organization of this book is based on the description of a path whose major characteristics are not as rigid as the constructing elements of categories. Our organization, therefore, reflects both different narrative styles and the elements of social experiences.

Borrowing from Forugh Farrokhzad (1934–1967), the most famous Iranian woman poet of the twentieth century, and from one of her poems, "Another Birth," we have selected the headings for the three sections. The title of the book is also inspired by a line from the same poem containing two symbols that were dear to her.

Farrokhzad, undoubtedly more than any other contemporary literary figure, insisted on woman and her representation in society. The significance of her observations can be seen in many of the stories in this collection, and indeed it seems that all of them can interact with these symbols. Each one of these stories projects a picture of a unique artistic individuality, and when they are brought together, it seems that stories and authors, by looking at others' images in the mirror, create a gathering and begin a conversation with each other. How pleasant it is to gaze at, listen to, and take part in this *Feast in the Mirror*.

> Travel of the body in the line of time
> Impregnating the barren line of time
> A body aware of the image
> Returning from a feast in a mirror

TRAVEL IN THE LINE OF TIME

The first part of the book consists of stories that do not necessarily correspond directly to a specific component of the existing reality. This dissociation is sometimes accomplished through the use of the same reality as a pretext to go beyond it. One of the best examples of this style is Shiva Arastuyi's "I Came to Have Tea with My Daughter." The story begins with the narrator's passing reference to her separation from her husband. Then different times, spaces, ideas, stories, and legends immediately rush into the text and the narrator's mind. Every moment of the text seems to represent an independent sphere wherein the narrator tries to find and redefine herself, in relation and in reaction to her husband and to men in general, to the legendary lovers, to the symbols of resistance, to her family, to her mother, and to different historical moments and social events. On the surface all these challenges seem to be creating tangled threads that blur and make vague the atmosphere of the story. But in fact every one of these threads has its own progression. More important, the outcome of all these narrative threads invites the reader to share the narrator's literary consciousness, and from this vantage point it is possible to observe not only the narrator but also other aspects of the story's universe.

Fereshteh Sari's "The Absent Soldier" opens with a familiar subject, war. Those familiar with the Middle East's recent history no doubt remember the bloody eight-year-long war between Iran and Iraq. The narrator, a young woman whose husband's name is on the list of Missing in Action, gives us, however, an unfamiliar look at the war. The whole story is the recounting of the narrator's dropping by at her mother's house with her small daughter, and her memories of her childhood alley. In this once busy and lively alley now only women and children are left, along with a single middle-aged man who has spent all these years inside the house with his mother to avoid the war. Through such interaction between the past and the present, the text suggests different or, rather, unusual meanings for such concepts as love, motherhood, childhood, even war itself. It depicts women as directly active in the war; despite the fact that the war has ended, it nonetheless is still going on for them.

Aside from the technical preferences of the authors and their choice of literary styles and devices, limiting social elements—that is, censorship—have occasionally influenced a piece. In such instances, the author's conscious approach could take a work beyond a mere metaphor or allegory and provide multiple possibilities for interpretations and readings. Farkhondeh Hajizadeh's "Contrary to Democracy" is one such example. Drawing on the stereotypical perceptions of woman's roles as mother, wife, and sister, it seems that, explicitly trying to explore these categories, Hajizadeh feels compelled to use ambivalent language and atmosphere in order to respect certain regulations. But by defining a particular logic for the story, she succeeds in turning those limitations into linguistic and conceptual freedom. Within this form, "strange" events, such as making a man so small that the narrator can hide him in her bosom and take him to the women's public baths, do not defy the "logic" of the story. Indeed, and ironically enough, conceptual and linguistic freedoms resulting from the author's challenging of limitations not only sneer at limiting taboos but increase the number of possible readings of the story.

A similar linguistic and conceptual freedom can be seen in the story "Cling to Life with Your Whole Body." In this case, Khatereh Hejazi, by emphasizing the sheer power of imagination, seems to be completely dissociating her story from reality. Characters with strange names such as the Eons and Hertakh, and events such as interplanetary travel and the conquering of Earth by Martians, are clearly reminiscent of the science fiction genre. This atmosphere, however, serves the formation of the transparent symbolism of the story. In fact, the first reading that comes to mind is to consider this story as an allegory or at least a metaphor of present-day Iranian society. But there are details, such as the torture practices of the invaders and the narrator's love for a man or for a flower, which problematize the simple allegorical reading of the text and demand a closer reading.

The same problematization is seen in other stories in this section as well. Chista Yasrebi's "Love and Scream," which begins with the description of an "old maid," suddenly moves on to themes such as love, fear, sexual desire, and repression through an extremely strange relationship between a woman and a crow. "Smile!"—a very short story by Farideh Kheradmand—describes the efforts of a young woman to take a picture smiling despite the force of her sorrow, and does not relieve the reader's perplexity.

The nonlinear, at times fragmented text of "The End, a City," by Mihan Bahrami, combines colloquial speech and poetic elegance. Her narrative style fits well with the polyphonic portrayal of the prostitutes who are the major characters in her story.

The two stories "Disappearance of an Ordinary Woman" and "The Fin Garden of Kashan" go even further in their formalist experimentation. In "Disappearance of an Ordinary Woman," Tahereh Alavi tells the story of a woman who, one day, while flipping through the newspaper, sees a picture of herself in the "Missing Persons" column. Once she calls the phone number printed under the picture, she begins a parallel life whose major components are searching for oneself and giving in to the desires and pleasures of living. Like many other stories in this collection, there is no closure. At the end there are only questions: Which one of these two parallel universes is more real, the "real" one or the "imaginary" one? Is the protagonist trying to gain control over her environment by favoring imagination?

The theme of control is one of the major concepts in Sofia Mahmudi's "The Fin Garden of Kashan." She begins the story from the point of view of a child who sees the life of her father, a truck driver, as a constant confrontation between him and road signs. Through her narrative style, these signs are intermingled with punctuation marks, which later on define the protagonist's decision to become an editor—in control of signs!

It can be said about these stories that because of their narrative complexities and their defiance of being simple reflections of the immediate nonliterary environment, they do not lend themselves to a single interpretation; but also, they often reject any traditional reading altogether. One of the few common denominators of these stories is their authors' confrontational purpose, which is demonstrated not only through rejection of social institutions such as taboos, norms, and traditions, but also through the rejection of narrative conventions.

IMPREGNATING THE BARREN LINE OF TIME

Probably the only common characteristic of the stories in the second part of the book is that each one of them focuses on one or more societal subjects, and the resulting textual reality, formed on the basis of these topics, is closer to the conventional reality. From the point of view of the subject matter, the story "Sour Cherry Pits," by Zoya Pirzad, is particularly unique, as it is the story of an Armenian community in northern Iran. The narrator is Edmond, a young Armenian boy whose best friend is Tahereh, the daughter of the Moslem school janitor. The story creates a small environment whose elements are so precisely tied together that there is no need for the author to underline any specific subject or dilemma. She leaves that to the simple function of the leitmotifs. Edmond and Tahereh are classmates and best friends. They come from different ethnic and religious backgrounds. It is then "natural" that the grown-ups would raise the idea of "incompatibility," and it is "natural" for the children to want to preserve their fluid identity through their simple everyday life and games and to resist the one-dimensional, rigid identities that most of the grown-ups argue in favor of.

Aside from "Sour Cherry Pits," Banafsheh Hejazi's "The Pool" is the only story in this collection whose protagonist is male. There are many tacit references to social issues such as poverty and class differences, but the heart of the story is the description of the man's sexual desires. Obviously the practice of censorship would not allow the author to be explicit, even if she wanted to be, about various aspects of this issue, but that does not seem to have caused any difficulty. Relying on a number of sexually charged symbols, Banafsheh Hejazi presents one of the boldest pieces in this collection.

The two stories "One Woman, One Love" and "That Day" deal in a more transparent manner with social issues and, more specifically, with women's issues. According to the author Farkhondeh Aqai, "One Woman, One Love" is based on a true story. At the center of it stands one of the most important Islamic laws concerning divorce. According to this law, a thrice-divorced woman should marry another man and consummate the marriage before being able to remarry her first husband. That law, which would normally represent a legal mistreatment of women, in this case provides an opportunity for her to experience love and pleasure for the first time in her life. She does pay dearly for it, but the ideas of resisting and negotiating such situations shine throughout the story. The idea of resistance is similarly referred to in Nushin Ahmadi Khorasani's "That Day." This time International Women's Day coincides with election day. Ignoring the latter, a group of women are determined to observe their day despite regulatory measures against such gatherings.

"Butterflies," by Mansureh Sharifzadeh, takes place in another space. Through the dialogues cover many subjects between two main characters in the story, the reader is exposed to the politics of the workplace, the dynamics of power, jealousies, and gossip. Furthermore, the work at times gives a sense of continuities as well as change before and after the Revolution, as demonstrated through bleached hair covered by the mandatory veil.

Contrary to the idea of challenging the status quo, the protagonist in "Lida's Cat, the Bakery, and the Streetlight Pole," by Azardokht Bahrami, insists on enduring in a relationship with her husband. She remains in a state of denial about her husband's betrayal throughout the story, securing her position as a married woman in the face of the appearance of a second wife.

AWARE OF THE IMAGE

Sometimes realities are so powerful that the most effective expression of them seems to lie in the use of a rather descriptive and quasi-documentary style. In these stories, therefore, traditional narrative

components such as the characterization and construction of space
and time become of extreme importance. These relatively simple
structures lend themselves more easily to traditional interpretations
and readings and thus provide a more direct relationship between the
reader, the text, and literalized experience.

Nahid Tabatabai's "The Lark" is a realistic depiction of social
differences in which the emphasis is placed on how women are used
within them. The narrative voice in the story, a servant girl, is forced
to marry the Master's son so that he can be exempt from military
service. Above all, her flesh and blood, her daughter, is taken away
from her to be raised by the second—"real"—wife of the Master's
son.

In Fariba Vafi's "My Mother, Behind the Glass," a young daughter constructs the narrative to understand the predicament of her
mother. A woman from the lower depths of society is forced to be the
second wife of an older man. Her prisonlike existence ends with the
husband's death. She enjoys a brief period of independence only to
end up in a real prison.

The powerful realities of events and experiences such as war and
abortion provide constructing dynamics in three of the other stories
in this section. "Downfall" by Nosrat Masuri describes the emotional
and physical traumas of a woman having an abortion. "War Letters"
by Marjan Riahi is the story of a mother who demands an explanation from the authorities, local and international, about the fate of her
son, who has been taken to the front during the Iran-Iraq war.
Farzaneh Karampur's "Refugee" deals with another aspect of war:
the harsh experience undergone by a woman during forced reloca-
tion.

Parvin Fadavi's "The Bitter Life of Shirin," the last story in this
section, depicts a woman who has to deal with a host of issues. She
has to deal with a traditional authoritarian father while also trying to
determine her own future. She has to deal with an insensitive husband, despite her ideals of romantic love. And when she decides to
break away, she has to think about divorce and custody laws. These
issues are debated by women coming from diverse social and genera-
tional backgrounds, in a unique space: the women's section of the
public bus.

The conversation that is taking place on the segregated bus can
be considered an analogy for the whole collection of stories in this

book. A reader not familiar with Iran has the opportunity to view a variety of life experiences through stories whose narrative diversity is presented in the three sections of this collection.

NOTES

1. Since the 1979 Revolution two other collections of short stories by Iranian women writers have been published: *Stories by Iranian Women Since the Revolution* (1991), edited by Paknazar and Sullivan; and *In a Voice of their Own* (1996), edited by Lewis and Yazdanfar.

2. In fact the quality and quantity of the writings by Iranian women in the past two decades have become so startling that once again the topic of women's writing with all its complexities has dominated many literary circles in Iran.

Part One

Travel in the Line of Time

I Came to Have Tea with My Daughter

❧ Shiva Arastuyi

I t was two years after our divorce. I was sitting in Mehran's office. Mehran was behind his desk and I was in the armchair. I was telling him, "You used to say I was not a good actress." The screenplay was on the desk. Until then, I had never seen Mehran in his office. At home he used to lie on the sofa, in his pajamas, his hand under his head, and he would fall asleep before I got to him from the kitchen. Between you and me, he was right. I was not a good actress. If I had been, I would have let him sleep till morning. If I had been a good actress, I wouldn't have gone and caressed his bald head so much, and put a pillow under his head, and covered him with a blanket, and kept the food warm in the oven so that whenever he woke up and said "I am hungry" I could set it in front of him and he could scarf it down and go on writing his useless screenplays. He said, "You are successful only if you play Leyli."[1] I said, "Cut! For which Majnun?[2] Aren't you the optimistic one!"

He looked at me as though he had found a Majnun. I am sure he had told him that he is successful only in the role of Majnun. I wanted to tell him that if he thought I would be a good Leyli, then why did he leave me? One doesn't walk out on Leyli. It seemed that from the look on my face he understood what I wanted to say. As always. He began, "There are many men who would enjoy Leyli-like women. I am not like that." I said, "There are many women who would enjoy philosopher-like men. I am not like that." He said, "One must have 'existence' to be a philosopher." I said, "How about being Majnun?" He said, "You have only a Leyli-like existence." Does that mean he has the existence of a philosopher and a Majnun, not to mention a whole bunch of other existences?

Ha! He thinks he majored in women. When I read his screenplay I realized he was dead wrong! It was the first time I read his screenplay. I haven't seen any of his movies. He never took me on the set. He never took me anywhere. On the last day, I stood in front of him and said that I wanted to be a film actress. He gave me one of his malicious laughs and said, "You want to register your face in history?"

I thought it would be nice to turn his own response against him. But I was not a philosopher. Somehow, in a clumsy way, I exaggerated the idea of his being an artist and I asked him why he didn't understand that I like being an actress, and I went on about the love of acting and such like nonsense. . . . While I was talking he was looking at me as the wise man would look at the fool; finally he said that what he understood perfectly well was that I was not a good actress. He went on to say that I lacked the skill to present myself as beautiful. He said that I didn't know how to walk properly, let alone try to act and imitate others. He said one word over and over; I don't remember it. He kept saying that I don't have "that." He said something else I do remember well: "Your beauty has no feeling." He said nobody would come and invest a lot of time and money just to show me. It was at this point that I blew up and said, "Shut up!"

Very coldly and calmly he said, "That does it! Do you understand, my dear? A woman who tells me 'shut up' should get the hell out of here. Go to hell and do whatever you want." He then left the house.

I didn't know which hell I was supposed to go to. I got scared. Wherever I looked, I didn't see any trace of Mehran. As if Mehran had never lived in this house. Nothing of him, not even a pair of pants or a sock could be found in the house. When I went into the kitchen, I saw it had become like me. I was amazed at the cleanness and order of the kitchen, as if it was the first time I was seeing it like that. In the dish rack there was one plate, one spoon, one glass, one cup, and one saucer, all washed. Of all the chairs around the kitchen table, there was only one that had been pulled back. There was a small pot on the stove and one small basket of fruit on the table. The small copper kettle was boiling on the burner. The stove was so clean that it shone. The flowered tiles of the kitchen seemed to be consoling me. How often I had scrubbed them! The checked curtain of the kitchen was standing kindly behind the window, as if it was on guard. The refrigerator seemed to be smiling at me and was offering me cold water. Even the red basket of onions and potatoes had become redder. Oh, you don't know, Parvaneh, that day I wanted to pick up a watering can and water the rug's flowers. Believe me, only a few minutes after he left I became a poet. It was not time for my period, but I started bleeding, and I was thrilled that my uterus walls had not been prepared to accept Mehran's seed and had collapsed. I am writing all this for you so that you know, and if one day you come back to Iran you won't question me. I did not even know that I could, one day, sit and write to you. Wait, Parvaneh. I want to fix myself a cup of tea of a pretty color and then write you the rest.

Since that day, I didn't see Mehran until the divorce court and then in his office. Listen. I had never enjoyed "The Blue Danube" so much! Mehran used to say, "You have no ear for music." He was right. He had cut off my ear, the same night that the film crew was invited to dinner at our place. They had decided to start a new movie. Mehran had never invited anyone home. They used to go to the restaurant, and at the end of the evening Mehran used to come home and sit at the dining table and write his nonsense. He was right. I was not a good actress. I thought I had married a philosopher who preferred writing to being next to me. I thought I was a low, illiterate woman who liked to be looked at by her husband. A philosopher's wife fixes tea for her man all day long, and watches her husband when he writes, and empties his ashtray. He was right, I was not a good actress. Because I really had shut up, and I didn't want anything from God. In fact, if I were a good actress, that night after the guests left, I would have pretended that nothing had happened. It is true that Mehran had touched the shoulder of that actress and kept flirting with her, but so what. An actress, especially if she is the wife of a philosopher, understands pretty well that there is a friendly and humane relationship between a director and his crew. Stupid people cannot understand that. I should not have thought that Mehran put his hand around the shoulders of that actress on purpose, or that that poor woman took Mehran's hand and laughed on purpose. But they didn't have to think that I poured all that salt in the salad on purpose. I had taken the saltshaker in my hand and was shaking it on the salad in order to not to hear anything. But it was useless. The actress spoke to me only when she liked the taste of a dish. From Mehran's description, I understood that she had a very difficult role to play in Mehran's movie. But it was obvious from her demeanor that she could not. The producer told Mehran, "I bet your own wife could act much better as a blind woman." Mehran was screaming, "Do you think that when two jackass producers said something nice about you . . ." and then one side of my face felt empty and my voice saying "Ow!" filled my head.

I fell on the table, on the ashtrays full of cigarette butts. The ash and dust went into my nose. I wasn't a good actress. If I were, I wouldn't take his hand and I wouldn't kiss it and I wouldn't place it on my slapped face to soothe the pain. If I were a good actress, I would have pounded all the ashtrays on his head, and I would have forced all those cigarette butts into his nose so that he would have choked. Parvaneh, if Mehran knew that I would not stay at your place, he would not have brought his guests to the house. If I were a good actress I would have pretended that nothing had happened so that Mehran would not take his guests to other places. In fact if I were a good actress I would have continued to be a pimp for Mehran and his guests.

You know, Parvaneh, I really had no ear for music. My eardrum was torn that very night. The doctor said, "It will heal by itself; just be careful that water does not get into it." How can water get into a slapped ear? Oh, I have never enjoyed "The Blue Danube" so much. Listen! It seems that the eardrum has healed. I am going to pour myself the tea.

This tea tastes like your teas, Parvaneh. Those teas that you said should attain their full flavor in order to become real tea. Do you remember? First, you would put the empty teapot on the samovar to warm it up and then you would mix tea with ground cardamom and orange blossom, and only you knew the proportions. And then you would pour it all in the heated pot. Then, you would pour a little bit of the boiling water of the samovar on the mixture just to make it wet, and then you would put it on the samovar to allow the tea to draw. You would put the beautiful teapot cover that you had sewed yourself on the pot so that the tea really drew. Oh, how much I loved the sound of pouring tea in those fat and clean teacups—how wonderful was your looking at the tea that you had brought into life! When you were drinking the tea, sip by sip, you were looking somewhere, as if you were talking to someone. When the smell of your tea filled the house, I used to sit next to you and then I kept talking. I was beginning to chatter and you would shake the one leg that was hurting you and you would move around on the floor. You took care to pour me another tea as soon as my teacup was empty. You used to say that anything sweet is wonderful with tea, except sugar cubes. You liked to have your tea with raisins, dried figs, dates, dried sweet berries, and such. There were always things like that on the tea table, on the small steel or crystal plates. When you were drinking you liked everything around you to be clean and orderly and you didn't want to rush. And when we were having tea you liked me to tell you about everything. You said you liked me to talk to you while you were looking at my white fingers and long nails as I was drumming them on the table. Because while talking I used to drum on the teacups, waiting for you to say something.

It was during my senior year at the university when, one afternoon while we were having tea, I told you about Mehran; that I had fallen in love with him and that I would like to become his wife. That day, when I had broken off what I was saying and was drumming on the teacups so you would say something, you didn't say anything. You were drinking your tea sip by sip and were looking somewhere else. I was in such a mood that the rug, on which we were sitting while we were talking about Mehran, seemed to me like king Salamon's flying carpet. The same rug that you used to sit on on one corner, busy sewing, while I was studying on another corner.

I was saying that Thursday is my friend's birthday. I was showing you a style in *Burda* magazine and I asked you to make that for me. When I would bring the cloth you would ask which day of the week it was. Then you would say the cloth should be cut on Wednesday, sewn on Thursday, and worn on Friday. I would laugh. I would say that from now on I would tell kids to be born on Fridays. You would say that on Fridays one should not touch the cloth with scissors, because it would be jinxed and would never be finished. By the way, Parvaneh, why did you let us get married on a Friday? When did you sew my wedding dress? Oh, how much you cried! Mehran, to whom I had talked a lot about you, was whispering in my ear, "It seems that Parvaneh doesn't want her cocoon to fly away!" I was looking at you. Stupid me! I didn't want to spoil the makeup on my eyes, so I was holding back my tears. And Mehran was whispering under my ear, "'It seemed that my mother had cried that night / The night I became the bride of acacia branches. . . .'"[3]

Later on when you would see me you used to say, "He stole your heart with these airs and graces." And I used to say, "Dear Parvaneh, I wasn't stupid!" And you used to say, "Well, I think you were! Forugh Farrokhzad herself was not as stupid as you are!" And I was in the kitchen mixing those poems with the rice, or placing them on the skewer and barbecuing them on the stove. "All my existence, all my existence" I used to say, and I didn't know whose existence Mehran was turning into a movie. Dear Parvaneh, I had never read any of his screenplays but I was sure at that time he wanted to make a movie of my existence. Get up, Parvaneh. Pour me a cup of tea so that I can tell you about it. I wish Shahab were here to sing for us: "Pari, listen to me / Get up and start the samovar!"[4]

Don't tell Shahab anything now. I am going to write him myself. No, I'll call him. No, I don't have money. Tell him to spend a few of those dollars he is taking from Imperialists on me and call me. I am sure he would ask about Mehran first. In the past two years I have always said, "We are fine."

"Are you good with each other?"

"Oh, wonderful!"

"Well, thank God!"

You know, Parvaneh, I was not that wrong. Since Mehran and I have separated, we are good. I know you are so wonderful that you don't ask why I haven't told you or Shahab anything in the past two years. Well, you weren't here, so the sound of your pouring tea in the cup would spread through the house and I would start talking. That day, in Mehran's office, as soon as he said that he wanted me to act in his new movie, that sound, the sound of your pouring tea, turned in my head. The smell of cardamom and the orange flower essence filled my nose and I had the craving to talk to you. The concierge brought two glasses of boiling water and two tea bags with four sugar cubes. The same kind that you don't like. I didn't touch them. I remembered how much you cried on the wedding night. You were not saying anything. You were smiling at everyone. But tears were coming down. The women were saying, "These are tears of joy!" "Mother and daughter are friends. Since the father died they have clung to each other."

I was sitting next to Mehran. Above my head, the women were whispering. They thought that since I put on a lot of makeup and my head was so wrapped up in lace, I couldn't hear them.

"She managed to raise her daughter with a sewing machine. She is right."

The sound of the sewing machine was mixed with the master of ceremonies' voice. I wish when I went to pick flowers I had never come back. The master of ceremonies said, "Dear bride, may I be your representative?"[5]

I was next to Mehran, quite present. But the women said, "The bride has gone to pick flowers." When I picked the flowers, the master of ceremonies repeated, "Dear and respected . . . bride . . ." I was going to give him the "yes," but the women said, "The bride is making a bouquet out of the flowers." When I made the bouquet, Mehran's hand was in mine. I pressed it and said "Yes." And the petals of the flowers out of which I had made a bouquet fell on my head. I felt a constriction in my heart. Women who go to weddings do not know anything other than tearing the petals off the flowers. You know, Parvaneh, whatever is happening to me is because of these women who go to weddings. They are all alike. They are all actors. I don't know who invites them. Wherever there is a wedding they appear. They come to take the flowers that the poor bride has picked and has made into a bouquet, and rip the petals off, and strike her head with them. I wish I had never gone to pick flowers. Damn all gladiolas! Have you ever seen such a rough, ugly flower, Parvaneh? It reminds me of the wedding women. They all wear similar clothes, put on similar makeup; they dance like each other and they eat like each other. Ah, damn all gladiolas. . . . Maybe if I had picked carnations or narcissi or even red flowers . . .

Mehran used to say, "A red flower is a red flower, is a red flower."

And I would say, "Don't cheat, Mr. Gertrude Stein! We have been at the university, too." But he would keep his composure. He would whistle and walk, and, very cool, would say, "Therefore the red flower is not a red flower. No, red flower . . ."

Dear Parvaneh, at the university, girls were taught to marry philosophers.

The first day of shooting, the red flower was not really a red flower. The setting, arranged by Mehran, was the wedding room. He had told me to put on the wedding dress and sit next to Ali. The wedding women, the gladiolas, everything was ready so that the red flower wouldn't be a red flower. Although Ali and I had practiced so that it would be. Mehran wanted the red flower to be a red flower at any price. Mehran had told me to not look up and to softly say the "Yes." I said it, and this time the petals of the flowers I had not picked and of which I had not made a bouquet were ripped apart and thrown on my head. The frightening sound of the wedding women was heard. I couldn't hear the sound of your sewing machine, Parvaneh. But I had read the screenplay attentively and I had practiced so that I wouldn't be afraid. Mehran had told me to smile at Ali when he takes the bridal veil off my face, "one of those smiles that he loved and that would drive people crazy." He had also taught Ali how to look at me. Ali was the best actor. Everybody knew him. He had practiced a lot in order to, as he put it, revivify his passionate tone. He looked at me and whispered, "So much beauty, for my eyes only!"

Ali was talking and Mehran came toward me with the camera. But I was the worst actress. I smiled for no reason and told Ali, "Thank you!"

Mehran yelled, "Cut! We don't have any 'Thank you,' Ms. Shahrzad!"

They all laughed. I wish Shahab had been there to joke with me a bit!

They started shooting again. Ali said, "So much beauty, for my eyes only!" And this time he said it much better than the previous time. Exactly as Mehran had taught him, too. In fact, he was like Mehran. So I forgot that this is just acting. I stared at Ali/Mehran. I didn't act. I said, "For you."

Mehran yelled, "We don't have 'For you,' Ms. Shahrzad."

Ali said, "Why not? It is very beautiful. It is much better than 'I have always been waiting for this moment.'"

Mehran said, "OK. We'll continue." And said, "Action!"

Ali picked up the ring box and put the ring on my finger. The sound of the wedding women was heard. It was my turn, Parvaneh. I had practiced so that I wouldn't panic. I turned the ring around on Ali's finger and moved it down. I kept my fingers on the ring. I didn't act. I looked at him. My face was burning. Mehran said, "That was excellent. Cut!"

They cleaned the table. People went about their business. We took off the rings and put them away. Mehran's voice was heard everywhere. Ali went to the locker room. No one was paying attention to me. I was sitting on the stool with the wedding dress, looking at the badly proportioned body of Mehran, who was moving about.

The next set was the living room. I went to the locker room and changed and came back. Ali was looking at the armchair that I was supposed to sit on and was practicing his lines.

I said, "Are you talking to the armchair?"

He said, "In a way."

And then, he turned toward me and said, "You were excellent, wonderful!"

The commotion of the wedding women was heard.

Shooting began. Mehran said, "Action!"

I was sitting in the same armchair and knitting and Ali was facing me, watching me and playing with a ball of wool. I said, "Don't you ever get tired of watching me so much?"

"Do you get tired?"

"I get embarrassed."

"My poor pullover!"

"I would never lose your hands."

"I should have become a painter, Leyli."

"Eh, why? You can draw on a computer and that is just fine!"

"A computer cannot draw such a beautiful Leyli."

Hell! I don't know what that lunatic Mehran thinks I . . .

Leyli said, "You have mistaken me for someone else, I swear."

Ali said, "Leyli, in the eyes of Majnun . . ."

I said, "Get up, Majnun. We didn't sleep last night either. If I don't sleep I'll get old."

We got up and Mehran said, "Cut!"

Mehran yelled, "Camera! Action!"

I began walking. I was rubbing my hands together and was walking in the salon. I looked at the clock. It was one hour after midnight. I went in front of the mirror. I returned. I waited for a moment and looked at the desk, which was in the corner of the set. Ali was supposed to be a poet as well, with an unfinished poem on the desk. I looked at the clothes stand; a piece of casual men's wear was hanging from it. I also looked at the men's slippers that were placed next to the armchair. I went and opened the door of the bathroom and looked at the toothbrushes. From now on I had to walk faster. I went and pulled open the drawer in front of the mirror and stared at the things inside. Then I closed it fast and went into the bedroom. I stared at the double bed. I went and opened the closet and began looking at the men's clothes, one by one. Leyli was supposed to take out the men's shoes from their boxes, one by one, and look at them.

Leyli was supposed to stare like crazy at a man's briefcase that was at the corner of the setting. I gazed at the bag and murmured, "His socks . . ." Leyli was looking for her Majnun's socks and I was thinking about Mehran's socks. He used to throw them away as soon as there was a hole in them. I used to tell him, "Let me sew them." He used to say, "Torn socks are not to be mended; they should be thrown away."

Leyli murmured, "No! His name!"

I would ask Mehran, "Why do people call me by your last name but you are not called by mine?" Mehran would say, "Is this all you have learned from women's rights?"

Dear Parvaneh, do you remember what you said? You said, "No, you have also learned all the poems of Forugh Farrokhzad."

All my existence . . . all my existence . . .

Leyli was supposed to jump toward the table next to the bed, open one of the drawers and pull out Majnun's birth certificate, flip through two or three pages, and then stop on a page and stare at it for a while and then say, "Then he? Where is he?"

I was not acting, Parvaneh. I was Leyli. I was supposed to calm down once the bell rang. And then I had to say, "He has forgotten to take the key again."

Slowly I put the birth certificate back in the drawer. I went and pressed the buzzer key and came back to the bedroom. Behind the door, I sat on the edge of the bed. Ali was supposed to come in and look at me, puzzled. I felt Ali's look on the back of my neck. I said, slowly, "Which one of your poems did you read tonight?"

"The Leyli one."

"Why didn't you take her herself?"

One does not take Leyli all over the place. She is too precious. But the poem . . .

"Majnun! You were here."

Ali said, "I am your Majnun!"[6] And laughed and came to embrace Leyli. But I stood up, quick and nervous. I went and took out a set of men's clothes from the closet. Ali was supposed, once more, to look at me, puzzled. I took the clothes and went toward the clock. I stood there and looked at the clock; it was past 2 A.M. Then I went and picked up the pair of men's shoes as well. Ali was supposed to follow me in a daze. I also picked up a pair of men's socks, and then stood in front of the clock with the clothes and shoes and socks and stretched my hands toward it. I told the clock, "Here he is! He came!"

Ali wanted to say something. I didn't let him. I went and took a set of men's underwear. I took it in my other hand and went toward the clock. I showed it to the clock and said, "He is always here! He!"

Ali yelled, "Have you gone mad?"

He had come next to me. I turned and pushed him away. I went and placed the clothes on top of each other, on the bed, in a very orderly fashion: first the underwear, then the shirt and jacket and pants; part of the pants fell off the bed and onto the floor. I placed the socks under the pants legs and put the shoes on the top of the socks. Ali was supposed to feel pity and come near me and take my hands and raise me up from the floor. But as soon as he came close I made a few moves and pushed him away. I looked at the clothes and said, "Take me in your arms! I feel sleepy!"

Ali sat next to me, on his knees, pounded his fists on his thighs and yelled, "Enough of this stupid game!"

Louder than Ali, I yelled at the clothes, "Take me in your arms! I feel sleepy!"

Ali picked the clothes up, one by one, and threw them all around the room. I was running after them and picking them up and taking them in my arms, saying, "Take me in your arms! I feel sleepy!"

Dumbfounded, Ali said, "Leyli, I am here, myself. Why are you doing that?"

I turned to Ali. I saw him for the first time. Can you believe that, Parvaneh? Until that moment I hadn't seen him. I didn't know what he looked like. I looked, and realized he was not Mehran. His voice, his tone, the way he said "I am here, myself"! His black eyebrows and pupils the color of coal and the line that this coal was stretching toward my eyes. I looked at him for a while. Mehran was following the scene worriedly, waiting for me to continue. But I was standing motionless, stupid, and could not continue. Mehran yelled, "Cut!"

I came to myself. Mehran said, "Ms. Shahrzad, the real fight begins just now. Have you forgotten the lines?"

I turned toward Mehran. I didn't know him. He was looking at me like an enemy. I didn't know him. I realized that two years ago— no, that very moment—I separated from him. You know, Parvaneh? I saw that I didn't even hate him anymore. I didn't know him at all. I kept looking at him and said, "No, I haven't forgotten anything."

He said, "Good! Look at Ali, the way you are looking at me, and say the rest of the lines!"

I turned toward Ali and said, "I can't."

The teas you used to make were always delicious, even when they were cold. Sometimes I would talk so much that the tea would get cold. You would say, "It got cold!" Now I always drink hot tea. I don't speak; my tea doesn't get cold. The second tea has gotten cold, next to the pages that I am writing for you. You call from America and say, "Don't stay alone, my dear. Anytime you feel depressed, leave Mehran alone for a while and come and stay with us for a while. Just tell Shahab; he will arrange it."

Dear Parvaneh, don't send me vitamins and aspirins anymore. I am going to send you orange blossom. I heard you pouring tea, from here. My eardrum has healed. My ears are filled with cardamom and orange blossom.

Mehran said, "Shahrzad, don't you listen? Hello? Are you still on the phone?"

I said, "This phone that you placed in my hand, Mehran . . ."

"Well, ma'am, you too are becoming a philosopher!"

"Let me do my own act in the movie."

"As soon as a couple of people say something nice about you . . ."

"I am not going to act at all."

"Go to hell!" And he hit the receiver on the cradle. My eardrum cracked.

Ali said, "Hello! Ms. Shahrzad?"

My eardrum was the leaf of orange blossom.

I said, "I can't."

"I am going to come over there, right now."

And the receiver slept over the leaf of orange blossom.

I had not finished my prayers yet. Ali had said, "Pray for ungrateful creatures like us!"

While I was folding my prayer chador,[7] I said, "Thank you, God."

I went to the closet. Do you remember, dear Parvaneh, what a beautiful pink dress you had made for me? I still have it. It brings me luck. The day that Mehran left me I had it on. Mehran said, "What is this? Pink does not become you at all!" And also that day that your hands were destroyed . . .

I put on the pink dress and went to the kitchen. My soup was boiling in my small pot. Mehran used to say, "Stay alone! Keep eating soup and salad and read Forugh's poems until you dry up!"

All my existenc . . . all my existence . . .

Parvaneh, he forgot to mention Yoga. Shahab used to pass his fingers through my hair and say "Yogi, are you all right?" Mehran always said, "Again you have put your head where your feet are supposed to be! Instead of these things, think a little bit!" But when I saw one scene of the movie he had brought home, I went to the bathroom and threw up. Mehran said, "Damn! What was I thinking! You know nothing about aesthetics. You don't understand at all." I understood, and I threw up. I was still throwing up until the following day when I came to see you. I couldn't look at myself in the store windows. When I got there, I ran to the bathroom and threw up. You said, "You got pregnant so soon?"

I yelled from the bathroom, "Get the tea ready, dear Parvaneh!"

"The Blue Danube" feels so good, like the sound of pouring tea into your teacups with handles. The eardrum does not tear, dear Parvaneh. You poured the tea and I talked and I cried like a baby. I asked, "Why did Mehran show me that movie? Because he wanted to say, 'We men are alike'?"

You poured yourself tea and softly said, "No. He showed you the movie because he wanted to say you are all alike!"

I ran to the bathroom and began to throw up.

Mehran was pouring himself a glass of vodka and was saying, "Stupid, I wanted to open your eyes and ears to new things. You don't know anything about the bed culture!"

You said, "Is this called culture to bring a bunch of strange jackasses home and show them to your wife?"

Parvaneh, I think I finally understood something about aesthetics. It means the loud moaning of a bunch of beautiful male and female dogs. The beats of our hearts apparently did not have any beauty.

It took me a while to realize that men are all naked and do not like that beautiful pink dress on me. I put on that loose, long pink dress and went to the mirror. I took my pink lipstick from the drawer and put it on, twice. I drew a fading line around my lips and then they became the same innocent lips that you liked.

You said, "Whoever said your lips are voluptuous is a stupid ass! Such innocent lips!"

Mehran used to say, "Mothers like to think that their daughters are innocent. She is jealous of me."

I was saying in a poetic tone, "I wish the rough face of my father would rub my cheek again. . . ."

Shahab would say, "Give me a kiss; that would make me feel better!"

I lowered the heat under the soup. In a small bowl, I diced tomato, cucumber, and lettuce. I poured some lemon juice and olive oil on it. I laid two plates for soup and one small basket of bread on the kitchen table, and waited. If Shahab were there he would say, "*The Feather,* by Matisson!" But Ali had already eaten his dinner. I could hear Mehran's voice through the wall: "Leave these things for the cat—let's go and have chelokabab!"[8]

"Since when have cats become vegetarians?"

"Since the time that the amount of leftover meats in the garbage has increased; the cats' cholesterol has gone up!"

I went to the kitchen to pour Ali a cup of tea. I heard Mehran's voice through the wall: "Wow, finally, you left the mirror alone!"

Tray in hand, I was in the living room. I said, "Be quiet!"

Ali said, "Who are you talking to?"

"Ah! To the cat!"

"Do you keep a cat at home?"

"Inside the home! Ah, no. Outside."

Ali stared at me. I forced myself to laugh. Ali began murmuring polite nothings; that I shouldn't be going to the trouble and . . .

I said, "You are less polite in the movies."

"In the movie I am Leyli's lover."

"Leyli's poet."

"By the way, Ms. Shahrzad, what do you think of this Majnun?"

"Which Majnun?"

I don't know what I said that made Ali very serious and polite. He said, "The only Majnun here is in the movie."

He had come just to say that. The rest was useless. But I decided to remain the Leyli of Mehran's movie in order to ruin the movie. When Ali left I had the craving to play with paper. It had been many years since I had played with paper and scissors and glue. Even when Mehran left I didn't play with paper. Do you remember, Parvaneh? Anytime you saw me playing with paper you used to say, "What is the matter again? Come on! I am going to make you a delicious tea, we'll talk a bit, you will feel better. Big girls don't play with paper!"

By the way, Parvaneh, what did you do with those gazelles I had made of paper? You used to show them to me and say that when Dad died everybody was crying and I was in a corner making paper gazelles and glued them to the walls and doors. You said that until the fortieth day after Dad's death, I had made four hundred gazelles and all the walls in the house were covered by them and nobody was allowed to touch them.

When Ali left I brought paper, glue, and scissors and got busy. I cut a piece like a man's shirt. Under it, with black marker, I drew a belt. I cut two black legs and glued them to a pair of big black shoes. A big head profile, with a rectangle on one side, like a mouth. I drew an eye right on top of the rectangle, as if he was looking outside. I blackened above the rectangle, for his hair; I didn't make a nose. I glued the rectangle with a tiny piece of paper to the shirt. I glued on the hands and legs as well. I took his hand and went on to the kitchen. The soup had burned and was stuck to the bottom of the pot. The dummy liked the salad very much. A cat's miaow came to the house. Neither the dummy nor I paid any attention. I heard Mehran's voice: "Cut!"

Mehran yelled, "Camera! Action!"

Quietly, I went and stood behind Ali and looked at the piece of paper which was in front of him on the table. Ali started and turned toward me. He pulled the chair out and threw it on the floor. Embarrassed, he said, "What are you looking at?"

"Nothing! I just wanted to say that dinner is ready."

"Leave me alone . . . go! Leave me alone. . . ."

I went to the kitchen and picked up a piece of cloth. I knelt down and began scrubbing the kitchen floor. I kept scrubbing until Mehran said, "That is good! Cut!"

Mehran said, "Action!"

I took the thermometer out of Ali's mouth. I looked at it and put it in the glass filled with alcohol. Ali had a fever and was lying down under a blanket. I pulled the blanket over him. I went to the kitchen. I picked up the cloth. I kneeled down. I gazed at the wall and scrubbed the floor. Exactly like the girl in that Kurosawa movie. Dumbfounded, confused. I kept scrubbing. Until Mehran said, "Cut!"

Mehran said, "Action!"

I moved the strip of my handbag on my shoulder and went into the shoe store. Leyli and Ali were not married yet. I came out with a shoe box. The gypsy woman was coming toward me from the end of

the street. There were many shoe stores and women in the street. I
was passing by the women's shoe stores and was getting closer to the
gypsy woman. Women were going to different stores. I was supposed
to be happy. I was. Between the two of us, Parvaneh, I was happy
because I had a beautiful pair of pink sandals in my shoe box. When
the gypsy woman came closer, she stared at me. Before I could do
anything she pulled me toward the street. She said, "Wait! I see
something in your eyes."

My eyes were supposed to shine. They did. I said, "What do you
see?"

"My God! My God, you have beautiful eyes and eyebrows! You
need a whole bag of salt to protect you from the evil eye!"

I laughed from the bottom of my heart.

She said, "Come and sit here. Let me talk to you. Thank God you
are nice! I have to tell you. If I don't, it will be a weight on my heart."

I let myself go.

The gypsy took me and sat me on the step behind the fences. She
said, "I swear to Hazrat-e Abbas,[9] you are so sweet. I like you and
that is why, of all these women, I just want to see your future."
Instead of looking at my palm, the gypsy was staring at my eyes and
around herself. "What is your name?"

"Leyli."

"Are you married?"

I was going to marry Ali. "Not yet."

"Let me see. You are lucky; you have good fortune, but you are
alone and sad. You don't know your friends and enemies. There is a
man who loves you. To him you are more than the whole world. You
scream a lot, you are moody, and a bit stubborn. If you want something you do ten things at once, but if you don't like something you
don't do so much as lift your hand."

She was talking so fast! I looked down and began laughing. I
was afraid that Mehran would say "Cut!" but he didn't.

I said, "Well, I am going to see him here. Before he comes, tell
me if you see anything good in my future!"

My hand was in the gypsy's hand and she was looking around.
"You are a noble bride, your friends love you, you flirt with gold,
you love to play with silk. Pretty soon your hand will be decorated in
henna. You are simple and don't distinguish between your friends
and enemies. I am telling you this because I love you."

"Get to the point. He will be here soon. I have to go." I laughed.

The gypsy said, "Thank God you are so sweet. Give me something; make me happy so I tell you the rest. Thank God, you are very nice. You are sweet, you have a garden in Vanak. You are beautiful, your eyebrows are like a lasso and your eyes are drunk. Put your hand in your purse and make me happy so I can tell you."

"I bought a pair of shoes. I spent all I had. If you want to tell, tell, and if you don't want to, don't!" I took the shoes out of the box. I put my black low-heeled shoes in the box and put on my pink sandals.

The gypsy said, "Thank god you have taste. Give me two hundred tomans so that I can tell you the rest."

"Then I won't have money to go home."

"The one who loves you will give it to you. The one who is coming here!"

I stared at her.

"You said it yourself, just now! The man who loves you is ready to die for you. Wherever you go, people love you. But not everyone finds the way to your heart. He says, 'I will give my head, my life, but I won't leave you.' Everyone is ready to sacrifice himself for you. Wherever you go, you are the sweetest one. But there are a mother and daughter who cannot see you so sweet. But he wouldn't listen to anyone."

"Eh! But who knows?"

"Many upper-class ladies asked me to write them a prayer so that they can take it to Europe. Many have asked me. But I haven't written. You are so sweet. God knows I liked you, that is why I told you all this. Make me happy now, and I'll give you something that will make you unique in whatever you do. I am going to give you a talisman of love that will work everywhere."

Before I could say anything Ali arrived from behind and put a bill in the gypsy's hand and said, "Give her a talisman so that she will never forget me, so that she will always be crazy about me!" And the coal of his eyes stretched toward me. Ali was supposed to be happy. He was. And I was supposed to laugh. I was laughing.

"God knows I am going to pour good luck in her eyes, just for you!"

The gypsy unknotted the corner of her scarf and brought out a few colorful marbles and showed them to me, one by one.

"Oh, talisman of love and affection, oh, Leyli and Majnun, oh, snake horns, go into a green cloth. May there be love. May there be affection. May my love be in everybody's heart!'

Ali interrupted her and said, "Oh, no! You should say that may the love of Leyli be only in Ali's heart!"

The gypsy didn't pay any attention and continued her words. "May whoever does magic to me lose their validity."

Ali said, "What are you talking about? What is magic? What is invalid?"

"Magic is bad; making it invalid is good. I mean it is good if these things are said. Take this and put it in a green piece of cloth and keep it with you always. Whatever you want in the world will come to you; you won't go to it."

Ali said, "None of these things would do me any good. Give me some of your magic potion!"

The gypsy didn't pay any attention to Ali. Ali was looking at me. The gypsy told me, "Don't forget the snake horns. Tell him, too. No one would talk behind your back. Everyone is ready to die for you."

Ali said, "I am dying for her; isn't that enough?"

Mehran yelled, "Cut!"

He blamed the gypsy and told her that she has talked too much. The gypsy said, "That's it! Movie or no movie! Whatever I said was true. Now you put your hand in your pocket and make me real happy. I can see your future, too. I am supposed to take a prayer to a lady's house, at ten sharp. I am late; hurry up, mister!"

Mehran said, "Camera! Action!"

I was sitting next to Ali in the car. Ali was driving. I pushed the back of the seat down. I slept. I was supposed to have a dream. Mehran said, "Cut!" I fell asleep. I began dreaming. You know, Parvaneh, I wanted to dream about a red star. I wanted to dream about someone's coming.

"Stay alone! Keep eating salad and soup and keep reading Forugh's poems until you dry up!"

Parvaneh, he forgot to mention Yoga.

In my dream everything was upside down. The world was upside down. People were walking on their hands, legs in the air, and asking each other, "Yogi, how are you?" And a big mouth was chewing lettuce. In my dream I saw Forugh was dreaming. Do you remember, Parvaneh? I told you that I would interpret Forugh's dream!

"You young people think you can change the world, with a few poems!"

Did you see, Parvaneh, everybody was upside down! The world was upside down. Did you see that we could walk on our hands? Mehran used to tape me and develop the films upside down so that I would stand straight and fall in love with him. I was walking and shouting in the street when I saw someone was videotaping me. I shook my fist in the direction of Mehran's camera and shouted louder. Mehran did not give up. You said, "What happened then for all your shouting in the street? Shout a little bit at Mehran! Didn't you want to change the whole world?"

Parvaneh, Mehran was always behind the camera. How could one shout at him? He found me from behind the camera and he lost me in front of it. With the camera, he followed me all through the demonstration until I got home.

I said, "Why did you tape me, sir? What use is it to you?"

He said, "Your tape is a nation's movie."

You said, "He is right! He has taken a nation into his house and is torturing it!"

I was at your place when we turned on the TV and saw people wearing black and crying. They had placed the old man on the ice and were carrying him.

How many years did it take me to fall in love with Mehran? You said, "As much as the time one needs to drink four hundred cups of tea!"

I liked the old man. I wanted to jump inside the TV and search the ice and find him. Oh, how much I liked talking to him! I went to my papers and glue and scissors.

You said, "Big girls don't play with paper!"

I said, "Dear Parvaneh, get your tea table ready!"

You went to make tea and I cut out four hundred flowers; five petals each. You were pouring tea and I was cutting out flowers and everybody was crying. The TV showed a woman who was taking her hand underneath her chador and hitting herself on the chest. I raised my head and poured the paper flowers on my head.

You said, "What the hell is wrong with you?"

I said, "I had dreamt that he would bring me tea on a tray."

And two small streams of tears passed my neck and went down on my chest. That day, the only thing I wanted to have with my tea was dates. After the war, Shahab always had chocolate. Mehran used to drink vodka before the war. He was drinking vodka after the war as well. I had gotten used to dates. Mehran used to say, "Hey, with that dark complexion it is quite becoming!"

Shahab was telling a story: "During the attack, we just had chocolate and water. A special kind of chocolate; one of them would give you four or five hours of energy."

Mehran used to drink four or five glasses of vodka and sleep fourteen to fifteen hours. And after waking up he would say, "Actually, Yoga is not that bad!"

And inside the TV was dark and the TV glass was wet! And the TV was hitting itself on the head and my paper flowers had been mixed with the flowers of the rug. It is great to become a poet overnight! Parvaneh, get the tea table ready! The poem of this letter has traveled from the time I had not been born yet and has come to the world of you, Leyli, and I.

I came home and told my dummy, "Action!"

And stuck my dummy to the wall with a thumbtack.

On the set, they took back my pink sandals. But I brought the marbles of the gypsy woman, put them in a piece of green cloth, and placed them under the chest of my dummy.

Mehran said, "Action!"

At the house of Leyli and Ali, there was a poetry night. The woman who was supposed to be a poet said, "I have written this poem for Ali." And read, "Your mountain-like arms . . ."

After she finished the poem, Ali smiled and told the female poet, "I have written this poem for you."

And he read: "'. . . and my hands always toward you . . .'"

Leyli was supposed to bring tea and offer it to the poets. I came in, tray in hand. I came in the middle of the poems and offered tea.

The woman said, "Thank you!"

I said, "No problem! It is just a poem!"

People looked at each other. Leyli was supposed to look at the woman's feet and see Ali's sandals on her feet. The tray was trembling in my hands. The camera was supposed to show the tray trembling in my hands and then focus on the woman's feet and show that she has her own shoes on and then once more show Leyli, who is looking at the woman's feet and this time sees her own pink sandals.

The tray and all the cups, except the one that the female poet had taken, had to fall down and be broken into pieces. Then Leyli was supposed to look down, to the floor, and say miserably, "Excuse me!"

I let the tray and cups fall on the floor. I was looking at the floor and at the poets. I said, "Excuse me!"

Parvaneh, I had never said, "Excuse me," not even to my teachers.

We could hear the demonstrations outside from the classroom. The teacher was giving lessons in algebra and trigonometry. He said, "$\Delta = b^2 - 4ac$."

I stood up. I was right in the middle of the class. I said, "Death to the king = Δ."

"What?"

"Sir, delta equals b square minus four ac."

"What are you saying! Sit down!"

"Now, delta equals death to the king."

"The hero of algebra and trigonometry is neither you nor Khomeini!"

"Sir, it is not delta either!"

"Delta is just a small triangle, stupid!"

"Like you, sir!"

"You should apologize right away, you stupid, emotional girl!"

"Sir, you are just a stupid triangle!"

A girl from the back of the class shouted, "Delta equals death to the teacher!"

Ali shouted at Leyli, "You idiot emotional . . ."

I said involuntarily, "You are a stupid triangle, sir!"

Mehran said, "Cut! What are you saying, stupid?"

I turned to Mehran and said, "Delta equals death to the king." And gazed at the camera.

Mehran said, "Do you know what you are saying, Shahrzad?"

Ali came toward me and said, "You are very tired."

I said, "You are a stupid triangle!"

I am alone like a student who is deeply in love with her trigonometry lessons. . . .

"Stay alone, keep eating salad and soup, and read Forugh's poetry until you dry up!"

Parvaneh, he forgot to mention Yoga. But we wrote 'king' upside down.[10]

Ali said, "It was excellent, Ms. Shahrzad! Your acting, your phrasing . . ."

Mehran said, "What are you talking about? She ruined it! We have to do it again."

And Ali kept insisting that everything was excellent. I wasn't a good actress, Parvaneh! I had to pick up the broken cups and the tray, pour tea again, and bring everything back. I had to empty ashtrays, serve potato salad and sausage and Chinese food for dinner, and keep telling the poets "Excuse me!"

Parvaneh, Leyli was not a good actress either. She had to listen to the poems that her husband wrote for other women and bring those women tea. Leyli had to pimp for her poet husband, and when Ali would finish his book of poetry he would write at the beginning of his book, "To Leyli."

Ali was talking to Mehran: "Let Shahrzad do her own acting. . . ."

Parvaneh, Ali was the best actor. Everybody knew him. They gave him many prizes and directors listened to him.

Mehran used to say, "As soon as couple of people say something nice about you . . ."

Parvaneh, "The Blue Danube" is so wonderful! I should remember to tell Shahab to put it on for you to listen. I am sure you will enjoy it, because my eardrum has healed completely.

Mehran said, "Action!"

I was sitting in the armchair, knitting. Ali, extremely happy, opened the door and came in. He showed me his book of poetry.

"Finally it is being distributed. See! I have dedicated the book to you."

He opened the first page and read it: "To my wife, Leyli."

The phone rang. I picked it up. "Hello? . . . Hello? . . . Hello?"

Ali was staring at the phone and at me. No one answered, and I hung up. It rang again. Ali came and picked it up. There was a woman's voice. Ali was pretending that no one was answering.

The woman was saying, "You can't talk? OK. Come out and call me!"

Ali hung up and said, "No one is answering."

I could hear the frightening sound of the wedding women. Gladiola was not a red flower. The carnation is a red flower. In fact, only my paper flowers are real flowers. Leyli told Ali, "After all, we too have learned something in the university, Mr. Gertrude Stein!"

"What? Gertrude Stein is not a man!"

"I am not a man either."

"What . . ."

I took the book from Ali. I brought a piece of green cloth out of my chest. I opened its knot. I took out the marbles that the gypsy woman had given to me and placed them inside Ali's book. I said, "May there be love, may there be affection. May the love of Ali be in the hearts of all women in the world!"

"Ah, no! May only the love of Leyli be in the heart of Ali!"

I was tearing the sheets out of the book one by one and I was throwing them out of the window. Ali's eyes were popping out of their sockets. He said, "Hey! Don't do that!"

"May the love of Ali be in the hearts of all women in the world!"

Ali ran toward me and tried to grab the book. But the book had no more sheets. I came slowly to the chair and sat. I picked up my knitting and began. Slowly. I repeated over and over to the knitted stitches:

"May there be love, may there be affection. May it be only in Ali's body."

Parvaneh, I was not a good actress. Leyli was a good poet. Ali had bent over the window sill and was looking at the sheets of his book.

Mehran said, "Cut! That was good! Cut!"

⁂

Dear Shahab,

I have not found your sister yet. Did you see! There was no hello or good-bye in her letter. You saw how restless I became when I read that long letter. My poor baby had poured her life into that letter and had sent it to me. Did you see how I lost patience! I came here right away, to see what these men are doing to my daughter. Poor girl, she wanted to change the world. Do you see, my son? She has changed herself. She has disappeared like a drop of water in the ground. What do I know? Maybe, as you say, she is traveling, somewhere. . . . After I received her letter, no one was answering her phone. Maybe she left after writing the letter. I don't know. But where the hell could she be, that we cannot hear from her or she cannot let you have news of her? She never did that, leaving us without any news from her. Now that I am here, I am going to stay here until I find her. You don't need me anymore. You have finished your school and you have a good job.

And I cannot cut myself in two pieces. When I arrived in Iran I saw that my baby's picture was in every movie theater. But she was nowhere to be found. She had locked up the house and left. I was happy thinking that I have a house here that can be my baby's house of hope. That if this jackass leaves her, she would have her own place. What else could I do? This man had his head up his ass. He kept talking about education and knowledge but didn't have a shack for his wife to sleep in. And you know Shahrzad; when she was in love with someone you couldn't stop her!

Anyway, after a lot of trouble, I brought a locksmith and opened the door. I wish I had never seen it! Her house was so clean and beautiful. Her paper dummy was still on the wall. That piece of green cloth and those gypsy marbles were still in his chest. I am sitting here, staring at the door, waiting for her to come. If it weren't for your phone calls I would have gone mad. One day the mailman brought a letter. They had invited her for a ceremony. . . . I don't know, it was for the movie, a celebration, I don't know what the hell that was! They also called. I said she was not here. They said that if she comes I should ask her to go.

I thought it might be a good idea to go to that address myself. I thought maybe I would see Mehran and maybe she would come, out of nowhere. I thought, even if she doesn't come, Mehran should have some news from her. What do I know! I got up and went to the theater. I thought I should see the movie first so that I can see the face of that other jackass, Ali, and then if I see him at the party I can recognize him and ask him about Shahrzad.

My dear Shahab, I wish you were there to see Shahrzad's movie. Twice I bought a ticket and I watched the movie twice. She had not described the movie properly. That pimp has turned my baby's life into a movie and has shown it to everyone. That pimp shows himself as well. As if this is art, to show a man who can torture women. What do I know? Truly, I didn't understand much of what they were doing!

I went to the party. It was like the Day of Judgment! What a big salon! There were so many people, there wasn't room for so much as a needle. How could I find anyone? I kept asking till I found Mehran and Ali. But how could I get there? They were sitting right in the front rows. I tried to remember their place so that afterward I could go there and talk to them. I couldn't move from my place. Finally everybody came in and sat down, and the room became quiet. Men kept going up to the microphone, and spoke, and went back to their seats. I don't know for how long I was there when I heard the word Shahrzad, Shahrzad on the microphone. They were saying, "The best actress . . . ," what do I know; "principal role," and things like that.

Everybody was looking for Shahrzad. They wanted to give a prize to my child. My heart was going to jump out of my mouth. I thought Shahrzad would fly and come there, like an angel. I thought because they kept repeating her name she would show up. She would go up there, she would bow and receive her prize.

Her childhood image kept appearing before me. I was seeing a little girl with a short pleated dress with socks and pink shoes, and a ribbon, who has flown and come up there to take a doll.

What do I know, my dear! I was hallucinating. They wanted to give her a statue. I was constantly thinking this was the same doll Shahrzad had thrown away. I was afraid. I hadn't seen my daughter for a few years, and now that I have come from the other side of the world, instead of my child they show me her movie and her doll!

They kept saying "Shahrzad . . . ," but she didn't show up.

People were shouting hoorah. They were standing up and applauding. But there was no sign of my Shahrzad. In my hallucination I thought, maybe Shahrzad has long since given up this doll, and even if she is there she won't go to take it.

I stood up, and went forward. I gathered my chador under my arm and, with the pain in my leg, I went up the stairs. I told the man who had the doll in his hand, very softly, "Sir, I am her mother. Shahrzad has disappeared. Give me her doll. When she shows up I'll give it to her."

The man gazed at me. And repeated in the microphone whatever I had said. People began to make such a noise that I got a headache. I took the statue and came down. Ali came running to me. He took my hand and sat me down next to himself. And shattered my hopes. He said, "Ma'am, where could she have gone?"

I cried and repeated, "I don't know . . ."

I came to have tea with my child . . .

NOTES

1. Reference to the story of "Leyli va Majnun"; she is one of the legendary figures in Persian literature who symbolize devotion to love.

2. Reference to the story of "Leyli va Majnun"; he is a legendary figure in Persian literature who symbolizes devotion to love.

3. Part of a famous poem by Forugh Farrokhzad.

4. The Persian original is actually a funny poem.

5. This is part of a traditional Iranian marriage ceremony when the master of ceremonies asks the bride to allow him to represent her in completing the marriage contract. According to tradition, the bride should wait for the master of ceremonies to repeat his question three times before she answers.

6. In Persian this line would also mean "I am crazy about you" because the word *Majnun* means crazy.

7. A woman's outdoor—and on occasion indoor—wrap, covering her whole body.

8. A famous Iranian dish made with barbecued meat and rice.

9. Hazrat-e Abbas is a religious figure who, for Shi'is, represents bravery and devotion.

10. During the days of the 1979 revolution, on many walls the word *shah* (king) was written upside down to indicate desire for his overthrow.

The Absent Soldier

Fereshteh Sari

T he taxi stopped in front of *Shahid¹ Amir Zamani* alley. The driver said, "Can a car go through the alley?"

I said, "No."

He said, "Do you want me to make a turn, from the other end . . ."

I said, "Thanks. But it just takes five minutes. Come along,
Alaleh, dear."

Alaleh had curled up in the corner of the backseat and had her
sleepy rabbit tucked in her arm. She was frowning. I knew she was
unhappy with me but I pretended I didn't see. I gave the money to
the driver. I leaned down inside the car, took Alaleh in my arms, and
brought her out.

She said, "What are you doing, Mommy? The sleepy rabbit is
waking up."

Before we left the house she kept me waiting for half an hour.
First she picked up her talking doll and wound it up. The doll started
crawling on the floor and crying like a baby.

Alaleh said, "Don't cry. When we get to Grandma's house I
won't put you down, not even for one minute, not even if I go to the
bathroom. You mustn't be scared, I'll keep you in my arms."

I picked up her yellow and red dress from the ironing board and
laid it on her bed. "Alaleh, dear, hurry up, put your clothes on.
Grandma has made a delicious lunch and she is waiting for us."

Alaleh picked up another doll and said, "Okay"; she didn't say,

39

as she always did, "I don't want to come." I opened the middle drawer of the chest and put all the folded clothes inside. I opened the sock drawer and began impatiently searching. I said, "Alaleh, where are your red socks?"

She picked up her black doll, took the red socks off of its chubby feet, and flung them into the middle of the room.

I said, "Why would you do that to your only decent pair of socks?" She put her black doll to bed and waited for me to leave the room so she could start talking to it again. Finally she said, "Leave my room."

I said, "Very well. But hurry up, take one of your dolls, put your clothes on, and come. I am ready."

She kept telling to every single doll she picked up that they shouldn't worry and that she wouldn't leave them alone at Grandma's house, as if she were going on a very long trip. And in the end, she didn't bring any of her dolls. Instead she carried her brown woolly rabbit with its half-closed eyes in her arms.

Once, when she was three and we had gone to my mother's house, she sat in the middle of the room bending over some drawing paper. I boiled her an egg and put it in a bowl with a small red flower on it and told her, "Alaleh, dear, eat it before it gets cold. I'll be back right away." She murmured, "Okay," but it was obvious that she was just paying attention to the drawing on the paper. I went up to the roof to drop a message at the neighbor's house. Mother had gone to the store at the end of the alley to buy some vegetables. I was coming down the stairs when I heard the sound. The sobbing was rising brokenly from her bosom. I felt an unfamiliar ache in my heart. I rushed down the stairs two at a time and ran to the room. She was standing in the middle of the room. She had the bowl of eggs in one hand and a teaspoon with a little bit of egg in it in the other. Her hand was frozen in the air halfway to her mouth. She was trembling like a chick just out of the shell. I rushed over and took the bowl and spoon from her, put them on the floor, and then hugged her and held her in my arms. I wiped away her tears and sweat and waited for her to recover her breath. I kept asking her jokingly, "What did you think had happened to me?" She didn't say a word. She must have been in her own world. Probably she had picked up the bowl and the spoon and had eaten a bit and then she had asked me something, thinking I was in the kitchen, and then the echo of silence and the eternal horror of being alone had shocked her. Even now when I remember that day my heart aches. Alaleh had forgotten all about it, but every time we went to my mother's she was in a bad mood. In the cab, I asked her, "Why are you frowning so? Don't you like Grandma?"

She said, "No."

The driver said, "If you want the truth, always ask the kids."

I asked her, "Why not, my dear?"

She said, "Because she is old, she is really old. Banafsheh says when people get old they get so small like this until they become like an ant. . . . Don't you ever get old, Mommy, okay? I don't want to lose you."

The driver said, "That's the trouble with kindergartens, lady. My daughter also keeps on—"

I said, "My daughter does not go to kindergarten."

Alaleh said, "Even if you do get old, try to get old just a little bit, just this much, okay?"

The driver said, "Excuse me, ma'am, but what does the child's father do?"

I said, "He was lost in action. He was sent to the front as part of the student's project.[2] He has been lost ever since."

The driver said, "Trust in God. Just the day before yesterday, both sons of our neighborhood pastry-shop owner—we thought they had been martyred seven years ago, and their father mourned them for forty days—they came back from the war, hale and hearty. The father gave away every sweet in the shop to the neighbors."

Alaleh said, "Mommy, what does my daddy do?"

I said, "I told you, my dear, when he comes back and finishes his studies, he will be an engineer."

As we were walking to the house, I bought two balloons, and when we crossed the street I gave them to Alaleh and said, "Blow them up when we arrive at Grandma's."

She said, "Mommy, I want a green one too."

I said, "Okay, wait here a minute." And I crossed the street again and bought a green one from the shop and came back and gave it to Alaleh and said, "Now, do we have Her Majesty's gracious leave to go?"

We arrived at the alley. Alaleh asked, "Mommy, what is the name of this alley?"

Amir himself was laughing at that alley sign and saying, "The girls can't play."

I said, "Amir. He was our neighbor's son. The one across from Grandma's."

Alaleh said, "How do you know, were you here?"

I said, "No, Your Highness. I have had the honor of waiting on you from the first day!"

She laughed. She loved to ask questions to which she already knew the answers.

Amir grabbed the cloth ball from Pezhman and began to knock it around.

Pezhman said, "Shall we begin?"

Amir said, "The girls can't play."

Pezhman said, "If you don't let Homa play I'll take back my ball."

The kids began chanting, "Go away, you German, with your cute ball." [3]

I said, "It doesn't matter, Pezhman. In fact, I don't like volleyball. I'll watch you play."

"Look at him, the mama's boy. He has cut his hair like German dogs. Here, take your ball and go and play with the girls. But first, let me stroke your face a bit, nice baby, cute baby . . ."

Smack!

Pezhman took his hand off where Amir had slapped him. The delicate white skin of his face was now the same color as his red cloth ball. Just as tears were about to fall from his big honey-color eyes he looked at me.

I said, "Let's play, Pezhman, just the two of us."

He said, "You just said you don't like to play!"

I said, "I do now."

I said, "Who cut your hair?"

He said, "My mom."

Pezhman's chestnut hair fell over his high forehead. The back of his head to his starched collar was shaven.

Pezhman said, "I told mom you think I don't need a haircut, but she said that I might have a sweat burn on the back of my neck."

"Pezhman, dear, come inside, it's time for your afternoon snack. Didn't I tell you not to go farther than the electricity pole? Come inside, dear."

The door was closed and the fragrance of recently watered geraniums wound in the alley.

Shahrbanu came out of Pezhman's house, with a bag under her arm. The geraniums were dried up and I was waiting, in vain, for the lost fragrance of those flowers.

Alaleh said, "Mommy, why are you standing behind the door? If Grandma isn't home, let's go back to our own house. My dolls are screaming. Listen, do you hear them?"

I said, "I am coming, dear, wait a minute, right here, behind Grandma's house, I am coming."

And I ran. Shahrbanu had reached the middle of the alley. In the old days she used to work in other houses too, but for many years now she has been working only for Pezhman's mother. As I was running after her, I said, "Why don't you tell Pezhman's mother that the war has ended? Why not?"

Alaleh was crying and running toward me, "Mommy, let's go home. Let's not go to Grandma's anymore."

My mother had come out of the house next to Pezhman's. "What is going on, Homa? Why are you going back? Why is Alaleh crying?"

Shahrbanu was now near the street. I shouted, "Why don't you tell them that the war has ended? For God's sake, tell them to open the door of that fortress. Pezhman has withered away in that house."

When Shahrbanu reached the sign with the name of the alley she turned.

I said, "Don't you have any conscience? At least tell Pezhman that the war is ended; tell him he's not a draftee anymore. Isn't there a radio or television in that house?"

Amir was laughing inside the frame of the sign and said, "Girls can play."

I wiped Alaleh's tears away and said, "All right, my dear. As soon as we eat lunch we'll go home. Are you tired? Do you want me to carry you?"

Alaleh said, "No. This sleepy rabbit is tired. I can walk."

Alaleh said, "Mommy, don't take my hand. I can walk by myself. My dolls aren't screaming anymore. See? They are playing. They know that we're going back to them very soon. They were just afraid of my becoming an ant. If I turn into an ant I won't be able to play with them anymore. How can I?"

I sat on the bench at the bus station. Pezhman, with his starched collar and his combed chestnut hair, was the first one who came out of the school yard. He waited next to the curb and looked attentively to his right until all the cars had passed. Then in the middle of the street he looked to his left; finally a car let him pass. I stood up and took my books and organizer in one hand and brushed the dust off my school uniform with the other. I said, "Pezhman, let's go home the longer way."

Pezhman said, "Mom will be worried."

I said, "Tell her your class had to stay an extra hour."

"I can't lie to her."

"Well?"

"You dropped your fountain pen."

"I'll pick it up myself."

"No, I'll pick it up."

Pezhman bent and picked up my pen. A spot of blue ink fell on his hand, like a broken star.

Pezhman said, "Is your pen leaky?"

I said, "Sometimes."

I said, "There's ink on your hand."

He said, "If Mom gives me permission, I will never clean the ink off my hand."

I said, "That's enough. Give it to me."

He said, "Wait, let me put it in your organizer so the ink won't get on your hand."

I said, "It doesn't matter even if I were to go home without a hand; my mom wouldn't notice."

He said, "You are making fun of me too."

I said, "No, you know I'm not."

He said, "Yes, I know."

I said, "Not always."

We were in the middle of the alley when Mother put her head out the door and, while putting her hand over her eyes to shade them from the sun, shouted, "Is this pint-size kid twisting you around her little finger again? Take her hand and bring her in. I am starving. Half of the rice is stuck together[4] by now. . . ."

Alaleh said, "Oh, good. I love crispy rice."

I smiled in her eyes and Alaleh placed her soft hand in mine and said, "Mommy, you love to come to Grandma's house."

I said, "Well, she is my mom, my dear."

She said, "Then why do you always go onto the roof and leave me alone with Grandma? I am scared of her. Let's go home soon today, okay?"

All around the vases of geraniums, there were little pieces of paper folded like airplanes. He hadn't opened any of my messages. They didn't even open the door to anyone. I used to go onto the roof and throw those letters into their yard. In one of them I had written the address of a smuggler I had spent a lot of time finding, and how they were supposed to contact him. He was very trustworthy, and the way he took people out of the country was very easy. If Pezhman's mother wanted to sell his inheritance, she could get him over the border. I knew that if I suggested that Pezhman be taken through the mountains, hiding himself in a sheepskin and crossing the border with the herd, or things like that, she would have had a heart attack. But this go-between was very easy. He would make a false passport and visa and take Pezhman nice and easy to the Mehrabad airport, and from there straight to Sweden.

But his mother had hidden Pezhman in an impregnable fortress, waiting for the war to end. None of them came out of the house, and the door was opened only to Shahrbanu. Once a week, the fortress door would open a little and Shahrbanu would carry the things she had bought under her chador⁵ and go in.

Alaleh closed the door very softly and said, "Shhh, the fish are sleeping." Then she bent over the pool and looked at the fish.

Mother came to the veranda and shouted, "Will this child let you come in or not? Lunch is already on the table. It's getting cold."

Alaleh said, "Now the fish are awake because of Grandma's screaming. They have to eat first; go bring them some bread."

Mother said, "God save us! I've never seen anything like this before."

And she frowned and went in and sat at the table. I took a piece of bread and gave it to Alaleh. Then I sat at the table and took a piece of crispy rice, put it on the plate and poured a spoonful of vegetable stew on it. Chewing the crispy rice was making a lot of noise in my ears. Mother was talking, maybe about the grocery man or maybe about the pain in her feet. In the middle of the sound of chewing the crispy rice, I heard a door close. I pause in the middle of a mouthful. I thought it was the door of Pezhman's house closing. I wanted to rush up the stairs and go to the roof and see who went to their house.

But Alaleh came in and sat at the table. I put some food on her plate and began chewing. My ears were filled with the noise again.

Mother must have asked me something, because she was looking at me waiting for an answer. I shook my head. Alaleh said, "Certainly not. After lunch we won't sleep. We want to go back home right away."

I pushed my plate away. Mother said, "I told you; after lunch you will sleep next to your mom like a normal child. In the evening, she is going to take me to the Ebn-e Babveyh Cemetery, to my mother's grave."

Then she looked at me and said, "When was the last time, Homa? I am sure my mom has been waiting for me all this time."

Alaleh said, "Certainly not. She is supposed to take me back to my dolls."

I stood up and took my plate to the kitchen and turned on the faucet.

Pezhman came to the bus station and said, "Let's go, Homa."
I said, "Why from there?"
He said, "Didn't you want us to go from the longer way?"
I said, "How about your mom?"
He said, "Today we really had an extra class. But I didn't stay."
I said, "Won't you tell her?"
He said, "She won't ask. We'll get home on time."
He said, "How is your fountain pen?"
I said, "It's better now. It doesn't leak anymore. By the way, do you know, Pezhman, that when I was a kid, once I got so afraid of my own dream that I went dumb?"
He said, "Really? What was your dream about?"
I said, "I didn't go to school for three years. I was ten when I went to the first grade. How old are you, Pezhman?
He said, "Fourteen."
I said, "I am three years older than you are."
He said, "That's good."

I turned off the faucet, but it was dripping.

"I told Mom you think I don't need . . ."

I tightened the faucet and came back to clear the table. Alaleh pushed away her half-eaten plate and took her sleepy rabbit in her arms and said, "Mommy, I am ready. I am going to see the fish. Finish the table soon, and let's go home."

Mother said, "What is this child talking about? You really want to go now? Didn't you tell me that you would take me to my mother's grave?"

I pulled the napkin over the tablecloth and said, "Alaleh is lonely. She wants to go back to her dolls."

Mother said, "God saves us. You listen to this pint-size kid?"

But sobs stopped her complaining. She put her head on the pillow. I gathered the rice grains at the corner of the tablecloth. I looked at Mother and then at the red line of Alaleh's skirt. I knew Mother would not forget this heartbreak and Alaleh, tomorrow, would forget everything. But there would be a dark spot in her memory, and many of these spots . . . I chose Alaleh, who was the future. . . .

Alaleh shouted from the yard, "Mommy, Mommy, come, hurry up. There is an old man at the door asking for you. Hurry up before he turns into an ant."

I shouted from inside the room, "Wait a minute, I'm clearing the table. I'll come and then we'll go home."

Alaleh said, "Hurry up, Mommy. He is very small. He is going to become an ant right now."

I put the tablecloth in the kitchen and picked up my purse. Mother was pretending to be asleep. I don't know why someone inside me said, "Life is the ground for continuous battles, and we are all unknown soldiers."

Alaleh was standing beside the door, saying, "Hurry up, Mommy, hurry up."

I thought she had made up the story so that we would go home sooner. Alaleh moved away from the door.

He was standing behind the door and on his pale hand there was an ink stain, a broken star. His white hair was cut German style. His starched collar had almost crept inside his bent back. The skin of his face was still as delicate as the cloth of his ball.

He said, "Shahrbanu is back and says that the war is finished. Is it true, Homa?"

I said, "No, dear Pezhman, war will never be ended. Hurry up and go back home."

From the sign posted at the corner of the alley I could hear Amir shouting, "The girls can play, too."

NOTES

1. *Shahid* means martyr in Persian. It was especially used to refer to those who lost their lives during the Iran-Iraq war.

2. The majority of universities in Iran are funded by the government. In return for free education, students in these universities are supposed to participate in various social projects.

3. It rhymes in Persian: "Boro baba almani, ba in tup-e mamani."

4. The word in Persian is *tahdig,* which means "the bottom of the pot" and refers to the thin layer of rice that is stuck to the bottom of the pot and turns nice and crisp.

5. A woman's outdoor—and on occasion indoor—wrap, covering her whole body.

Contrary to Democracy

Farkhondeh Hajizadeh

Yesterday, in the cab, you were sitting in the face of a man. I stared at your eyes. You looked at me. I laughed. You left. He winked. [No, this is not right. Do you understand? You must be honest.] I moved away. I grimaced. He shrugged his shoulders, "There is an abundance of women. Especially after the war." The driver removed his foot from the accelerator. Four girls passed by. He said, "God bless them. Look over there, Mr. Driver. After war, men are really lucky." My mouth dried up. I said, "If God willed it, your species would become extinct." He said, "Dream on."

The man was not like you. Let me tell you how he was. See! How should I say it, you know, he wasn't like you at all.

I turn the key in the lock. Your eyes laugh. You become pale. "Click"; the lock turns open. You turn red, gray, blue, khaki, purple. I laugh, "Hi."

"Hi."

I lie back to the wall. I look at your shoulders. My head turns on the wall. You stand right in front of me, bosom to bosom: "What is it? What is the matter?" My right cheek gets wet. You shake your head no. You take a few steps. You return: "Your eyes are red again!"

"I didn't sleep."

"You didn't sleep! Why?"

"Well, it is obvious. He is sick, he is crazy. He is not a human being. He has driven me crazy. Do you understand?"

You shrug your shoulders: "What do you want me to do? You women always act as if we owe you something. You asked for it."

"Yes, I asked for it, myself. But you are not on trial here, trying to be acquitted. I wanted that myself, yes."

"Well, who is sick?"

"That damn image of yours that comes to me anytime it cannot go to sleep and begins its night walk. It shakes me, the bastard doesn't even think that I am dreaming about you. It wakes me up. I sit in bed. As soon as I turn on the light it leaves. What would you do if you were in my place? Ha? What?"

The softness of your hand touches my cheek: "What do you do?"

"What do I do! I take my head in my hands, I clutch at my hair, I curse myself, I hit the pillow, I curse you. Do you understand? Leave me alone. I want to be myself, myself. I want to live."

"Well, live."

"Without you!"

⁂

Zhaleh said, "Say 'In the name of God,' Parvaneh, 'in the name of God'; force the earth to make a pledge. Then you won't have bad dreams." She is right, I shouldn't place myself into the hands of . . . I can. Anytime I want. He should understand that I too am a human being. Whatever the case may be, one from a creature . . . What did she say, I should force the earth to pledge? But then I wasn't having a bad dream. Oh, yes, I was. A dream that takes one's peace of mind is a bad dream, no matter what dream and whose dream it is.

One sheep, two sheep, fifty-nine sheep, two hundred and eighteen sheep, six hundred and eighty-six sheep, twenty-two sheep . . .

"What is the matter? Is it something wrong, Mother?"

"No, straighten your neck, you are snoring."

"You've got a screw loose again? Don't you want to go to sleep?"

"I cannot sleep, what do you want me to do?"

"Take a pill, it cannot be like this every night. . . ."

"That's all I need, getting addicted to pills."

I put the pillow in its original place. Who said that when you dream about someone, if you move pillow around he will dream about you. I don't want you to have a dream about me at all. You can't force me. I have to sleep. I know that tomorrow I'll be dozing off at the office.

※

Your fingers twist in my hair: "So, you want to live, is that so?"

I quiet down. I stare at your eyes. Your eyes do not speak. My legs are trembling. The side of my dress is crumpled in my hand. You laugh: "What is it? What is the matter?"

"I am afraid."

"Of hell?"

"No, of being finished. Do I exist at all? Did I ever exist?"

Your lips close my eyelids: "You are pessimistic again! Why are you crying now?"

"For the times that you were not, I was not."

"But now you are."

I laugh. Your look warms up. Your lips move. My veins are beating. Your name sits on my tongue. My hands fall down.

※

I see you. Your hand goes toward the receiver, you dial a number. My ears grow hot. My heart sinks. I have goose bumps all over my body. I pick up the receiver: "He— hello."

"Pushinehbaf?"

I throw the receiver away. I hit my head on the back of the chair. I am depressed. The numbers are turning under my fingers. Hey, who is he talking to, so early in the morning?

Then, why didn't you call me? You devil, you knew that I am at home, damn it.

The numbers are trembling under my finger. I slam the receiver down on the cradle.

I am not going to call, I don't care, why should I call? If he can resist, why can't I? No, I won't call. Zhaleh is right, men are like shadows. I won't call, I'll resist. Mother is not home, so I'd better at least make lunch.

One cup, two cups, is it four? No, five.

The hell with it. I'd better go to Zhaleh's. Should I go? If I go and then he calls, like that day . . . Oh, no. he won't call. That was a long time ago. All this time I sat at home, why didn't he call? In fact, let him call when I am not home. Let him wonder where I could have gone, let him wait.

I pass the stairs. "Oh, the phone!"

"Ye— yes."

"Hello, what a surprise, for once you are out of breath!"

It was stupid of me to think it was he.

"My breath, yes; I ran."

"Did you guess it was I?"

"Ah, no, I was waiting for a phone call."

"I want to see you."

"There is nothing to be seen about me."

"You mean you have no feelings."

"Feelings? How do you write that word?"

"No matter how you write it, you have none. Have you?"

"I had heard that if you water even a dried branch regularly, eventually it will grow."

"How do you know this branch has not blossomed somewhere else?"

"Stone doesn't blossom. Wood maybe. You are stone."

❀

Zhaleh said, "Is he beautiful?" I said, "Beauty is the moment of love's birth."

Yesterday his eyes were wet; his eyelashes were stuck together, had he cried? I couldn't ask, would he answer if I asked? No, I don't think so. When I got close, he went away. Why doesn't he speak? When I looked at him, a hand took hold of my heart. I wish I could understand why he has cried. Maybe he misses his mother; if I were his mother, I would miss him as well for sure. Oh, if I were his mother, when he fell in love at the age of eighteen, maybe even younger, I would put his head on my shoulder and I would say, cry as much as you want. Then, we would draw her picture, together, and hang it on the wall. So that he could look at her whenever he misses her. Or if one day he brought her home he could tell her, "Look, you have always been here!"

❧

Where did I put it? Eh, this damn memory! It was in this book. No, I had put it in my notebook.

"What do you want, dear? Why are you making noise?"

"A picture, Mother. Where did I put it? Did you see it?"

"What kind of picture was it?

"Just a picture! I should take it to the office tomorrow."

"Make a knot at the feet of the devil and you will find it."

Maybe he really has fallen in love and that is why he cried? Who could she be? Their neighbor's daughter? Yes, that is her, she is very beautiful, but beauty is not everything. How about his cousin? What were they whispering about, that day at the party? I wish I knew who she is! Whoever she is, if he loves her I can love her too.

❧

Maybe you were tired. Here your eyes are laughing. Were you depressed? Do you want me to be your mother? If I were your mother would you speak? No, you can't, you are shy. Do you want me to be your sister? Your little sister to whom you can give your letters; at noon when Mother is asleep, she can go and put her hand in front of her mouth, and call the neighbor's daughter, and put the letter in her hand and say, my brother sent this. Don't make a face. You don't like it. Ha? OK, do you want me to be your friend? Anyone; I can be anyone you want, just tell your eyelashes not to stick to each other. OK? Tell them to always laugh like they are in here.

"God help me, the girl has completely gone crazy, she is eating paper."

❧

I say, it is good that you are here, otherwise I wouldn't dare go home this time of night; it is good like this, isn't it? I don't have to get stuck in traffic, or be careful and make sure that nobody would see me, and at the party keep an eye on everyone so that I can look at you, just a little bit.

"Taxi, stop right here."

"Do you see what you did? Are you happy now? What should we do now?"

"You are right, what should we do now? Don't leave, don't leave me alone with these, oh, God, wait a minute."

"No, I can't. You know that I have problems."

"Oh, don't worry."

"What you mean, don't worry? The problem is that . . ."

"I understand. I'll hide you."

"Where?"

"In my bosom."

"In your bosom! How?"

"I'll make you small. Very small. And then I'll put you in my bosom."

"Stop! How many passengers do you have?"

"Three in the back, one in front."

"There was another one in the back; what did you do with him?"

"Where could he be, brother!? When did he get in? There should be a mistake. Where is he then?"

"You mean we couldn't see!? She was sitting on his lap."

"You are imagining things. God knows there wasn't anyone."

"Come down."

I get off. I pull my scarf down over my forehead.

"What happened to that man?"

"Which man!?"

"Shut up, you dirt! Who? Ha! The same one on whose shoulder you had rested your head. Where are you going this time of night?"

"I am coming back from class, I am going to night school."

"What did you put in your bosom, was it a flyer? Bring it out, let me see."

"That was nothing."

"Search her."

※

"I didn't see anything."

"Open your purse. . . . So, you smoke, too!?"

"I bought it for my husband."

"So, you have a husband, too."

"Yes. I have."

"Your ring?"

"I have a husband, not a ring."

⁂

"You will sign this and will get out of here."

"Why should I sign? I haven't done anything."

"To begin with, your socks are thin, you have makeup on, too, you lie, too, you don't have a ring, you are addicted to cigarettes, too, and you are on the street at 9 P.M. To tell you the truth, we are still suspicious."

⁂

"Mother, what happened to this bathroom?"

"They'll come and fix it tomorrow. Wait another day."

"I can't. I stink. Since last night, the smell is in my nose."

"Go to the public bath. It is down the street."

⁂

"Go and take a walk round here. I'll be back soon."

"What do you mean? I am not a bum."

"I can't take you there, in the middle of all those women."

"I say, how about putting a blindfold on you."

"No! Not at all, no way. A blindfold is contrary to democracy."

"Get out of here; for a long time democracy acted contrary to us, now for once we will act contrary to democracy."

"In general, I am against any kind of blindfolding."[1]

"So, what do you say we should do?"

"What should we do? Well, this is one way we could—"

"I know. There is a library right here. How about going there and waiting for me there."

"No, not at all; waiting causes anxiety, and anxiety makes you upset. I disagree. You know what? The public bath reminds me of my childhood and my mom. You know what is my last memory of the public bath? My mother and I had gone there . . .

"OK, don't be emotional. Come. But promise . . ."

"OK, I give you a manly promise that I will not look at anyone but you."

"It is not right to look at me there, either."

"So, you want me to go blind?"

"No, why blind, there are a bunch of things over there that you can watch."

"For example?"

"For example, the water, a mirror . . ."

"Why don't you say pumice, facial scrub . . ."

❦

"I say come, come and sit behind this column. Here is water and soap."

"I don't like it. It is dark in here."

"Wasn't it our deal that you wouldn't bother me?"

"Come on, now, you have brought me to the bath for once, and you keep nagging. Look at this girl who is sitting behind you, how old do you think she is?"

"I don't know, seventeen, eighteen years."

"No, her body is bigger, the tip of—"

"Stop it! Didn't you promise?"

"Come on, didn't you say that you won't be jealous?"

"Well . . ."

"Don't make a face. OK, I won't look. Smile, smile a bit. Now close your eyes, close them, you'll have shampoo in your eyes."

"You want me to close my eyes so that you can keep looking people over?"

"Again this feminine jealousy! Don't close them. Look at that woman, her legs are more . . ."

"Remember. You gave me a manly promise that . . ."

"Well, I am acting manly now. I just wanted to show them to you. Otherwise, I wouldn't want you to think I want to look."

"Go to the locker room. OK?"

"Yes, it is hot in here."

"No, I don't want you to go. There, women . . . Why don't you go out for a walk?"

"What do you mean? I want to stay here. Is this any of your business?"

"No, but now that you are being stubborn I know what to do with you. I am going to make you small and put you in my bosom."

❧

As soon as I step out of the bath you stick your hand out of my bosom. You slap me on the face. You laugh: "Did you see that woman? The one whose layers of belly were twisting and falling on each other?"

"You know what? We cannot reach a mutual feeling. I give up."

❧

"It is not possible. Until yesterday there was no visiting. And today is only for members of the immediate family."

"Five minutes, only five minutes, I will run in and come back fast."

"Only members of immediate family; are you his wife?"

"His wife! No."

"Then what is your relationship with him?"

"I am his mother."

"What? His mother!"

"No, I mean his daughter, his sister."

"Go on, my sister, don't bother me, there is no way."

"Sir, could I wait here, behind this wall, until his sentence is finished?"

"She has gone crazy, poor thing. Hey, soldier, take her right there and hand her over to the madhouse."

❧

Zhaleh said, "I am worried about you, Parvaneh. Don't be stubborn. I am your friend, after all. It is not a question of one or two days. In the middle of this nowhere, behind this wall, how can you . . . all these years . . .? You know that waiting . . .

Waiting causes anxiety, and anxiety upsets people.

❧

"Oh, my baby, what a terrible insomnia my baby went through. Are you her friend, sir?"

"Yes, her body is cold. It is freezing. Her pulse does not beat. What does the doctor say?"

When you put your hand on my forehead my veins start beating.

I see the tip of my nose getting red; my cheeks fire up; my body warms up. As soon as I open my eyes you say, "What is it? What has happened? I told you that waiting causes . . .

I laugh: "Waiting . . . there is hope in waiting."

※

"Where?"

"Emergency."

I run up the stairs. In front of the emergency room door: "It is not possible, madam."

"Why not?"

"We set the hospital regulations, not you. This patient is in quarantine."

"Well, I have the same sickness."

"This should be diagnosed by the doctor and the lab, not you."

"At least the cause of his sickness."

"Pollution, madam; polluted air has contaminated his breath."

"Doctor, can one change one's breath, like blood? I can—"

"Don't make so much noise, my girl. Be sure that my goal and that of all employees of this hospital is the health of the patients. This patient needs a long rest, healthy air, and fresh milk. Go on, my dear; I promise that as soon as possible I will let you visit him for a few minutes."

※

I am in front of the hospital's door: "Hello."

"Where are you going, madam? So early in the morning."

"I have come to see him."

"It is not possible."

"Why not?"

"Well, it is not possible."

"What do you mean?"

"I mean you are late."

"Please sir, I beg you, five minutes."

"We have responsibility, my sister, responsibility. Go and come back later, visiting hours begin at eight o'clock."

"I will come out right away, before eight."

"No, my sister, it is not possible, you came late."

"You told me to come at this time. Yesterday, because we are from the same city."

"I am sorry, sister, I can't. Go and come back later, with one of your relatives."

"That's him, let me go and see him, just for a second."

"It is finished. He is gone."

The hospital bells are ringing. My head is turning on my body. My hair is suddenly long and has come out from underneath my scarf. The smell of cedar disseminates in the air. The guard throws his big body on my eyeballs. Blood boils under my skin and becomes round as a bullet in my veins. A voice is heard: "Blood, blood, hey, come here, nurses, run, someone's veins have exploded, hurry up, blood!" People come and step on my head and pass. The veins in my breasts are swollen. I hear the sound of milk pouring. Milk leaves a white dry spot on my long dress. Mosaics become white. Someone says: "Stop her, she has a lot of milk, like a cow. All this milk in such small breasts!? Just like a cow!" My head does not turn anymore. It goes in a dark well, my breath is drowning. Your name sits on my tongue. I want to call you, your name is broken in pieces. My voice is not there; it has drowned. Like the day that word broke in pieces on my lips. You laughed. You said, "You'd better say nothing, you can't talk. But the color of your face, the tics in your cheeks."

❦

"It is five over eight."

"Hurry up. Sugar IV. Hurry up, Don't let her go into a coma."

Once the softness of your hand rests on my forehead, I open my eyes. The doctor says, "That is not right, dear girl. Are you feeling better?" A voice says, "They have taken him to Behesht Zahra."[2] I pull the IV out of my hand; I jump down from the bed. A few black drops of blood drip on the nurse's clothes.

In Behesht Zahra someone says, "Aren't you ashamed of yourself, wearing red clothing with your white hair! And here, in Behesht Zahra." I roll up my sleeve and show him; I say, "See, I have black clothes on." He says, "What is his relationship to you?" I say, "He is my child, I won't let him die. I will give birth to him again. On the highest peak of the mountain, in healthy air, my blood will become red again; then I'll give him to young mothers to pour their first milk in his throat; he will grow up, gradually, gradually, his eyelashes will not stick together; young girls with scented hair, daughters of the fairy king come and fall in love with him and take him to the sea. I will not be there, but from far away, very far, I will see his eyes laughing; his eyelashes are not stuck.

NOTES

1. In this text the Persian word has a double meaning. The original meaning of *cheshmbandi,* which we have translated as blindfolding, was the creating of illusion.

2. The name of the most famous cemetery in Tehran.

Cling to Life with Your Whole Body

❧ *Khatereh Hejazi*

O nce the ozone layer was torn, ugly creatures who resembled hexagon plates and were called Eons entered the earth and occupied it. Of course, before the crust of being was ripped, the head of the Physics Institute, through the huge God-granted telescope that he had in his illuminated eye socket, had spotted these creatures, who had enveloped the wound around the earth like an infection, waiting for a signal from their collaborators on Earth to start their domination. With the green light projectors, their collaborators on Earth had made radiant slides and glided a group of Eons to Earth each night.

In a short span of time, the Eons succeeded in learning millions of languages and dialects spoken on Earth, assimilated earthly traditions and customs, and finally established their rule with a massive assault.

The Eons were against warmth; that is why they deceived the sun with a candy and drove it out of orbit. And the sun, like a giddy little girl, was gradually fading to disappear in infinity. Thus . . . the earth got cold.

The rich lit their fireplaces and the poor gathered around bonfires in the streets. Later the Eons issued a new rule stating that "no one is allowed to make fire!". . . Thus the earth got darker. . . .

Even that was not enough for them, so they ordered the arrest of anyone who thought of warmth; members of different societies such as physics, philosophy, literature, music, mathematics, and charitable organizations, those who worked for churches and mosques . . . were among the first to be arrested and to be forced to build pyramids out of huge blocks of ice for the Eon leaders.

The last to surrender was the Physics Society, which the Eons conquered after a series of bloody fights. They dragged the last person, the head of this society, out of the observatory, where he wanted to sink with his ship like a devoted captain. Before his arrest, out of intuition, he turned the eye of the huge telescope of the observatory toward the sky and its opening toward the earth, wished for something to happen to turn the events around, and with his hands held up, went with the Eons. The Eons, of course, were too wily to execute anyone; they would, instead, put their captives under special suction tubes to suck warmth out of their bodies.

Once the cold chilled her bones, Hertakh took a big knife and, screaming with pain, skinned her head off. Creeping along, she made it to Mirak's room and covered his head with her own head skin. But the Eons tracked down Mirak and finally captured him. Instead of crying, Hertakh tried to follow the path Mirak and others had taken. She knew perfectly well that she would be arrested as well if she repeated Mirak's words in her mind. Mirak's words, however, were so sweet that as soon as uttered, they would find a place in the heart of his addressee, so that even Hertakh would wonder if these words were his or her own. In his absence, one sentence . . . only one sentence of Mirak's words would make her heart fill with compassion. Mirak had said, "Cling to life with your whole body," and Hertakh was determined to do just that, without any fear of Eons. She approached the only tree on earth that had not yet frozen completely and still had some life left in it, unbuttoned her shirt, and with her shirt wrapped around the tree embraced it, buttoned her shirt, and remained still. She became one with the tree.

Three minutes later the Eons arrived and arrested her for committing a warm and heartfelt crime of embracing the tree.

Upon her arrival in the frozen prison, Hertakh was glad. She was under the assumption that she would be able to see Mirak there. The Eons, though, aware of the thermogenic contact between men and women, had separated them in the prison. Among her fellow inmates, whose warmth had already been sucked out of their bodies, Hertakh felt deeply lonely.

In the freezing cell, no one was permitted to talk to anyone. No one was to touch an inmate. The prisoners had to sleep, distanced from each other, suspended in the air in a supine position. If a prisoner was caught with her hands under her head or over her body, she was immediately put under the suction tubes and punished for the crime of generating heat and refusing to follow the Theory of Suspended Being.

Hertakh pretended to be adapting fast to her situation. Meanwhile she tried to use all her talent for finding ways to generate warmth. She remembered the ways in which she would establish contact with Mirak outside the prison by passing through the antennas, frozen windows, and cameras to greet him with her eyes, to invite him to herself and to travel through him. No one could see a drop of the flowing stream between them. Now she was determined to find the expressive eyes of someone without letting Eons discover her plans.

Hertakh's first tactic in prison was to look indifferent and try to gain the Eons' trust. This helped her succeed in her plan. She was appointed head inmate. Hertakh would fulfill any task she was assigned to do. She had two reasons for her firm discipline; she believed she could observe things better from above, and she adhered to the principle of accomplishing any task with great care, even in prison. She despised carelessness.

Hertakh's hard work in the prison caught the curious eyes of an inmate called Nires. After that, one could find Nires wherever Hertakh was. In Hertakh's opinion, Nires had the warmest eyes in the whole world, as though pure honey were dripping from her pupils.

With the language of eyes, the two would read poetry to each other. They would talk about their memories outside of prison, would laugh and cry with no tears. They had become so friendly that Hertakh would worry and think, "These days when I make friends I feel I have been so close that it is time for betrayal." And one day . . . Nires told her that those who had been deported to Mars were coming back to rescue the earth . . . it was time for them to escape from prison to show these people the way. The news gave Hertakh palpitations; the prison thermometer was on the rise until she controlled herself.

Since Nires and Hertakh had more freedom compared to others in the prison, this made their plan for escape easier. The first thing they decided to do was to pretend they were dead so that the Eons would move their bodies out of the prison. Until the arrival of the deportees, they had to make a big and warm quilt out of all the earthly shirts to keep the earth warm and alive.

So . . . one cold earthly night, they sat cross-legged opposite each other and pretended to be dead. According to their plan, Nires had to cut Hertakh's pulse and hide it under the bone of her ankle; she would then hide her own pulse. The thought of freedom had made Hertakh so anxious that like an intoxicated elephant she would not submit to Nires. She had to remind her that it was necessary to co-operate.

Once Hertakh came back to life, thinking she was outside the prison, she quickly got up. But to her surprise she heard the prison alarm. The doors opened and the Eons entered the solitary cell and started beating Hertakh with icicles.

When she became conscious, Hertakh realized that she has been betrayed by Nires. The pain of this heartlessness threw her into the depths of a coma.

But Hertakh was a strong woman and was able to struggle with death. With the help of affectionate and tender vibes Mirak was sending from the men's prison, she was able to soar up from the depths of nothingness and ascend the thread of life.

Once she reached the surface of survival after passing through the last knot on the thread, she determined to stay alive with all her power. Her toys as a child had been fire and snakes; she had never played silly games. How could she submit to death now?

After a few nights, the Eons took her to the public cell again and entrusted her to Nires to keep an eye on her. Hertakh decided to hide her feelings from Nires. This indifference and coldness was driving the treacherous friend, Nires, to the edge of insanity. As a result, Nires was restlessly jumping up and down and pulling the prison alarms with the pointer of the prison thermometer still showing a thousand below zero.

Then, regardless of her collaboration, the Eons came and beat Nires with ice pipes and left her there.

Days passed and the rumor of the arrival of the deportees was making the Eons worried. They were showing less cruelty and getting softer in their control of the prison. They permitted the prisoners to leave their cells for three minutes each day to take a walk in the prison yard.

Hertakh, like the others, would go out for walks in the prison yard, but she was too sad to notice anything. She was getting weaker every day. However, she was determined to stay alive. Her passion for life, like a piercing gaze, revealed the existence of a yellow being by the prison walls that was at the climax of its hidden life. Finally, that persistent gaze penetrated the pearl drop of Hertakh's eye and she was able to see that yellow being, which in fact was a small, lovely daisy. This daisy, perhaps, was the only surviving flower on earth. For Hertakh there had never been a flower as beautiful as that one. At first sight, she fell madly in love with it.

Pretending to feel faint, she sat by the prison wall and glanced at the flower from the corner of her eye. She looked passionately at the flower as if she wanted to devour its vitality and make it part of her own being.

The daisy was very fragile, and it had sprouted so innocently that it brought tears to Hertakh's eyes. Its height was about two centimeters. It had nine petals and two leaves, and one of the leaves was turning yellow. This withering state made Hertakh so sad that she thought she should find a way to cure the flower. To protect the flower from the night wind, she arranged a few pieces of ice around the flower, and once sure the flower would be safe, she caressed its petals with her fingertips and felt as if she was caressing the chin of a babe. She felt happiness because of this sudden joy. She remembered the days before the attack of the Eons when she would run around carefree and see the earth differently.

She took a piece of ice and put it in her mouth. The ice melted immediately. Pretending to tie her shoes, she bent and spat the water in her mouth around the Daisy. The anticipation that a mean conspiracy would ruin her efforts to water the flower made her so anxious that she was sweating all over.

Only a minute was left of their time in the yard. Hertakh wondered what else she could do to protect her flower. She had to be quick. She tucked her hand under her shirt, pressed her heart with her fingertip, and waited until her fingertip was filled with her pulse. She then, carefully, put the panacea on the wounded leaf and hoped deep in her heart for life to come back to that part of the flower.

With sorrow, she looked at the gray sky; what was going to happen to her flower? How could this flower grow in the prison without sunshine? As a substitute for the warmth of the sun she licked the daisy's body with warmth. She felt the flower sigh out of relief. . . . But, what about when she was not around? Who would bring light to the flower? Suddenly a thought came to her mind; she tore the hem of her skirt, took Mirak's picture out, and put it next to the flower with such care that no one could see her. For the first time in her life she did not ridicule the idea of "mental existence." The whole world seemed to look more familiar now, and she no longer felt the heaviness of any wall pressing her heart. She could see herself on top of the world. She felt a deep attachment toward God.

The alarm went on; the three-minute break was over. She had to go back to the cell. Getting up she noticed with surprise that her feet were not touching the ground. She looked at her shoes and noticed she was hovering about five centimeters over the ground. What could she do? If the Eons noticed she was free from sorrow, her secret would be revealed. Cautiously she reached down and grabbed a few pieces of heavy ice and put them in her pockets so her feet could touch the ground again. Once her feet were on the ground, she decided not to let anyone discover her deep secret. That is why, like a mountain of ice, she joined the other prisoners and walked toward the prison building. At the entrance of the prison building, one of the Eons, who had noticed her bulging pockets, stopped her. Hertakh was trying to pretend she was calm. The Eon shrank and entered her pockets. When he found out she had pieces of ice in her pockets, he let out a loud scream. He got out of Hertakh's pockets and left her alone. But Nires would not let go of her. She knew Hertakh very well and could not believe her to have become so attached to ice as to be putting pieces of it in her pockets.

After that day, Hertakh was followed constantly by Nires. She noticed after a while that Hertakh's footprints were not as deep as they were before. She had become light.

Her time in prison had made Hertakh very tough. She was not going to break under any circumstances. She was aware of Nires's plans against her. She had to do something. Though she did not want to stain her hands with Nires's blood, there was no other way. Hertakh decided to kill her in a quiet corner on one of the nights they were taken to the ice farms for hard labor. Before Hertakh could put her plan into action, Nires, who no longer possessed any warmth at all, was freed. Earth's order to get rid of her was issued and as she was leaving the prison door, she was struck by a meteor called "Akdendrit" that had been wandering in space for the last two million years, and her brain was smashed.

After that incident, Hertakh would attend her flower freely during the three-minute breaks. She would water it. She would collect the soil on the statues, which were installed to prevent the prisoners from escaping, and put it around the flower. She would lick its petals one by one. This ever-increasing love was making her lighter and lighter every day, to the point that the Eons were thinking Hertakh had lost her mind walking around with pieces of ice in her pocket. That's why she was convicted of madness and was put in a special cold cell for lovers.

One day when the Eon doctor came to give her an ice-cold-water injection, he was surprised to see Hertakh was not on her frozen seat. Looking up, he saw her floating in the air close to the ceiling, still asleep. He immediately, turned on the prison alarm and started to analyze Hertakh's dreams. In her deepest dreams he saw the daisy and discovered the reason for her lightness.

A few seconds later, the Eon Special Army entered the prison yard with a very big suction tube and, directed by the doctor, went to the area where the flower had grown. The daisy was uprooted and sucked into the tube.

When Hertakh was transferred back to her old cell, she noticed a big change in the prison and guessed something must have happened. She passed the night in great anxiety until the three-minute break time. Then she approached the flower cautiously. Instead of the flower, she faced a lake of frozen blood. She felt as if the sky was so low that she could hold her bosom against a deluge of beatings. It felt as if she did not have a heart, any eyes, that she did not exist at all. To prove her existence she kept slapping herself, but she felt nothing.

She stood there for a while and started screaming and sliding on the daisy's lake. Her screams made even the rusted alarms go off.

Hertakh could see the Eons approaching her in a big circle. After all that had happened, she had no strength left in her to fight them. She knelt down and looked up to the sky. She saw big eyes gazing at her through bright circles. She thought she was dreaming. She screamed, "God, don't leave me alone!" She then unbuttoned her shirt and touched the empty place of the daisy with her skin. She opened her arms, put her legs together, and remembered Mirak saying, "Cling to life with your whole body." She smiled, and closed her eyes so that the thought of death and the approach of the Eons would not disturb her concentration on melting into life.

When she opened her eyes again, she noticed a daisy had grown on each of her long fingertips. She thought she had to be either dead or dreaming. She carefully looked at the left hemisphere. It was all green and fresh. There was no trace of ice. Far away by the meadow a fawn was playfully following a butterfly. She smiled. She was about to look at the right hemisphere, when she felt the heaviness of a body on her shoulders. Without touching it she recognized Mirak's head. Once again the rainbow of her smile was reflected in the sky. To feel his breathing, she slowly turned back and held the man's head on her left shoulder and let her ears feel his breath.

Mirak held the woman's hand, kissed her wrist, and as he was touching her hair with his head, he said, "With the telescope of the Physics Institute, the deportees, guided by your shining heartbeat in absolute darkness, found the earth. . . . All is saved."

Love and Scream

❧ *Chista Yasrebi*

F riday evening, Golbas Khatun, Aqa Bozorg Khan's eldest daughter, was sitting by the window in her flowered purple dress, looking out. The sky was leaning on the neighbor's rooftop, resting. She thought, "Perhaps it's because I did the laundry." She had washed several loads of laundry that day and had hung them in the backyard. She was now watching the sky and thinking, "Well, I'll be darned! Look how dirty the sky's sleeves are; if I were his wife, I would wash them. Poor sky! He has no one to do his laundry for him."

She yawned and leaned her head against the window. She felt a sharp pain in her right hand and thought she needed a nap. But first she had to serve her father's dinner. The tall green pine trees were lined up outside the window. Winter was unable to overpower them. Golbas liked the pines. In her mind, they defended her rights against winter and cold. Doing the laundry and washing the dishes was very difficult in winter. They didn't have hot water, and the cold water made her hands ache. On snowy days, she had to call someone from outside to clear their rooftop. Ever since her father had become disabled, all the responsibilities were on her shoulders. Golbas wasn't complaining, not as long as the pine trees were on her side. She yawned again. The steam coming out of her mouth blurred the view. With her aching hand, she wiped the window. At that moment she saw the crow. . . .

It was sitting on the tallest branch of the pine tree, beneath the gray evening sky, staring at her.

Golbas thought she was making a mistake. She looked around and looked at the crow again. There was no one else there. The crow was gazing at her. Golbas turned her eyes from the crow to the sky. The sky was now puffed up like the wet sponge in their kitchen. She felt like stretching out her hand to grab the sky and squeeze it dry. Golbas didn't want to look at the crow. She knew the crow was still looking at her, and she didn't like it. She thought, "What a rude crow!" and spontaneously tightened the knot in her red headscarf. At that moment, she remembered her younger sister's, Golbala's, wedding. That night also she tightened the knot in her headscarf as soon as anyone looked at her. Her eyes turned to the pine tree again. Not that she wanted to. It happened accidentally. The crow was still sitting on the last branch, gazing at her with its black eyes. It gave her goose bumps. She remembered she was afraid of the dark and of anything that reminded her of nighttime. She had had a fear of the dark since childhood, and this fear was still with her. The crow's black eyes reminded her of the dark, damp closet in their old house where her father locked her up whenever she did something bad. She couldn't breathe. The smell of mold and mothballs was stifling her. She extended her arms, as if she wanted to open the door of the imaginary closet. Her hand struck the window and opened it. A cold breeze filled the room. Golbas closed her eyes, massaging her right arm; she exposed her face to the winter breeze. She had done the same thing thirty years ago when she was a child. She was remembering it now. She could still feel her mother's warm, coarse hand that smelled of parsley under her chin, as well as the burning pain on her face. She remembered her mother had slapped her on the face. But she didn't remember why. That time, also, she had opened the window, had closed her eyes and had felt the cold winter breeze caressing her face with its finger. She had enjoyed this feeling then, and had wanted to cry. But she didn't cry this time. She opened her eyes. The crow was still there, staring at her. Golbas suddenly panicked. The window was open and the crow could attack her at any time. She closed the window quickly. The window wasn't completely shut when the crow flew away. Golbas followed it with her eyes. The crow got smaller and smaller in the sky. It shrank to look like a small black napkin, then like a bead; later, like a black mole, a small black mole. But Golbas couldn't remember where she had seen it. Probably on someone's face. She had forgotten. She just knew she had seen it somewhere, and that time too, she had frowned and pulled her head-scarf down. She put her hand on her cheek. It was hot. She didn't know why. She thought, "Probably it was offended by my closing the window." Her father's gloomy voice brought her to herself. It was a weak voice, as if he was out of breath. Golbas closed the curtains and left the room.

Ten years ago, when Golbas announced that she did not intend to get married, nobody was surprised. Her brother secretly had softly remarked to his wife, "She didn't have any suitors anyway." Her sister had taken the news with a sigh of relief, for she could marry her cousin and didn't have to wait for her older sister to marry first. Her father had not opposed the idea. He had actually welcomed it. Being a good cook, Golbas would take care of him in his old age. Perhaps if her mother had been alive, she would have reacted to the news by saying, "It's not good for a girl to remain at home. Whatever will neighbors think?" But she couldn't say anything, for she had died five years earlier. She died of a severe cold after she gave up hope of marrying off her eldest daughter. Golbas had no one to oppose her, not even someone to ask her why. She had made her decision and nothing in the world could make her change her mind. But why had she made this decision? Did she know why?

Holding the barbari[1] bread with one hand and her bag with the other, Golbas secured her veil on her head by holding it in her teeth. She jumped over the creek and thought, "Of course I know why! I didn't want to get married because there was no one to fall in love with. I waited until I was thirty, then I was sure I couldn't find anyone. If there were someone, someone I could like a little, I would have married. I would definitely have done that. I searched well. On my way to do the shopping, in the line for bread, the movies, even at Aqa-jun's store. There was no one to fall in love with. There were many men around, but one could not die for any one of them. Let alone dying, one could not remain alive for them. One could not stay up all night thinking of them until morning. Not only that, one could not even distribute charity for any of them. There was something wrong with all of them. My presence didn't matter to them. It didn't make any difference to them whether they married my sister, the

neighbor's daughter, or me. One could not work around the house for
them, cook, wash their socks, or sweep the dry leaves in front of the
house. Love is necessary for all these tasks. I wasn't going to a doctor to sit in the waiting room for my turn to come. I wanted to get
married. I wanted to sacrifice all my love and life for someone. This
is a sacred act; one should not take it lightly."

Golbas was deep in these thoughts, holding her veil in her teeth,
when she felt she was very tired. Too tired to take another step. She
sat right there on a bench in the bus station and put her load down.
She felt a pain in her neck. It felt as if all her joints were falling
apart. She covered her face with her veil and leaned her head back.
At this moment she noticed the crow again.

Standing by the creek a few steps away from her, the crow was
gazing at her. Golbas took a look around. Except for a few school-
boys, there was no one there. And they were not paying any attention
to her. Golbas's face was covered with her veil; only her bluish-green
eyes and joined eyebrows were visible. She looked worriedly at the
crow. No, she was not mistaken; it was the same crow. She noticed
her palms were sweating. She felt as if her heart were beating in the
middle of her palms. She held her veil tighter. She felt her heart was
about to burst out of her skin. She had felt like this before. But she
didn't remember when.

She thought, "I don't know why this rude male crow is not leaving me alone! What does he want from me?" The crow got closer.
Golbas swallowed her saliva and felt as if her feet were dried up like
pieces of wood; she was unable to stand up. She told herself, "If it
attacks me now, I will scream. I will call for help. Someone will
surely come help me." Then she imagined the crow was flying
toward her wanting to gouge her eyes out. Instinctively she covered
her eyes with her hands and looked at the crow through her fingers.
The crow was gazing at her and Golbas noticed a sneer in that look.
A wet, viscous sneer! She had never seen a crow laugh. She was now
sure the crow was laughing at her. It seemed as if it was saying to
her, "Stop resisting, you can't do anything, I can do anything I want
to you." The crow's sneer disgusted her and gave her goose bumps.
She had never seen a rude crow like this; the crow was gazing at her
in front of many eyes, in daylight. Golbas wanted to scream and say,
"Help, people, the crow is a man and it's not leaving me alone, it's
following me. As if he has inherited me!" But she didn't say anything. Instead, she stood up, picked up her bag and her breads and

quickly headed toward home, running fast, like playing tag when she was a little girl. She had taken a few steps when she felt a funny sensation on the back of her neck. She knew she was being followed. With her eyes down she tried to look behind her. There it was. She could see the crow's shadow behind her. It was flying above her head. She panicked. She wanted to scream. But how could she allow herself to scream? How could it be possible for Golbas Khatun, Aqa Bozorg Khan's eldest daughter, and the pride of the great Ali Khan Khan's family, to scream in the street? She was the Golbas who was literate, who read books, who always read the newspapers wrapped around the vegetables. She was the one who was a great cook, whose soup, whenever she sent it as an offering to the neighbors, was so delicious that they wanted to lick the bowl. She who was once told by a fortune-teller when she was a child that she would grow up to be a great personality. She who was once told by a tall man with black eyes, and a mole on his face, who was the librarian, that she chose interesting books to read. In response, Golbas Khatun, Ali Khan Khan's granddaughter, had pulled her veil down and had glared at him. That black-eyed man, whose voice reminded her of Arous soap, had never spoken to her again. Yes, how could the modest and respected Golbas Khatun scream in the street? And to scream for what reason? For a worthless male crow who was following her? Above all, to scream in the street the day she was turning forty-one? It was impossible. So Golbas remained silent. She just held her veil tight with her teeth and quickly looked above her head. She suddenly felt like her heart was coming out of her mouth. She let go of her veil. The crow was watching her from above with its flaming black eyes. Golbas felt she could go no farther. Her veil fell from her head. She put her bag down and pulled her veil up. The crow landed on a branch close by. Holding her head up toward the tree, Golbas said, "What do you want from me? Don't you see I am busy? I have to go prepare lunch for my father. And tonight my brother and his family are coming over for dinner. I want to make fesenjun.2 What do you want from me? Why aren't you saying anything? Don't be afraid. Speak up." The crow was silently looking at her. Golbas felt as if all the words that she had piled up inside her since childhood were coming out and getting stuck in her throat. She felt like she was suffocating. For an instant she forgot she was Golbas Khatun. That she was Ali Khan Khan's eldest granddaughter and that it was her forty-first birthday. She even forgot to put her veil in order. Golbas felt as if she was falling in a swamp of tomato sauce, with no one around to help her as she was struggling to come up. She heard the dripping sound of the worn-out kitchen faucet. She smelled the smell of the burned lentils. She put her hand over her heart and said to the crow, "I am afraid of your eyes. Don't look at me like that. If you have something to say, say it. I am late. My father is waiting for me at home. I want to make qormehsabzi[3] and then I want to sew my father's shirt. These are not so important. I have to finish reading *Les Miserables* tonight. After my mother died, I raised my younger brother and sister. I sometimes sing in the shower. My right arm is aching. You see, we don't have hot water at home. I have to call the plumbers. I like our yard to be filled with laundry. I like our laundry to be colorful. Like in Agdas Khanom's yard. In our neighborhood, only our laundry is not colorful. Our laundry is only my clothes and my father's. I like the laundry to consist of all kinds of clothes; pajamas, underwear, children's clothes, aprons, tablecloths, diapers, curtains, jackets, and handkerchiefs. So why aren't you talking? Don't mind my pale face. I would feel better if I took a nap. I usually pluck my eyebrows. I look much nicer when I use eyebrow pencil. Well, you still won't say what you want?" The crow was still. Golbas was waiting with her mouth open. The crow moved. Suddenly it opened its wings and flew toward Golbas. She wasn't expecting this. At once everything in front of her eyes got dark. She only heard her own scream and felt the smell of the Arous soup that fell out of the crow's beak.

✺

When she opened her eyes, her head was in the arms of Raziyeh Khanom, their next-door neighbor. Rosa, Raziyeh Khanom's new daughter-in-law, was fanning her. Golbas spontaneously checked to see if her veil was over her head. Rosa's newlywed scent was very strong. Golbas was still dizzy. A few people were standing around them. She heard the voice of Mashdi Akbar, the grocer in their alley, who was saying, "God was with us that I got here soon, or else anything could have happened." Raziyeh said, "Golbas, dear, you have become weak. Mix some rock candy with water and drink it as soon as you get home. I can send Rosa to get you some rock candy if you don't have any." Golbas tried to stand up. Her legs were weak. Raziyeh and Rosa helped her. Rosa took her breads and Raziyeh her bag. Golbas fixed her veil and quietly asked, "What happened?"

Raziyeh answered, "May God be with Mashdi Akbar, for he found you in time. It looks like you fainted and slipped on the snow." As he was looking down, Mashdi Akbar, said, "May God protect you. I was behind the scale when I heard Golbas Khanom scream, and then she fell down. I ran over here. Golbas Khanom had fainted and a black crow was sitting next to her." Golbas looked at the sky in astonishment; there was no trace of the crow. She asked, "What happened then?" Mashdi Akbar said, "What happened to what?" Golbas said, "The crow, what happened to the crow?" Mashdi Akbar responded, "I threw a stone at it; it flew away. The crow brings bad luck. It is not good if it gets close to someone." Raziyeh said, "Golbas, dear, Mashdi Akbar is right. May you always have good luck! But it is said that if a crow sits next to someone, that person would never have the good fortune to get married."

Mashdi Akbar continued, "That crow looked very rude. It probably scared Golbas Khanom. I threw stones until it flew away." Golbas took her bag and bread from Raziyeh and her daughter, held her veil in her teeth, and headed home without saying a word.

Raziyeh turned to Mashdi Akbar and said in surprise, "As if she were dumb; not even a word of thanks!"

Mashdi Akbar said with a sigh, "So much for our good deed. They are just like the crow."

Rosa whispered to her mother, "Looks like she has a screw loose!"

※

She opened the door. Put her bag on the floor and the bread on it. The barbari breads had Rosa's newlywed scent. Her left hand was now in pain as well. Before checking on her father and giving him his medicine, she rushed to close the window and pull the curtains. The pine tree was still covered with the white snow of the night before. The crow's place on the tree looked empty, empty like her heart. It felt as if all the snow in the world had been poured in her heart. She felt a sharp pain in the left side of her chest. She put her hands over her heart and sat down on the cold floor next to the window. She put her head on her knees. As she had years ago when her mother had slapped her, saying it was customary. She started crying, first quietly and then out loud. She felt as if a mountain of ice were melting in her chest. Nobody would believe that Golbas Khatun, Ali

Khan Khan's eldest granddaughter, could cry. So loudly, like a child, as if she wanted the entire world to hear her. She heard her father's voice calling her, " Gol . . . . bas." But she didn't answer; she didn't have any answers.

NOTES

1. A kind of flat bread.
2. Stew of pomegranate and walnuts.
3. Stew of fresh herbs.

The End, a City

❧ *Mihan Bahrami*

They divided the city among themselves, depending on opportunities to do business. Before, when Yadollah was in charge of them, the ability to attract customers and make money would determine their pitch. After the accident, the women cut loose and stood wherever they wished.

Blindness made Yadollah inactive. Before he got used to it, he would yell and scream for any reason and throw whatever he could get his hands on; he would beat the hired kid who carried the cane and he would swear at Heshmat, but gradually he calmed down. He would sit by the verandah and his dark vision would focus on a scene that he had never seen in the time of light.

The courtyard was square, paved with brick, with an octagonal stone pool made of stone and two small gardens filled with weeds and camomile and four-o'clocks and a pomegranate tree with flowers the color of the sun's blood.

The breeze would sweep the old dust from the end of the alley, get mixed with the muffled roar of the swelling, monstrous city, and bring some ambiguous, distressing news as a gift to the blind man.

Yadollah seemed confused; he would act differently; he would blink continuously for no reason and unconsciously cock an ear toward some sound.

He would hear the whispering and laughter of the women, the sound of their high heels, and would utter a bitter curse that would not be voiced as time passed and would stay in his heart. Yadollah was becoming gradually withdrawn; he didn't want to be a laughing-stock. Lately, even Heshmat had started to beat him up, and the few times he had not been able to get to the lavatory on time and had wet himself, she had scolded him with reproaches and punches and had not even given him clean underwear.

Yadollah felt that something was reaching its end, and the monotonous routine of his existence was broken off. He was getting softhearted and willing to accept whatever was said to be the end of being a pimp. . . . But if he had not rescued the women from bumming around and given them shelter in this house and protected them against the double-crossers, thugs with knives, hoodlums and hooligans, if he had let Shamsi face torment in different houses . . . alas! Behind his darkened eyes, apparitions were passing, with names old and strange. Names so lasting that in the prolongation of an eternal night, at times he would hear the rhythm of those words, as if they were new. . . .

Ashraf with the Aleppo boil was a twenty-two-year-old woman from Shahpur, Mehdi Kalehpaz Lane, one of the immigrants from the South, tall and dark-skinned with light brown almond eyes and arched eyebrows; the round Aleppo boil on her right cheek made her look cute. Straight of body, strange and masculine, strong and valiant. She worked alone and at night. Yadollah had assigned Lalehzar and Toupkhaneh up to Karamat's café to her.

As a hot-blooded southerner, Ashraf only knew the way to the stall like a donkey. Every evening she would put on light makeup; no rouge and no powder. She knew her dark complexion was beautiful enough. Besides, once when she had felt like putting on makeup like Batul, after a while the powder had smudged around her nostrils, the wrinkles around her mouth and the corner of her eyes, and according to Yadollah she had turned into one of the masks at the door of the baths. She would leave a lock of hair out of her chador, give a delicate motion of her shoulder, and enjoy the sound of her high heels on the broken tiles of the alley. She could recognize a pocket loaded with money, and as soon as she spotted one, she would open her chador before the man. She would come back alone at the end of the night, tired, and in the darkness she would not think about the nothingness inside her, and lately she would not worry about the crowd that would gather at times in front of the theater in Lalezar, the good-looking boys, pederasts, pimps, peddlers, pickpockets, strangers, truck drivers, ticket sellers, the vagabonds of Rah Ahan and Khaniabadi swindlers and dealers.

She had seen few women among them, except accompanied by a man who was following wife and the children like a rooster, looking after them. Meters away, a gathering of boiling breaths, and far from her . . .

Ashraf just had to find someone. She had to go down the stairs in Karamat café, eat the hot Caucasian kabab that she liked, or chelo kabab kubideh,[1] not touch drugs, be careful with venereal diseases of the foreigners, ignore those who are wearing scarves, then go to a basement or an upper floor room or the back of a store, refuse to stay overnight, and return home on time.

But Batul, who was in her forties, was a watcher herself. She had lost all her beauty. She would walk around in the dim lights of the passageways to be picked up by bachelor cabbies or peddlers from the sticks.

When it came to Shamsi, the blonde, the drum would beat in Yadollah's tired mind. Shamsi the blonde was indeed something else, alas a thousand times. Shamsi had come to Tehran from the North with her aunt's husband to work as a maid. She was a young girl, fourteen or fifteen years old, with an elongated face and a yellowish complexion. Dreamy eyes under thick blond eyelashes; it wasn't clear what color they were. And a bony, weak body.

The aunt's husband had met Yadollah at the Pachal Teahouse and asked about a safe home to send Shamsi to work as a maid. The girl was an orphan, the aunt's husband himself had five daughters and a retarded son and a wife who had tuberculosis, and he was a fisherman, a job that was not permanent.

He entrusted Shamsi to Yadollah, together with a superb smoked fish based on an agreement that he would come every six months to check on her and would bring a sturgeon for Yadollah to eat with his booze. It was now about three years that there had been no word of the aunt's husband or the fish. Shamsi had nobody except him, and besides she was no longer the Shamsi of those days. The person moving before Yadollah was a young woman like a branch of jasmine. With eyes the color of emerald and a rounded body in full blossom, wine-colored silken curly hair that was in combat with her pink face. She was a treasure!

In summertime when she was a child, hungry and barely dressed, she had searched so often in the black mud with the kids of God-e

Akhtar Kur hoping to find a penny. In her early youth in the hope of finding a treasure she had searched the low-lying land of Chaleh Karkoshi and the ruins around Gar and the road to the trolley car.

He was searching for a middle-aged rich man to whom he could sell Shamsi, and his determination was so strong that it was stopping Yadollah from giving in to his desire, and having calculating dreams. He desired Shamsi, but first he had to turn her virginal flower into cash. He would head toward some destination and come back half-way until the day he saw Asghar the puny behind him in a Ford. That day his decision was made. Love for that car started in his heart and covered his entire mind. His sweet dreams were mixed with the cherry-colored Ford, but the watching snake! With brown eyes, round face and tanned skin, erect on a strong short neck and a strong body. Squatting by the verandah. Watched this house for twenty-eight years, a loyal watchdog defeated by barrenness.

She used to sweep and clean house, her hands with rough skin over strong bones, so delicately as if playing the *Tar*2 would comb and braid Shamsi's hair, would tie it into a bun behind her back and secure it with hair pins or ornamented combs, and when finished, she would kiss the hair, take a deep breath. As if relieved of a heavy weight.

"She is not a kid, let her do her stuff herself."

A teardrop would sparkle in Heshmat's eye, "She can't, Yadi! She can't reach her back, and besides . . ."

"You want to flirt with her; why don't you say so."

A light blush would appear on Shamsi's face, she would hold Heshmat's hand, and put her head on her shoulder. Their faces would stay next to each other. A freshness of a light would cause the old fatigue of Heshmat's face to have a poised sadness, a woman who had created motherhood alone and her love, like an erect cypress tree, was standing in the barrenland of this house.

Yadollah would notice this change in her, but would tolerate it with pity and stubbornness. Heshmat had such a temperament that she had made a one-month *sigheh*3 with him last for twenty-eight years. With closed eyes and without being nosy, she took care of the house. She eased things for Yadollah. She kept face in the neighborhood. She could keep secrets, she did not stand at the door, she was honest with accounts, she was a good cook, and when she found Shamsi, she turned into a complete mother and embraced her daughter like soil embracing a seed.

"She has grown up and become mature; I have to think up a plan for her."

Heshmat was peeling fava beans; she was splitting them in half and putting them in the strainer. Without raising her head she said, "May God protect her, I hope she ends up in a good marriage. Don't let her leave the house, especially with these others."

Heshmat shook her head: "Not her, she wouldn't raise an eye to anyone, she is chaste to the core."

Yadollah pointed to the rooms: "Don't you let them open her eyes, then no one can stop her; be careful they don't fool you and take her gadding about."

Heshmat raised her head and looked grave. "What kind of talk is that? They treat Shamsi like their own daughter."

Yadollah sneered, Shamsi entered, and there was silence. She was carrying dill weed in the strainer, and Yadollah glanced at her again.

He was deep in heavy thought; he tried to free himself. He picked his jacket up from the coat hanger, left two twenty-toman bills on the mantelpiece, and went off.

It was the first time the women were taking Shamsi out secretly. Heshmat was going to the monthly baths and Yadollah was planning to go to a distant relative's house in Varamin, an overseer whom Yadollah had recently been reminded of after many years.

The sound of the door shutting was heard and all heads became visible through the opening in the curtains. In the yard there was an obvious silence, the buzzing of the bees, wavelets of the pool water under the pomegranate tree, the bright light of the afternoon through the shadows of the plastered wall, the cooing of the pigeons, and the mild sleep of the afternoon siesta in the house.

Two women were going, followed by Shamsi, who was scared and undecided. The way was opening to them with colorful, varied, and hazy imaginings. Although Ashraf hadn't given them a clear description, she had said so much that it had made them curious. She had charisma, stemming from her southern charm and the fermented fervor of her heart that she poured into her story.

"It's about three months that they are showing it. Friday nights it gets really crowded, people fight over tickets." Batul had asked and Ashraf had answered, "I went once! I went and asked, they said the best seats are five tomans!"

Batul sighed. "Those days I went once with Reza. Tafakkori was in the play. I went. Reza liked him a lot. The tickets were only two tomans. They even had an opening number."

She sighed again and Ashraf said, "Nothing can match this, no matter how much I tell you about it, it wouldn't be enough. They wear such costumes, they have created such a palace scene, with jewels, and it sparkles before your eyes! It looks like a dream. But him, nobody can match Yousef."

Batul was worried; she called the women and said, "Well, we will see it ourselves. Stop telling us about it!" Shamsi looked pale. She didn't have the courage to look around; she had pulled her chador over her head and was just looking down at her feet.

In Lalezar, Ashraf turned to her excitedly and nudged her. "Look around, kid, why are you so glum? Look around, so that you'll have at least seen something in your life; that bastard doesn't let you . . ."

Shamsi raised her head. Before her eyes she saw colorful neon lights, lighted signs above the stores, and the merchandise in the store windows. And a wave of fear of strangeness. She clung to Batul's arm, who herself had a deep and frozen look, and didn't raise her eyes until they reached the front of the passageway. Shamsi felt all those who saw her would inform Yadollah.

A joyous melody whose clarinet sound was irritating to the ear was accompanying the sad voice of a woman. . . .

Let me die . . . oh . . . let me die. . . . I am tired of you . . . oh . . . I am tired of you . . .

Faces were laughing, looks were bright, teeth were chewing, and the crowd billowed. By the column, a pockmarked, blind man was playing the flute, and a young, weak, and pale girl wearing a head-scarf was collecting money in a cardboard box.

Batul came back from the ticket booth; she was carrying two bags of sunflower seeds and a bag of popcorn and toasted almonds.

They got away from the crowd. A man passing behind them touched Ashraf's behind and she turned and made an ugly gesture at him. Two young men who had seen it started laughing and made a snide remark, "Let go, Assdolah." This line had become popular in those days and would make people laugh.

Batul said, "We'd better go in."

The heat of the alcohol-stenched breaths, the stench of tobacco and body sweat, and an air like the lavatories in the public baths, behind the thick velvet curtains that were once crimson red, sent a shattering blow to the sanctity of their thoughts about the theater and what Ashraf had been talking to them about in the past few months.

The discovery of the theater was a visit to another world that could only appear in dreams, bringing with it good news that would never turn into reality. The sign of what should be but is not.

Ashraf was stirred up. On a quiet Saturday, she was fed up; with the excuse of having her period she skipped work and went to the play *Pir-e Pare-duz*. It was a slow, simple play and she could not make any sense of the dialogue and movements on stage. Pompous words and advice; she was bored and she was scared of the darkness of the theater.

There was no other woman in the theater but her; the few other people there were talking and making suspicious noises. She checked around her.

"In an empty bus, especially late at night, they picked up a woman, took her outside the city, three or four of them, and then they beat her up with a belt and left her right there half-alive. . . . In the quiet back alleys of Zanburak-khuneh, a few guys tied up an old woman. On the way to Abali they found a young girl; she was deflowered and they took the skin off her face so nobody would recognize her. . . ." Yadollah's warning voice in the theater faded and Ashraf got up in the middle of the play and left the theater. She escaped the bald villager who followed her to Sepah Avenue and got home in a cab.

After that, she lost her eagerness to go to theaters. The days following, she would stand behind that place, and whether she ended up with a customer or not, she didn't set foot in the theater.

One cloudy and quiet evening when, as always, she felt melancholy, she entered the bazaar with Abdollah.

The scent of roses from Qamsar, the odors of dust, kabab kubideh, and new chintz. Her heart was beating.

Perhaps Abdollah wanted to go to the shrine, to pour the water of repentance on her head, and then marry her. Abdollah had been dating her for a couple of months; Ashraf wouldn't so much as look at or pay any attention to anyone else.

In the middle of the bazaar, Ashraf stood in front of the sacred drinking fountain; she splashed some water on her face, and Abdollah watched her. He had rushed into the kabab restaurant. Ashraf had asked, "Aren't we going to visit the shrine?"

Abdollah had answered, "What for? Why do we have to go there? If you and I set foot in that shrine, we will be damned by the saint." Ashraf was so embarrassed that she didn't touch her kabab.

What greenery it was, what a beautiful green color it was and the river water that would pour over the rocks, that time they had gone to Sarband. They had sat on a bench by the river and Abdollah had ordered kabab.

The food hadn't arrived yet when two guys appeared, Esmail Aqa Ghab Kesh and Aqa Nasrollah. Abdollah had kissed them both and had invited them to join them. Ashraf had pulled herself together and sat in the corner. The cry of the water was causing the voices to fade away, the allusions, allusions were fading farther away, the cry of the water stopped suddenly, the voices came nearer and Aqa Nasrollah, as if talking to Ashraf, made a fist and crushed a bunch of grapes.

"By the life of Abdol, I've never seen a chick like her, she was something. . .! A jewel, her face was like the full moon."

He shook his head, "Alas, she had lost her heart, as if she never once had a heart. . . . By the life of Esmail Aqa, when she sat down to drink, as soon as she saw black grapes, the tears would roll down her cheeks like pearls. . . . She would pick up the bunch of grapes, look at it, kiss it and say, I could just die for your black color, you are black like my Reza . . . then she would squeeze the grapes into her glass and drink the juice along with her booze. . . . I have never seen a chick like her. What fidelity . . ."

Esmail shook his head, "Yes, I remember, wasn't she in love with that same black Reza they sent to Bandar?"

Nasrollah nodded, "That's right, God knows what happened to him there, but the woman, Moluk, always thought about him, until one night she went to sleep and never woke up; she had swallowed a handful of pills with her drink."

"If ever there was a woman, it was her."

"I say fidelity is better than chastity!"

"Fidelity is chastity!"

In the silvery flash of the water something leaped, like a fish. Green, the green of greenery, what a green it was.

That silent cloudy evening, suddenly something shook her, the sound of the loudspeaker announcing the title of the play. *Yousef and Zoleykha:*[4] *A magnificent, historical spectacular, starring . . .* Ashraf's heart sank.

Yousef? Yousef, the boatman, dark-skinned, with frizzy hair.

Checkered shorts, water touching the body of the boat, the strong sun of the Gulf and the salty smell of Yousef's body and a waiting that sank in the bottomless pit of Tehran. Emotions rose inside her. Tired, aching at every step in those high-heeled shoes she had to wear, she reached the windows. Colorful photographs and faces. Outfits made of silk, velvet, lace and tinsel. And Yousef's portrait, and another picture of him among the women of the royal court in Egypt. A made-up face with attractive colors, the icon of a being so unreachable moved her heart, and as if in sleep, she found herself in front of the door. The lights were off and the loudspeaker was quiet, and the silhouette of the photographs in the window. How many times was it that she had been here? She didn't know.

It was the first time they were coming in as a group. They sat on the wooden chairs and Batul put the bag of roasted seeds on Ashraf's lap, and the raising of the curtain amazed them.

The throne and the royal court, golden pillars, tasseled purple curtains under the colorful velvety lights glowing from the ceiling, the begemmed throne and the tinseled colorful costumes of the women lying on the cushions, all was glittering. Zoleykha, with a small body and dark skin, had rings on her fingers and on her bosom a splendid necklace. As she ascended the stairs to the throne, her anklets gave off the cheerful sound of Indian silver chimes. The women bent their heads down and put their hands on their bosoms. The pleasant sound of a dulcimer added to the spectacle.

Zoleykha was calmly sitting on the throne; she clapped her hands and the chamberlain entered; he bowed and waited; Zoleykha's command was heard.

"Let the musicians play."

Immediately, the musicians entered bringing drums and flute and tambourine; the stage was filled with music. A young girl with a fringed brassiere (it wasn't clear what it was supposed to hold) and a skirt hung all over with silk and sparkling frills; it kept slipping down as she danced, and she kept having to pull it up in the middle of the stage.

Batul's eyes were full of tears. She was taken on her wedding night, she went calmly and peacefully off to the desert of Garchak. A group of musicians had been brought in from Tehran. They had sacrificed calves and had invited people from several villages. She was to become the bride of the village head. After all those years she had suffered without a mother and getting beaten by her father's new wife. The girls around her had raised such a clamor that nobody could hear anybody talk, but she was apprehensive, and it was as if she was sinking in a well. The words of the women giving her guidance were making her nauseous. They were giving her advice left and right; she shouldn't give in easily, she shouldn't unveil before getting a present, she shouldn't let the groom come to her drunk, and she knew that Qorban Ali was a drunkard and nobody could stop him when . . .

"Oh, Mother!"

Younger sisters had gathered round her like kids and lambs; the women relatives were all strangers; her mother had died while giving birth. Her aunt had refused to come to her wedding, because she had fought with her stepmother. Helpless, she looked around; before her eyes was mayhem, as if everyone had gone mad. She lifted her head toward the deep sky of that night; one star with silver rays connected with her. In the sky, there seemed to be no other star, and that star was familiar with her. She felt better, the same as she did years later, after Qorban Ali died and she turned into a vagabond and finally ended up in Yadollah's house; this was her only safe haven.

Once again that dark feeling that was sometimes far away from her came back to her amidst the joyous music of the dulcimer and tambourine, but now it was as if it didn't suit her; it didn't fit her feeling old and tired. In Zoleykha's behavior she could see something comical, she had seen the reality of her own face, and her beauty, elegance, and honor the night of the wedding. She was comparing the two situations, and an ambiguous conclusion was puzzling her.

Ashraf's fingers pressed her hand and she heard her excited breathing and her eyes once again opened to the stage.

The curtain was raised and Yousef entered the great hall bearing a decanter. He was of a medium height, dressed in white silk, with a belt ornamented with gems and with a jeweled buckle; he had a square bony face and almond eyes. His long, curly hair flowed down to his shoulders from under a white headband with designs on it; his narrow short beard framed his fair, rosy face. Slowly he walked from the curtain to Zoleykha's throne and began to sing a pleasant song that impressed the audience even more. Nobody was paying any attention to the cutting of the women's fingers in Zoleykha's palace; the singing dominated the stage and the audience clapped so much that Yousef had to do an encore, and the play turned into the singing of the song. The women in the play were sitting idle with knives in their hands holding spongy citrons and lying on the cushions, and Zoleykha was yawning out of boredom. Yousef became the entire play all by himself. With the cheering and clapping of the audience he stretched out the song. Finally when there was nothing left to be sung and a few people started complaining, the curtain fell, and the lights went on. The audience did not let go; they cursed and booed and threw chairs.

A few people had gotten into a fight. Batul rescued the women from the mayhem by pushing and shoving and screaming. But if the play had ended as it usually did, it would not have left such an impression on the young woman.

Through the latticed windows, Shamsi could be seen watering the potted verbena and humming; noticing this, Heshmat had been experiencing strange and unpleasant feelings. A different Shamsi was sitting by the pool in the yard. Her recent mood was related to these solitary moments. Her eyes were restless, her smiles meaningless, her staring off at a single point, her lack of appetite, and her humming of love songs. Heshmat reflected on the events of the past few weeks and other than the change in Shamsi she couldn't think of anything else. "Oh God, if Yadollah finds out, he will raise hell."

Yadollah had ordered them so often: "Don't open the door for anyone." He would watch the women like a cat. They would not even drink water without his permission. He was proud of this. He had the power of possession, and in his absence, Heshmat was his eyes and ears.

But passion, like air ever encompassing and invisible, filled the house. As Heshmat grew more careful watching and safeguarding Shamsi, her initiatives for escape took more complicated forms, until they bewildered Heshmat. She would eavesdrop, she would come back midway if she had gone out to run an errand, she would search Shamsi's belongings and, embarrassed at her suspicions, she would lie to her and offer excuses and keep wondering how to prevent this course of events from moving toward a downfall. Hadn't she heard from Batul all the time:

"Everything depends on one's fate; nobody can stop fate, not even the Simurgh. Whatever is written in one's fate will happen; my fate was for Qorban Ali to die so young and for me to turn into a vagabond. This unclean Tehran was also my fate. May God bless his soul, my father used to say: It is written in the books, the northern cities and Mashhad will go under water, Esfahan and Shiraz, the cities of the South, will go under the earth, but Tehran will go under the sewage, to Hell! This was my fate: to get up from a corner in Varamin and come and wander in this godforsaken place. If Aqa Yadollah had not rescued me, the dogs of Sabun-Paz-Khuneh would have torn me apart. Maybe I would have fallen in the sewage, who knows?

"That accursed of God, who brought me to work, why did he leave me in God-e-Akhtar Kur and go off?

"Why did the one who made me his Sigheh sleep with me only twice and got lost? Why couldn't I last in any house more than two nights before the man of the house would come to me in the middle of the night and the woman of the house would throw me out in the morning? Why wasn't it my fate to have children and put down roots somewhere? By the Mother of the descendents of the Prophet, if Aqa Yadollah had not found me that night . . ."

Batul would shake her head and laugh and suddenly feel free. In that defeat she was free, like a child. But Heshmat did not have that opportunity. There was a harsh and cruel feeling in her that was in conflict with what one desires for another person. Whatever her fate, it was easy and agreeable. She had stayed and aged with Yadollah by her own choice. She considered Yadollah part of herself and she would never question his doings; she would not ask any questions of herself or of Yadollah. Shamsi was a God-given miracle to her, she was the daughter she had always wanted but could never have. In the corner of her heart was an image, and Shamsi the reality of that image, like an apple blossom. With a calm temperament and a modest nature, like a lady. She would never believe she would one day look someone straight in the eye. Perhaps she had seen someone in her dreams.

Heshmat was bewildered. Is this part of the fate that Yadollah is off somewhere these days more than ever?

"Don't let the women run around loose." He would always say this as if Heshmat was not a woman, or as if he was hinting at something. A few nights with the absence of the man of the house and one day of Heshmat going to a doctor; despite her insistence that Shamsi accompany her, the girl had refused. She had a headache and she was sleeping and Heshmat knew that this too was a result of her recent condition.

They had taken the doctor off to a patient, and Heshmat had to wait for hours. When she returned the women were standing at the door worried, but Shamsi was not there; she was not in the house; later at night, she appeared distressed in the bend in the lane and ran to the back of the room. As she ran she gestured to the women and they closed the door to the lane. No sooner had the women stepped inside the house then Yadollah came.

Heshmat was standing in the middle of the room, amazed, thinking about the question the answer to which she knew beforehand. Bits of what she had heard up to that day and at times aggrieved by the distant voices of others were reaching her inner voice.

"The more you pull it, the faster it escapes; bind the chick's leg; don't call your neighbor a thief; the drunk has no tolerance for drunkenness."

Yadollah entered in a good mood with a small bag of fruit fastened with a rubber band; he stuck it behind the bundle of wrappers for bedclothes. He was in a childlike mood, something Heshmat had always thought about and could never picture. Some people have never been children; they come into the world adults and late. Now Yadollah was showing his boyhood, bright and lively, and Heshmat didn't want to ruin this facade.

Quickly he went out the door without uttering a word. Heshmat heard a few honks of the horn; she listened carefully—the sound of kids playing in the alley could be heard and the repeat of the honking. She put on her chador and went to the door. Yadollah called her; he wanted to take them on an outing.

A clean Ford stood in front of the door and Yadollah's face behind the car window had a fresh, youthful expression.

At night when they returned home and Yadollah came to bed, Heshmat knew what was about to happen. Seeing the car she had been startled, during the outing she had remained silent, and now also, she closed her eyes and tried to endure.

The childhood state had evaporated. Skillfully and calmly, Yadollah raised the subject of Shamsi, and in Heshmat's silence found strength and at last felt content and in the right.

Heshmat, who had drawn her chador over her face, was crying quietly, and Yadollah was felt happy inside; he knew this crying meant surrender. It only remained to get Shamsi's consent, and that just for Heshmat's sake.

"Don't fret. This car of mine is for taking you to her whenever you feel like seeing her. It's not a long distance, only twenty farsangs.[5] She'll be rolling in dough instead. At least it's better than getting stuck with one of those good-for-nothing playboys. Who knows, he might extend her sigheh for ninety-nine years and make her the lady of the house. After all, he doesn't have a wife who could make trouble."

The women were standing by the wall, crying. All but Heshmat, who, with a frozen look and lips shut tight, was not uttering a word. Yadollah opened the back door and tossed the suitcase onto the seat. He opened the front door and Shamsi got in. Heshmat turned away and left. The sound of the women crying rose, and with one fast move the car took off and left the alley.

Shamsi raised her head. It was a bright morning. Before her tired, bleary eyes, the crowd of people and things appeared, ambiguous and unknown. The city was alien and she didn't know where she was heading. She didn't grasp where the city ended and the road began.

Yadollah was having fun driving, but every little movement of the car was a painful blow to Shamsi's injured arms, legs, back, and side. They were both silent, and as they drove on ahead, some internal distress would make Shamsi's condition worse. She felt nauseous and had a twisting pain in her lower abdomen. Whatever had happened before was very far away.

Moments of joy, moment of compassion, moments of the blossoming of body and soul, moments like the sparkle of a star in an unlit world, a bright feast in the monotones of her meager, unbearable life. Yousef's fragrance, from the roots of the grass beside the road, or the coolness under the shade of a tree. The ambiguous, unknown smell of the green in the trunk in the corner of the verandah, and the warmth of his hands, the warmth of his breath, it was life. All these had faded away like volatile perfume. When Heshmat cried out and threw herself on Shamsi and was in every agony possible, she snatched the belt from Yadollah.

But he seemed to grow crueler using his bare hands. The first kick, under the belly, was the effective blow, and then there was no other sound. Not a sound. It was Heshmat's wild scream and her cries of supplication that were continually getting the blows in Shamsi's place, and saying, "My child . . . my child is dying, Yadi have mercy . . . Yadi for, for the sake of the Prophet's family, for the sake of mother's soul . . . for the life of anyone you love . . . Yadi have mercy."

"I don't love anyone, you bitch. Understand? This ungrateful one has enjoyed my support and betrayed me; like a snake she has gathered around and poured her venom on me. I will teach this mule driver a lesson, I will show this low-life loose pants, he has to pay for it. . . ." Shamsi, crumpled up against the wall, did nothing but moan.

The great pain was separating from Yousef and leaving. For someplace she didn't know where. To someone who was older than Yadollah. And it had collapsed on her head like debris. "No . . . as soon as Yadollah leaves, I will run away, I will reach Tehran, I will go to Yousef. . . ."

Having made this decision, she had put up with the blows. Something cracked, a thread was severed, on the other side, whatever it was, it was holding out the hope of freedom. The hope of being on her own with no one watching her. For she had suddenly realized, she was too young, optimistic, and defenseless. Suddenly while taking the blows she had realized that her dearest Heshmat was Aqa Yadollah's stooge and she, who had believed herself a daughter, a dependent stranger.

"Oh my God, Batul, dear!"

She had run to Batul, whom she thought of as an aunt, because of her being older, and Yadollah had put her in her place as well.

"Sit down, you old bitch, your stink would drive away the dead. You aren't even worth as much as an old ass; an ass's skin would be worth a penny for tanning, but even syphilitic strangers wouldn't have you, you should see your wrinkles."

Batul, who had a white floral chador on, withdrew, she went back, she bent over and silently left the room. She had come to mediate, to help; she had held Shamsi under her chador. Heshmat, alone and desperate, said, "Oh God, I wish Ashraf were home at least . . . "

Yadollah yelled, "Just wait till I get my hands on that mother . . . I will tear her apart. She showed her the way, it's all her fault, I took her away from the street corners, and this is how she pays me back. I should have let that Armenian dog do it to her, I should have let her get torn up to her mouth in the Arab quarter. Damn me, she didn't deserve it that I made her a lady, I gave her shelter, to get a manicure and wear blue jeans, to swing her hips following the tramps. It is all that bitch's fault; if I just get my hands on her . . ."

He would say this as he was swinging the belt. The buckle of the belt had struck the side of Shamsi's lip, her ear, her neck, and torn them. She saw Heshmat as she was leaving; she had a bruise under her eye and the belt buckle had ripped her cheek down to the side of her lip.

An intense pain doubled her up. A weak moan came from her closed lips. Yadollah turned instantly. Shamsi saw him, his dark, frozen, irrational, simple and wild look, and his habitual mercy.

Yadollah was thinking of the promise he had given to Mash Beman Ali for Shamsi's virginity and thousands of hidden sensations; he was trying to find a way to resolve it. He heard the moan; it was the moan of a woman.

A woman who was becoming a mother, weak and middle aged, after giving birth to seven girls, humiliated and intimidated by the possibility of a second wife, was giving birth to a boy and saying, "He was sent by the hand of God." She moaned and said, "Yadollah." And she did not rise from the bed where she had given birth.

Yadollah was hiding this moan in the deepest corner of his being. It was the mother's moan; it was Heshmat's moan. Desperation, helplessness, complaining, the last word, over all a great pain, a black wish and death. The smashing sound of rock and of glass. The truck loaded with melons came right up to the Ford, and overturned. As they carried Shamsi away, blood was dripping from the stretcher.

Heshmat was sitting in the corridor on the floor in the corner, banging her swollen head against the tiles. Ashraf was following the injured. There were no wounds on them. She asked; they didn't answer her, all the way to the operation room; a female nurse came up and said, "It's nothing serious, go to the waiting room, you can't stay here."

Ashraf entreated, "Then what about all this blood? For God's sake tell me, it's as if a sheep has been slaughtered!"

The nurse laid her finger on her nose. "Don't make a scene; she had a miscarriage. They are taking her for an abortion."

The door closed; Ashraf, stunned, stared at the round, immovable window of the operation ward. Heshmat's sharp wailing rose, and a frightful feeling moved Ashraf. Without looking at Batul, who was going to get valerian for Heshmat, she ran out.

It was a bright morning; the pedestrians crossing on the one-way Sepah Street, she ran straight to Lalezar. In front of the passageway it was quiet; the shoe-shine man and the nut vendor had not come yet.

The door ajar, and the corridor dark. There was no sound. She stood and listened to her heartbeat, in the dark. There was the dormant smell of smoky soil in the air, and farther away, suffocating and ambiguous sounds. She went toward the sound; a few iron stairs at the end of the corridor and the sound was clearer. She went up the stairs, to an old, wooden door and a broken dirty glass. From the ceiling rags of burlap and wool were hanging, and rays of light from under the opening of the door reached her; she looked. She saw a small room with fallen walls, with a mirror on the wall in front of the door and a coat hanger hidden under the clothes next to the mirror. Yousef was sitting on a stool in front of the mirror. He was wearing a sleeveless sweatshirt and dirty striped shorts; he was smoking, and his face was contorted. Behind the door a woman was standing and talking; she was talking continuously and had an accent. Her voice was trembling, and her hand, which wanted to strike Yousef. Yousef hit her on the chest, and the woman fell on her face.

"Don't let me get up and smash you; if I get to that point I'll do something so even a dog won't want to piss on you. . . ."

The woman got up and cursed, madly, her voice choked by a lump in her throat. She swore by her son's life she would kill Yousef.

Yousef threw the cigarette on the floor and got up and now he was standing in front of Ashraf. Black, round eyes, with no sparkle and unfocused, surrounded by wrinkles and plucked eyebrows and puffy bags. A yellow skin, wrinkled and full of holes and spots reminiscent of youthful pimples and a round Aleppo boil next to the lip that had stopped the growing of hair there and dark lips and tobacco-stained teeth. He turned and the crook of his back became visible, it was a saddle like a hunch. That hood he put on over his cloak hid the hump. Ashraf, stunned, thought that whom she sees is another person; but when Yousef with a calm and indifferent tone, like talking on the stage, raised his voice and advised the woman who was sobbing to mind her business and leave, Ashraf believed the person before her is a person who has destroyed not only his own joy and heart but Shamsi's chastity.

It's him, the stripped, real self of Yousef, the lover of this middle-aged woman who is the mother of a boy, who has saved Yousef from being a chauffeur's assistant and taken him home, and after eleven years of care and financial support from her, he now fancies someone else. Ashraf was staring at the curly wig on the dummy's head on the counter in front of the mirror and heard that this someone else to whose house Yousef has been going is one of those old, newly rich, opium-addicted women from the provinces.

Yousef's voice was heard: "You, leftover of the Chale Silab, what do you want from me? You spent money on me, the hell with it, nobody would look at you, you sucked my blood . . ."

The woman's screaming and cursing interrupted him: "Damn you, you bastard! . . . Have you forgotten the syphilis and gonorrhea all over you? I had to pay for your medication!"

Yousef's hand holding the stool went up. The woman, writhing with pain, crumpled on the floor. Ashraf slammed the door and pushed Yousef, who was still about to strike. Stunned and shocked, Yousef crashed into the mirror and broke it into thousands of pieces.

The stool was thrown to one side and before Yousef had a chance to get up, Ashraf's punch hit his face; a few blows on the left and right and a pulling of his hair that made him scream. Ashraf's hand wrapped around his hand like a handcuff and she dragged him toward the stairs. "You . . . scoundrel, come and see, you son of a bitch, come and see what you have done to this innocent girl!"

The woman was dumbfounded. Yousef pulled himself together on the stairs and their struggle started: "Who the hell are you, you monkey-faced bitch? Who let you in here. . . . Hey, Mashd Abbas . . ."

Ashraf turned and kicked him hard between the legs. Yousef bent over with pain and lost his breath.

"Shut up, you son of a bitch, or else I will call a cop and send you to the jail! Who do you think you are dealing with, you low-life?"

The woman had dried up tears on her eyes. "And you, go get the clothes of this wretch whom I hope I see dead. What do you think? This is not like other times; I know you well, just come with me quietly."

Yousef got dressed with no argument and held his head down in front of Mashd Abbas, and the janitor came out behind Ashraf.

They passed Batul, who was sitting at the door holding her head.

In the small and dirty room at the end of the hallway was an iron bed with a mattress and torn-up sheet and a gray army blanket. Shamsi had just become conscious, pale like the moon and weak, her wrinkled dress stained with blood, she lay on the bed. She opened her eyes and closed them again. The nurses, the doctors, Heshmat, and Batul were all by her bed.

A doctor whispered, "A strange case, inconsistent conscious-ness!"

Heshmat asked, "Will she be all right, for God's sake?"

"We can't tell yet."

Heshmat moaned, "Oh Mother of the Descendants of the Prophet . . ."

No one was paying attention to Yadollah, whose eyes were band-aged, sitting quietly in a corner, and no one looked at Yousef. They didn't know him. Heshmat saw Ashraf; she burst into tears, and in a weak voice she mourned, "Do you see what has happened to me, Ashraf? Yadi's eyes . . ."

It was as if Ashraf didn't see her. She stood by Shamsi's bed and kissed her pale, wet forehead and quietly whispered, "Dear Shamsi, it's Yousef. . . . I brought him."

Shamsi let out a moan; Ashraf's face contorted. She had to lie: "He has come to see you."

Shamsi breathed deeply and for a moment opened her eyes; her eyes turned without expression and didn't recognize the apparitions around the bed; she closed her eyes again. Heshmat's crying voice rose again: "Dearest . . . for God's sake open your eyes, look, what misery has befallen me. . . ."

A moment of silence and the nurse held Heshmat's arm. Shamsi blinked a few times and suddenly sat up. The nurse ran and held her and fluffed the pillow under her head to hold it up. Shamsi opened her eyes and cast a confused look at the people around the bed. A shivering smile.

The doctor gestured and the nurse gave her an injection. Shamsi looked and laughed. The doctor's face became sulky. Shamsi looked at him and this time laughed louder. The doctor went close and stretched his hand to close Shamsi's eyes, Shamsi held his hands. The doctor did not resist; Shamsi bit her lips, made a childish gesture and laughed, she laughed loud and guffawed. The doctor shook his head, "An injury to the brain . . ."

Ashraf didn't understand. Yousef moved closer. The nurse was trying to put Shamsi to sleep. The doctor ordered a tranquilizer injec-tion, but nobody could calm Shamsi. With a movement, she pushed the nurse and laughed. As if she was playing, her face became open and her eyes sparkled.

Heshmat had put her head on the blanket and was crying. A vague fear stole up from Ashraf's depths. For a moment her eyes met those of Yousef, who was standing next to Shamsi's bed.

In Yousef's wild, black, irrational and innocent look, one could find a compassionate control that wanted to replace Yadollah's dark gaze.

NOTES

1. A famous Iranian dish of barbecued minced meat and rice.
2. An Iranian stringed instrument in the guitar family.
3. Shi'i Muslim form of temporary marriage.
4. Joseph and Zuleika (Potiphar's wife).
5. Unit of measure equal to 6 kilometers.

Smile!

❧ *Farideh Kheradmand*

Ms. Saburi angrily put the envelope containing the photographs on the counter. The photo shop clerk, who was meeting her for the first time, noticed the client's anger and asked, "Is anything wrong?"

"Take a look at these pictures!"

She started walking around the shop. On one wall was the photograph of a little girl in a golden frame. The little girl looked neither happy nor sad. It seemed as if she was waiting for some news to show an expression on her face. On the other wall, there were two bigger framed photographs. One of them was the picture of a smiling man.

Slowly, the clerk took the photos out of the envelope and looked at them.

There were six, six-by-four colored pictures of Ms. Saburi. The clerk raised his head.

"Forgive me, but what seems to be the problem here?"

Ms. Saburi asked, "Is Mr. Mokhtari in?"

"No, but he should be here any minute."

"You are not aware of this problem!"

"What problem?" the young man asked.

"Look, mister, I don't know your name. Last week, I had my picture taken here three times. But each time . . ."

At this moment, a tall broad-shouldered man with glasses

entered. Ms. Saburi interrupted herself and turned to Mr. Mokhtari. "Here . . . take a look at these pictures . . . for the third time . . . for the third time!"

The clerk handed the pictures to Mr. Mokhtari.

Mr. Mokhtari looked at the pictures.

"I don't know what goes on in your dark room!"

Mr. Mokhtari was about to say something when Ms. Saburi continued, "How could it be possible for the photographs to have the same problem every time. Tell me where in the world one takes a picture three times, and each time . . ."

Mr. Mokhtari raised his eyebrows and shook his head in disbelief.

"Look, Mr. Mokhtari, you know how important this picture is to me."

"Yes, I remember you had mentioned that you want this picture for . . ."

"For the magazine."

"Believe me, I tried my best to develop your ideal smile, but . . ."

Ms. Saburi tightened her scarf under her chin and mumbled with a scornful smile, "My ideal!"

Mr. Mokhtari passed his hand over his thinning hair. With a pensive expression on his face, he pushed his glasses up his nose and said, "I am sorry."

"Thank you. But your being sorry will not solve my problems. Please think of a solution."

Mr. Mokhtari put the pictures back in the envelope. Ms. Saburi paused for a second and said, "Tomorrow is the deadline for sending the photo to *Woman* magazine. Do you understand?"

"Yes . . . yes, madam."

The clerk was sitting on a leather chair following the conversation closely and staring at a spot on the floor. Mr. Mokhtari said, "If you agree we can try one more time."

Ms. Saburi said with a long sigh, "One more time! But this time please try your best."

Mr. Mokhtari nodded and said, "I promise."

Ms. Saburi breathed a sigh of relief. Mr. Mokhtari said, "Please get ready to have your picture taken," and waved his hand at the next room.

Ms. Saburi went into the room. She stood in front of the mirror and tightened the knot of her scarf. She tucked in a few strands of her hair that had come out from under the scarf, fixed her eyebrows, and practiced her smile in front of the mirror. Before entering the room Mr. Mokhtari asked, "Are you ready?"

Walking toward the stool, Ms. Saburi answered, "Yes."

"Please sit up straight on the stool. Very good. Look at the camera. And now smile!"

Ms. Saburi looked straight at the camera lens and smiled.

"Finished."

"Thank you, when should I come back to get the photographs?"

"Tomorrow evening."

⚜

The following evening, Mr. Mokhtari wasn't in the store. He had left a note for Ms. Saburi, to be given to her by his clerk. The young clerk gave the note to Ms. Saburi.

"Dear Ms. Saburi, I didn't know how to give the picture to you in person. I therefore decided to write you a note and apologize. Please don't hold me responsible. Believe me, I don't know what goes on in that damned darkroom. Sincerely, F. Mokhtari."

Ms. Saburi's face turned pale. The clerk slid the envelope on the counter toward her, his head lowered. Ms. Saburi carefully took one of the pictures out.

"No . . . this is impossible!"

Her new photograph was showing her with teardrops on her face.

Disappearance of
an Ordinary Woman

❧ *Tahereh Alavi*

I sit in the kitchen in front of the window. At times, I watch the windows across the way from me for hours; one window is so close that I can hear their radio clearly, and the other is so far that only a halo of the window frame and the curtain is visible to me. Then I try to imagine the lives behind these windows; the fears, apprehensions, joy. . . . This is my hobby.

Outside the kitchen is filled with the noise of five-, seven-, eight-year-old kids. Two of them belong to my downstairs neighbor, one belongs to my neighbor on the right-hand side, and the other two are mine. The kids are gathered in my place because we have a turtle, and chickadees, and all different kinds of spiders and roaches.

The noise of the run-down motorcycle fills the alley; it's the newspaperman. I count to twenty-five, a click is heard; from the top of the door, he throws the paper in the yard. I get up immediately. I go down the stairs quickly. I am now standing in the middle of the yard; our yard is about three by five meters. Taking a big step, I reach the paper. I pick it up and look at the large-print headlines on the first page. Then I go to the *Incidents* page. It is full of reports. I am glad; this is my other hobby. I go up the stairs two steps at a time. I finish my work as quickly as possible and go to the back room, where noise and light can't penetrate. Then I turn the light on and open my favorite page and devour the items. Usually after reading these types of news I get a strange feeling of fear and anxiety. If the news happens to be about a strange, hot incident, I look at the people around me in a different way for a long time, especially my husband and my children. I avoid everybody and everything. This is the major part of my hobby.

The *Incidents* page today is full of reports, but nothing special. Report of an accident on the road to Hamadan; the suicide of a sixteen year old, and the quarrel of two friends that has led to the death of one; that's all. I prefer the domestic topics. I am about to put the newspaper aside when I notice a woman's picture. Above the picture it says, "Disappeared," and under are given the details of the disappearance of the woman. The way the report is written is different from the way these kinds of reports are usually written. *A husband comes back home after a few days on a trip and finds no trace of his young kind wife.* He is now seeking help to find her. Then there is a phone number that starts with 538. "Why should a woman leave her home?" I examine the photograph closely; it is not very clear. All of a sudden my heart wants to stop, my eyes are blurred, and my temples are hot. I throw the paper aside and hold my head in my hands. I press my head with my fingers and reproach myself, "Calm down! Calm down!" But I'm not calm. I look at the photograph again. God, how is it possible? I get up, walk around the room, and leave. The kids are still there. They are playing. To me, they now look like big dolls that move around. I go into the kitchen, wash my face and fill my lungs with air and breathe out a few times. Then I return to the room. I look around. My past flashes before my eyes: marriage, buying the house, the birth of the children. . . . I have known this room for a long time. I know the place of everything in this room so well that I can find the most minor object blindfolded.

I pick up the newspaper again; I stand under the lamp and examine the page. Once again I read the report about the vanished woman and this time I look at the photograph more carefully. That's it; I mean, that's me.

This is the same picture I took a few years ago for my insurance card. I had a few extra copies left. Quickly I go to the picture album; I have one copy of the photograph in the album. In this picture I am wearing my maqna'eh,[1] and only the shadow of my hairline is visible. I am staring in front of me; my left eyelid is down. This is because of my eyebrow and the scar that splits it. I put the pictures next to each other; they are the same. My heart beats fast. I put my hand on my heart and try to calm myself. I have a cold sweat on my forehead and my breath comes up only halfway. I breathe fast and feel there is no oxygen in the room. I tear out the page and hide it together with my picture under the sewing-machine table. I leave the room. A burning smell and smoke have filled the kitchen. The children have gathered around the chickadees' cage and watch their fast movements. I rush to the kitchen, turn on the ventilator, and try to clear away the traces of crime as quickly as possible. I hide the burnt pot under the cabinets and put another pot on the stove. I sit in front of the window again; I want to divert my thoughts to whatever happens behind the windows in front of me, but . . .

I don't find free time to look at the picture again until the next day around five in the afternoon when the kids go to the zoo with their father. When I'm finally alone in the house, I lock the hallway door and go to the room. I get the newspaper and the picture and return to the living area in the hall. I have to look at it in the light. I don't know exactly how I feel; do I want to be that woman or not?

I said the way this report is written is very different from the way reports like these are usually written. It is obvious that someone who is highly educated and cultured has written it. I put my picture next to the picture in the newspaper and look again; exactly the same. I quickly write down the phone number. But I don't go near it until a week later. I hardly go out of the house, and when I go to do shopping, I try not to run into anyone. I examine the daily paper eagerly, page by page; I want to see if the report is published again. No, there is no more report. Perhaps it's been published in other papers.

When no one is in the house, I sit in front of the phone. I dial the number, and I cover the speaker with my hand trying to stop the very sound of my breathing from being heard on the other end. I hear a man's voice coming from the other end of the line; a respectable and dignified man who has a warm voice that keeps repeating, "Yes, please?" I hang up immediately; I am embarrassed. I have never done anything like this before. He won't hang up if I don't. We both remain silent, and I start to feel anxious; I am afraid of his being able to trace down my number with a special machine. Until one day when he goes ahead and says, "Please talk. Why don't you say something? I know you are not a nuisance. I am sure you have something to say. But you hesitate, please put hesitation aside. I won't harm you. If it has anything to do with the report in the paper, you must know that I am waiting desperately . . ."

I hang up immediately; it's him, the man who is looking for his wife. His wife? Wife? I have been married for years, to a teacher; a teacher who is all thumbs, and according to my mother, mediocre. His job, his income, his looks, his level of education, his behavior, the way he loves, everything about him is mediocre. I have no intention of playing games with anyone, and I keep telling myself that people are not toys and should not be used for one's amusement. If you are bored, start working, at home or outside. Hassan has suggested that several times. It's you who don't want to work. If you prefer to stay home, don't waste your time with the telephone. Knowing all this, I am again sitting cross-legged in front of the phone. My hands are shaking; with the fourth number I hear a busy signal. I put the phone down and decide to go do my chores. It's late; it's ten o'clock. I pick up the phone again; with the seventh digit, I am ready to hang up again. But I don't. With the third ring the man answers the phone. His voice has the usual warmth and dignity. Before I get a chance to think, he says, "Please, don't hang up. Please!" In his voice, there is such pleading that I feel for him. He speaks for half an hour. His words are at times joyful and at times so sad they bring tears to my eyes. He finally says, "You can hang up now, I think I have tired you out. But call again, okay? At the same time; and let me talk just for half an hour with you. I don't know anything about you, and I don't want to know you. I just want us to chat as unknown friends and pour out our heart to each other, that's all."

He says good-bye, but he doesn't hang up. He is waiting for me to do it. I do hang up and look at the time; it's ten-thirty. No, this is not betrayal. I tell myself a thousand times, this is not betrayal. But I can't tell Hassan about it; I mean, it's too late for that; it will cause trouble. He will definitely want to know why I didn't tell him earlier. He is right.

About two months have passed since the time of that report in the paper and life goes on as usual. But my phone is busy every day between ten and ten-thirty. I am totally disconnected from the world outside. I sit cross-legged every day in front of the small table where the phone is and dial the number. After a few seconds, that is, by the third ring, his warm and resonant voice is heard: "Yes, please?" Then time stops and the clock stops ticking for thirty minutes. It's always he who says, " It looks as though I've tired you out." And it's always me who always wants to scream and say, "I am not tired. I am not tired at all." There is not one day that he doesn't have something interesting to talk about. One day he talks about collecting donations for the earthquake victims, another day he talks of an incident that has happened in prison. His life is very different from the lives of ordinary and boring people like us.

I only speak a little. Once in a while I say something and give an opinion. I try to make my sentences short and meaningful. After all, he is an educated person, and I lose my confidence in front of such people. I mean, I don't want to say something and make a fool of myself. After each conversation, when I think of what I have said, I want to melt with embarrassment. I am worried that his judgment of me will be the same judgment that I have of Hassan: a mediocre person. I hate being mediocre; if I have to be mediocre, I prefer not to be at all.

He is different from others. He looks at any subject from a new angle and says things that I haven't heard from anyone else. The way he says a thing is different from others, too. His other difference is that he doesn't force me to do anything I don't want to do. He doesn't insist on getting my phone number, or my address, or anything I don't want to tell him. He only suggests that we see each other once in a while, but he never insists. He lets me get used to it slowly. It's not much, what he asks, a visit, from a distance. I finally accept. I have to wait under a tree in Vali-Asr Square while he is waiting on the other side in front of the Tejarat Bank. But we will each go our own way after a while.

He is tall. He has gray hair and a face that shines in the sun. I have gone wearing my black scarf and black overcoat. I want to pass without paying any attention to him. After seeing his face, I feel sorry for him. Then I wait a while under the tree. Just until he looks at me and smiles.

I come back home quickly. I want to stop calling him. What does he think of me now? A loose woman who can be taken out of the house with the slightest signal? I, however, call him at ten o'clock the next day. His voice vibrates with excitement. He speaks with a special intimacy; more intimate than the other days. He is eager for us to see each other today.

From then on the Modabber Café is our meeting place. Once, when he opens his wallet to pay the bill, I see the photograph of a woman; it is the same picture in the newspaper. It is the same six-by-four picture that I took for my insurance card. He then suggests that I look at a few pictures that he has with him. We walk side by side and look at photos. Next time when I see him from far away he looks much more familiar to me; I feel I have seen this person many times. Perhaps it's because of the pictures. In the taxi, I hold my head against the window and think I should take a cold shower and an aspirin with codeine to get rid of my headache.

For two days I can't lift my head from my pillow. I can hardly recognize myself. When I finally get up out of bed, I am pale; my eyes are puffy and my hair is disheveled. I rush to the phone. As soon as I hear his voice my mind is filled with thousands of images. It's me, there, in every single one of them with the outfit and makeup that is mine. Everywhere with the same frozen looks and smile. It's as if everything is happening for the first and the thousandth time. Everything is as familiar as it is strange. The degree of my knowing is the same as of my not knowing. My knowing and unknowing are so close that they are one.

The next morning I am standing in front of an old house, a house in a long and narrow alley, a bit farther up from Amiriyeh Square. "What am I doing here?" I ask myself. I want to return, when all of a sudden a big iron door is opened. He comes out; "How wonderful that you came, welcome to your own home, come in, what are you waiting for?"

It's getting dark when I stop the first taxi I see. "Three hundred tomans to Engelab."

I go back home and promise myself not to call again. The next day I don't call, as well as the week after. But I can't help myself. I can't wait until the time to sit cross-legged next to the phone and dial the first digits, 538. I do that as soon as I find myself alone at home.

"Excuse me, madam, whom did you say you wished to speak with?"

"Mr. Javad."

"He is not here."

"Where is he?"

"He has not lived here for years."

"How could that be possible, sir? I spoke to him a few days ago."

"You are making a mistake, madam; he has been living abroad for a long time now."

"Abroad? You are talking nonsense."

"Please, madam, don't insult me."

"Then give him the phone. I need to speak to him. I have something important to tell him."

"Madam, how can I convince you? It's been years since he has lived in Iran, and I don't have any number for him."

"Dear sir, don't bother me, please. If he has told you to tell me he is not home . . ."

"No, madam, it's not what you think. He is not here, really."

"Would you at least give him my message?"

"I can't; how can I do that?"

"You are lying, I'm sure. But I want you to know that you are making a big mistake. A mistake that can't be corrected. Do you know why I am calling? I wanted to speak to him about the report in the newspaper. I wanted to tell him something very important."

"Which report?"

"The one about the disappearance of his wife."

"Oh, yes, now I remember. Well, that was long time ago, many years ago. It's old news now."

"I don't understand. Do you think you are dealing with a crazy person? I don't want to hear your ugly voice. I don't . . ."

I hang up. I get up; the newspaper, I have to find the newspaper, the one with the report in it. That's my only token of remembrance.

NOTE

1. A short veil.

The Fin Garden of Kashan

❧ *Sofia Mahmudi*

M y father was a truck driver. Every morning instead of roasted
seeds he would pour a handful of questions marks in the pocket of his jacket and leave the house. He would sit in his metal cab and
accelerate toward the street. As soon as he wanted to speed up, poles
and road signals and commanding and preventing signs emerged in
front of him one after another, from left and right. Warnings, danger
signs, and attention signs assisted him in not reaching his destination: "Do Not Accelerate, Brake!" Then "Stop!" As soon as he would
start moving again: "Do Not Enter!" "No Crossing!" "No Parking!"
"No Left (or Right) Turn!" "Do Not Honk!" "No Passing!" "Dip!"
"Caution!" "Dangerous Slope!" "Slippery Road!" and . . . and . . .
and even when he would give up and wanted to return he would face
the sign "No U-turn!" He would make the turn somehow; and at
night when he parked the truck in the last dead-end alley in front of
the house, he would be in a bad mood.

He would put his hand into his pocket to find the key. But the
key was the only thing that wasn't there. Other than a few handfuls
of the morning's question marks, his pocket was full of various signs
of caution and danger!!!

Father would be surprised, and so an exclamation point would be
added to the signs. Strange!

Then he would ring the bell, very hard! Quickly, my mother
would open the gate of the Fin Garden of Kashan[1] and say "Shhh!

109

The child is asleep! No Honking!" And she was right; I was asleep in the cradle, waiting. I was waiting for milk or hot sugar water.

Father would tiptoe across the hallway, enter the yard and sit next to my cradle. Mother would pull forward the tray of tea, pick up the teapot, and then the whispering of the creek would begin. Birds sang and Father drank his tea. Then he would take his jacket off and shake out his pockets, right there onto the tray.

Ever since his marriage Father had lived in the Fin Garden of Kashan. Of course they had not really moved to Kashan; they were in their own city!

I heard this story many times from people around me: "When Mother opens the door, her open face has no less pleasance than the gate of the Fin Garden of Kashan. Her voice is lovely; when she speaks a thousand melodious birds begin singing from the branches of her cypresslike figure, exactly like the springtime in the Fin Garden of Kashan. . . ." People around always said that! And there were many people around. After all, for them that place was like a Fin Garden of Kashan and people, both for its pleasant weather and its inspiring tranquility, frequented it often. Every day, people, one by one or in groups, from far or near, took their various signs under their arms and poured into the Fin Garden of Kashan. One would bring his life's regret sign in a handkerchief and would wipe away his tears. Another one would hold a question mark between his fingers and would sit and smoke it and throw the butt away right there into the limpidness of the water! And another one would open an envelope, a letter full of dashes, separation lines . . . and Mother would sigh and sigh. . . . A breeze would blow softly in the yard. And signs from people's hands would scatter all around . . .

I was seeing all those people and all those wandering signs being whirled around by the wind. I saw them and thought, fall has arrived!

My mother would stand up, sweep the yellow dry leaves, and open a parenthesis in the middle of the fall and gather the signs and place them in it so that the chaotic garden would come upon a bit of order.

But how is it possible to keep up with the fall and the falling of the leaves?

Then one day Mother left that place! She left everything and left! I think she went to the mausoleum of a strange Emamzadeh[2] in an abandoned village and fastened a strip of cloth for a prayer to it, forever!

And the following day, my father picked up a big question mark, put it in his inside breast pocket, got into his metal cab, and went to the desert. This time without any fear or any paying attention to the desert's road signs, such as "Wild Animal Crossing!" "Danger, Landslide!" "Dangerous Downhill!" "Dangerous Uphill!" "Danger of Falling into Gully!" "Danger of Fog and Storm!" "Twisting Road!" and . . . and . . . and thousands of other signs.

He left anyway and never came back.

Now I was left alone in the cradle, with a ton of periods and commas and parentheses and exclamation points and question marks, which were my inheritance.

That was why I stood up. I grew up fast and slung my purse over my shoulder. I put a handful of my inheritance in my purse and went to a publishing house. I told the head of the publishing house that I knew the signs pretty well. He sent me to the chief of the editorial section. He was a tall man named Mr. Farhadi. He hired me. Now I am an editor, an editor from the Fin Garden of Kashan!

NOTES

1. A famous garden in Fin, a region near the city of Kashan.
2. Literally, "born to an Emam." Emamzadeh is a mausoleum where it is believed a descendant of an Emam is buried.

Part Two

Impregnating the Barren Line of Time

Sour Cherry Pits

❧ *Zoya Pirzad*

M y childhood home was right next to the church and the
school.

The courtyard, like all the courtyards in the small seaside town,
was full of orange trees. In front of the porch on the ground floor
there was a small rectangular garden where during spring and summer my father planted flowers; in the fall and winter it was always
full of rainwater.

The ground floor had large rooms with high ceilings and wooden
columns. The rooms got light only from the courtyard, and in the
evening they were completely dark. Nobody lived on the ground
floor. Effat[1] Khanom, who came once a week to do the laundry, put
the washtubs and soap there, and in rainy weather she would hang
the washing on the ropes that were fastened to the columns of the
rooms. My mother stored things that she didn't use but didn't want to
throw away either on that floor. My cradle, my scooter, her bicycle
from when she was a girl, the two-door mirrored closet she said was
left over from her mother's trousseau. My father's hunting gear was
also in one of the rooms. Every time my father said, "Why do you
leave this floor empty?" my mother shrugged her shoulders, saying,
"I don't have the patience for tenants."

In order to go to the second floor we would go past narrow
wooden stairs that went from the courtyard to the balcony on the
upper floor, which was bigger and wider than the porch on the

115

ground floor. The second-floor windows on the one side opened onto the balcony, and on the other side they looked out onto the courtyard belonging to the church and the school.

The church was a rectangular cube made of gray stone with six tall, narrow windows that I had never seen open. Grandmother said the first Armenian immigrants built the church and the school in our seaside town.

The school was two stories high, with a facade of white, square stones. On every other stone an embossed four-petaled flower was carved. When I was very small, I used to bring a chair to the window, sit on it cross-legged, and look out at the courtyard of the school and church. I couldn't figure out the games children played during recess. I gazed at the embossed flowers on the school facade and thought, When I go to school, during recess, instead of yelling and screaming and running around, I would take a handkerchief and clear away the moss in the middle of the four-petaled flowers. I thought, When I grow up, I'll be tall and I'll reach even the highest flowers on the ground floor. I couldn't think what to do about the flowers of the second floor. When I was in the second grade, one afternoon I was playing with Tahereh in the courtyard at school and she said, "We'll build a tall ladder! Then we can reach every single flower!" Then she read my mind. "Since you are scared, stay down here and watch the ladder! I'll go up!"

The courtyard of the school and church was the only place Tahereh and I could play in the late afternoon. Tahereh never came to our house. Perhaps because she knew that my father didn't like it. Tahereh and her parents' room, one of the rooms on the ground floor of the school, was very small, and there wasn't enough space to play in. Besides, if my father were to find out that I had gone to the school janitor's room, he would hit the ceiling, and my mother and I would have to listen to a long, repetitive lecture about class, religious, and tribal differences.

Behind that church was the graveyard. There was no fence between the graveyard and the school. Maybe because there was no need. The school principal had forbidden children to go into the graveyard, and for us his words were the highest and strongest fences of all. For many years nobody had been buried in the graveyard behind the school. The Armenian graveyard was a few kilometers from the city, on the Tehran road.

Grandmother said that the last "one at eternal rest" in the graveyard behind the school was Anahid, her childhood friend, who at the age of twelve caught meningitis and before they could take her to the doctor . . .

Grandmother never talked directly about death.

I was not going to school yet when, one rainy evening at Grandmother's house, I heard the story of Anahid for the first time. Staring at the fire in the cast-iron heater, I thought about my grand-mother's childhood friend; I don't know why I was certain that she had been a thin blonde girl with a large mole on one of her cheeks.

For a long time I kept asking my mother and my grandmother and my paternal aunt and any older person who was around, "When I'm twelve will I catch meningitis and die?"

Nobody's "No" convinced me.

My mother would jump on my father: "Why does your mother keep talking about death in front of the kid?"

My father would defend his mother and it would lead to a fight, and I would sit in a corner of the house, with a lump in my throat, and cry about my death at the age of twelve.

Until one day Grandmother took me in her arms and sat me on her lap and said, "Listen, Edmond! Anahid caught meningitis and left us because she was a girl. Boys never catch meningitis."

My parents stared at Grandmother, and I, who considered the explanation convincing, was relieved and never again thought about death at the age of twelve.

Before I went to school, playing in the empty rooms on the ground floor among the washing and useless things filled my days. From late afternoon on, I used to play with my toys in the living room or flip through newspapers and magazines and blacken the let-ters with holes in them. At bedtime, from my room, which was next to the living room, I would listen to the sounds. On the nights when we didn't have guests, I could hear the static-filled voice of Radio Armenia or Mom and Dad arguing.

I was twelve.

A few days before Easter, in the early morning, I stood on top of the balcony stairs and ran my hand over the banister. I thought, Today I shouldn't slide. The banister was still wet from the rain the night before. I went down the steps one at a time.

My mother yelled from the kitchen, "Don't drag it on the steps!"

I put my backpack on my shoulders, stood on the last step, and looked at the courtyard. The trees were in blossom. In a few days the whole town would be full of the smell of orange blossoms. I went to the garden. The snapdragons had grown so tall since yesterday! And then, suddenly! I closed my eyes and searched for a wish to make.

Mother always said, "Every spring, when you see the first ladybug, close your eyes and make a wish."

I didn't have any wish except to see the ladybug. I opened my eyes. The ladybug was climbing the stem of the snapdragon. Its red color and black spots on the pale green stem were so beautiful. I put my finger in front of it; it got on my finger and climbed up.

Mother always said, "When you make a wish, let it go. Your wish will come true before Easter."

I told myself, "Since I haven't made a wish, I'll keep it."

I threw my backpack down beside the garden; I made a cup for the ladybug with one hand and put my other hand over it and ran up the stairs two at a time. I reached the balcony upstairs. I passed the kitchen, then the dining room and then the living room, begging God that Father or Mother wouldn't appear.

For sure Father would have said, "A big boy like you!"

Mother would be happy to see the ladybug but this was not the time. I was late for school.

Once in my room I picked up one of the thirty or forty empty matchboxes I had collected, opened it, and dropped the ladybug inside and told it, "Stay here, till I come back!"

When I reached the stairs Mother came out of the kitchen. "What are you doing? They rang the bell!"

I slid down the wet banister, picked up my backpack and ran.

I was late.

The children had formed lines and were reading the morning prayers. "Our Father who art in heaven . . ."

I read "art in heaven," with the other children and thanked God that the eyes of Mr. Principal were closed and didn't see me coming late.

I stood at the end of the line, behind Tahereh.

Tahereh's eyes were closed, her palms pressed together, her head down, the tip of her nose touching her fingertips.

She murmured, "What did you find?"

I put the backpack down, crossed myself fast, looked down and read, "Forgive us our trespasses."

I whispered, "A ladybug."

Tahereh turned. Her eyes were shining. "Did you make a wish?"

Mr. Principal said loudly, "Sixth grade!"

Our line set out for the class.

As I was going upstairs I thought, How did she know that I had found something?

I wanted to ask her, but I changed my mind. There were a few children between Tahereh and me. Even if I had asked, she would have made her eyes wide and crossed them and said, "I am a sorcerer!" or she would have made another face.

The first hour we had Armenian history. I had studied the lesson, and when the teacher called "Edmond Lazarian," I was not afraid at all.

The teacher asked, "Which king of Armenia was called 'The Beloved'?"

As soon as I opened my mouth, I forgot everything about the lesson and the class and the teacher and all the kings. I remembered that I had forgotten to make a hole in the matchbox and for sure the ladybug would suffocate.

The teacher loudly demanded, "I said, which Armenian king was called . . ."

Tahereh whispered from the front row.

Looking at Tahereh's mouth and thinking about the ladybug, I repeated whatever Tahereh said: "Sultan Hamid the Second!"

The children burst out laughing and the teacher said angrily, "Stop that nonsense!"

When the bell rang Tahereh came over to me, as if nothing had happened. "Where did you find it?" she asked.

I put my index finger in my mouth and then took it out and shook it aiming at the ground, meaning, "I am not talking to you." Tahereh's chin shot up; she turned so fast that her two braids hit me on the face and head.

During the second recess, cheerless and bored, I leaned against the wall and watched the first-graders playing *Amu Zanjir Baf*. Tahereh was distributing the dictation notebooks. I was looking at her out of the corner of my eye to see when she would reach me. I was still sad.

She came over to me and smiled: "You got nineteen."

I put my finger in my mouth, took it out, and this time I shook it twice toward the ground, meaning, "I am really not speaking to you.

Till the last hour, Tahereh didn't even look at me, and when the bell rang she left before everyone else.

Sorry and angry, I began collecting my stuff. I was angry that I had refused to speak to her and sorry that I hadn't met her halfway. I tried to think of my father's words; he always said, "A man has one thing: his pride." I remembered my mother saying, "Men call their stupidity pride."

I went out of the class and I was trying to figure out which one of them was right when someone suddenly jumped in front of me: "Boo!"

I was scared.

Tahereh laughed. "Are you scared?"

She didn't let me speak. She stomped on the ground and said, "For Christ's sake, let's make up!"

Then she placed her hand on my shoulder and turned her head sideways: "You are my only friend."

Being Tahereh's only friend was my dream. Every single boy at school and a few girls who were not malicious and jealous wished to be Tahereh's friend. I held out my little finger. Tahereh held out her little finger too. Our fingers grabbed each other; we shook them three times toward the ground and said, "Peace!"

I was thinking how wonderful it was not to have any sorrow, and then I remembered the ladybug. I ran.

In front of the stairs I shouted, "Late afternoon in the courtyard!"

Through the railings on the second floor Tahereh looked at me. When I left the school I ran into my father's chest. "What is happening?"

I said, "Nothing! Hello! Nothing!"

I wanted to pass him, but he caught my arm. "We will go get a haircut."

The sadness of the world poured into my heart. I was sure the ladybug would die.

I tried to find an excuse. "Can I go home and come back?"

"What do you have to do?"

"The thing is, I want to take my backpack to my room."

My father opened the door, took my backpack and put it behind the door and said, "Let's get a move on. I have a lot of things to do."

I didn't dare say a word about the ladybug. If he had found out about it he would have gone there, and if it was not dead by now, he would have killed it. Then he would have said, "How many times have I told you I don't like it when you act like a spoiled kid?" And then he would have a fight with my mother: "It's your fault! You are the one who teaches this big boy such girlish stuff!"

Aqa Reza the barber gave me a close crew cut. My father and Mr. Abraham were sitting on the shop's rickety Polish chairs talking.

Mr. Abraham was the father of my classmate, Anush, a fat, frizzy-hair girl who fought with everyone and always called Tahereh "the Muslim janitor's daughter!" behind her back. She didn't get along with me either. Last week during recess, we were playing *Chahar Gush* on the pavement in front of the church. Anush got into a fight with Tahereh, and when I defended Tahereh, Anush yelled in front of all the children, "Mama's boy loves the daughter of the Muslim janitor." Tahereh slapped her hard and Anush's nose started bleeding.

Mr. Principal and the teachers came out to the courtyard. One of the teachers laid a wet handkerchief on Anush's forehead. Mr. Principal asked what the matter was. Anush, screaming and crying, said that Tahereh had hit her. Mr. Principal turned to Tahereh. Tahereh had locked her hands behind her back; her head was down. No matter how much Mr. Principal and the teachers insisted she tell them why she had hit Anush, she wouldn't say a word. That day, for the first time, Mr. Principal punished Tahereh. That Tahereh was punished was so astonishing, the children forgot the original story.

Mr. Abraham was whispering in my father's ear. I could see them in the mirror. Suddenly I was afraid. Did Anush tell her father what had happened? Was Mr. Abraham telling my father the story now?

I was relieved when Father burst out laughing. Still laughing, he put his hand on Anush's father's knee. "You are lying! Swear by Christ!"

Mr. Abraham laughed. "Why should I lie? There is a witness."

"Who?"

Anush's father pointed left with his head.

To the left of Aqa Reza's barbershop, right across from the school and church and our house, was the lemonade shop of Khanom Gregorian, the close friend of my grandmother, who lived on the floor above her shop.

Aqa Reza yelled at his apprentice, who was sweeping in front of the shop, and swore at him in Gilaki.[2]

My father said, "But the shop is shut at night."

"She saw it from the upstairs window."

"What did the janitor's wife say?"

"First she cried, then she told him, 'You ought to be ashamed! You could be my father!'"

"What did Khanom Gregorian say?"

"She has said 'I spit on you! You could be my father too!'"

My father and Mr. Abraham slapped their knees and burst out laughing. In the midst of his laughter, my father said, "Then Simonian still . . ."

Aqa Reza unfastened the white cape from around my neck.

My father put a bill in Aqa Reza's hand, looked around at me and said, "You go home. Tell your mother I am invited out tonight."

I don't know how I got across the street. The house door was open. I kicked my backpack away, I ran through the courtyard and up the steps two at a time. I saw Mother and Grandmother through the open window of the kitchen. Before they could say a word I went into my room.

I opened the matchbox. Then I took my head in my hands and my tears came pouring down.

When the door was opened I was scared for a moment. If my father saw me crying he would make fun of me. My father always said, "Men don't cry."

It was my mother. My mother never made fun of me for crying. She would cry herself every now and then, when nobody was in the house. Whenever I put my hand on her shoulder and asked her, "Why are you crying?" she would force a smile and say, "I just feel sad."

My mother put her hand on my shoulder. "Why are you crying?"

I showed her the ladybug.

She picked up the matchbox. "Poor little thing."

I was crying harder. "It was my fault! If only I hadn't picked it up from the garden! If only I hadn't put it in the box! If only I had remembered to make a hole in the box!"

My mother stroked my head. "We planted 'if' but not even a cucumber grew.[3] Everybody dies in the end. Get up, get up and go say hello to Grandmother. If you don't get a move on, again, we'll have another fight tonight."

Grandmother was sitting at the kitchen table; as always, very erect on the edge of her chair, as if she wanted to get up and leave that very minute. Her white embroidered handkerchief was sticking out of the sleeve of her black dress. The sadness of the ladybug faded. I thought what a pity I wasn't home when Grandmother came and I couldn't see her dusting off the chair.

Whenever Grandmother came to our house, before she sat down, she would pull her handkerchief from the sleeve of her black dress—she always wore black dresses—and dust the spot where she wanted to sit.

My father would laugh: "My mother is compulsive."

My mother would get angry. "Then why doesn't she do such things in her daughter's house?"

And I would always think of the Indian magician who, a few years before, at the end-of-the-year school party, pulled colored handkerchiefs from the sleeve of his black coat.

When I said hello, Grandmother sighed as she always did, and laid her hand on my cheek. "Why is this child getting skinnier day by day?"

Then she looked at me as if I was going to die soon. Then she turned the same sad look on a pile of grape leaves on the kitchen table. "What leaves! Like velvet! Yesterday I took some for Shakeh. She made wonderful dolmeh![4] Small and uniform like strands of pearls. I don't know if you have the patience to make them or not. If you don't want these . . ."

Grandmother patted the leaves sadly, and my mother's lips tightened in a thin line. She turned to me and said angrily, "Haven't you got homework to do?"

In my room, I closed my Persian notebook and began thinking about the subject of the Armenian composition I had to write: What is our Duty to our Motherland? From the third grade on, when we began to write compositions, every year we wrote about our duty to the Motherland. The first years, our sentences were simple and our duties were limited: learning our native language well, not forgetting our national identity, and asking God in our prayers for the freedom of our country. I thought, Now that I am a sixth-grader, I should write more difficult sentences with more duties.

Like all the other Armenians in our small city, I had seen Armenia only on maps; the old maps in our classrooms or in the big books that the older people had. On the wall of Grandmother's living room was a large map of old Armenia, a gift from Khanom Gregorian. •

Khanom Gregorian was the only Armenian in our city who had actually seen Armenia; and she commanded ever so much respect on that account! She was invited to every engagement party and marriage and baptism, and her place was always at the head of the dinner table. After dinner the guests would sing in honor of the host, would wish the young couple or the child good health and happiness, and then they would ask Khanom Gregorian to tell them her memories about Armenia. Khanom Gregorian, short, and thin, and blue-eyed, would straighten the collar of her dress—her dresses were always milk-white in color—cough a few times as she waited for absolute quiet, and would stare at a saltshaker or a fork or a piece of bread on the tablecloth.

I knew all of Khanom Gregorian's memories by heart, and as soon as she began I knew it would be, for example, the story of the pilgrimage to "Ajmiatsin" Church that lasted forty days, or it was the description of grape-harvesting ceremonies in the vineyards, or stories about her eventful migration from Armenia to Iran. The original plots always stayed the same but the details changed every time.

One night before I went to sleep, Grandmother was reading me *Little Red Riding Hood.* She got to the point where the wolf swallows the grandmother and every time, right at that point, I cried and said, "What if the wolf doesn't eat the grandmother?"

Grandmother laughed: "We mustn't change the story."

I looked at the wolf on the cover and said, "Then how come that Khanom Gregorian, she always changes her stories?"

Grandmother's small eyes grew large. "Don't say 'How come,' say "Why," and it's not 'that Khanom Gregorian,' it's plain 'Khanom Gregorian'! Besides, Khanom Gregorian's memories are not stories! You will understand when you grow older! And let this be the last time you call an older person a liar!" Then she threw the *Little Red Riding Hood* book on the bed and left the room.

It was not the first time that Grandmother had blamed me for speaking colloquial Armenian, but she had never gotten so angry. I picked up the book, trying not to touch the wolf's picture, got off the bed, and put it under the bed, face down. At night, if the picture of the wolf was faceup, I would be afraid and I couldn't sleep. I got under the blanket and thought, When did I call Khanom Gregorian a liar?

I thought I would begin my composition with one of Khanom Gregorian's memories that had a patriotic finale; then you could make the circumstances more colorful and dazzling. If Khanom Gregorian could add more details to her memories every time she recited them, why couldn't I? Then I would finish the composition with a few slogans and some long and difficult words. The teacher of Armenian literature loved long and difficult words.

I began the first sentence a few times and crossed it out. The first sentence was always difficult for me. I thought, I wish Tahereh were here helping me. Like in her other subjects, Tahereh's Armenian compositions were better than those of the rest of the class. In our school there wasn't a single kid who hadn't been scolded by their parents, at least once, after having been compared with Tahereh. "Aren't you ashamed of yourself? The daughter of the Muslim janitor knows your mother tongue better than you do!"

I thought, What would Tahereh write in her composition? Our Motherland was not her Motherland.

I went and stood over by the window and thought about my first sentence. From where I was standing I could see the trees in the graveyard and, among the long weeds, a few tombstones.

The graves behind the church were mostly small, short rectangles with stone crosses. There were bigger graves also, of cut stones, with memorial statues. The only grave whose shape and location were different from the others was a rectangular cube, like a high platform, in the front yard, under one of the church's windows. Nothing was written on the stone. Even Grandmother and Khanom Gregorian didn't know why this isolated stone was called the priest's grave; but on the Day of the Dead, on this grave too, as on the graves in the rear yard, they burned mastic.

I had rarely gone to the rear yard. Once I went with Grandmother after I got over the measles, because Grandmother had vowed that I would go around the church seven times after I get well. I also went a few times after school, because of Tahereh, who insisted, "Playing among the graves is so much fun."

Playing among the graves was not fun for me at all. I was afraid of being questioned by Mr. Principal, and the musty smell and the sight of the moss-covered crosses would make me feel bad. The only thing that could tempt me to go with Tahereh was the statue of the merchant's wife.

On a grave larger than the rest was a life-size statue of a woman sitting on a platform, her head bent over a book she held in her hand. Grandmother said that many years ago, the wife of an Armenian merchant erected this memorial statue on the grave of her husband. The husband was doing business between Iran and Russia. When he died, his wife invited a sculptor to come from Russia and commissioned him to build this statue, which, they say, looks exactly like the wife. One year after the death of the merchant, they placed the statue on the grave, and a few days later the merchant's wife went to Russia forever, with the sculptor.

Time, humidity, and rain had disfigured most of the tombstones, but the marble statue of the merchant's wife was still in very good shape. A few times, Tahereh and I had touched the woman's stone shawl, which covered part of her stone hair and one of her shoulders. The statue was so natural that sometimes I thought I should pull the shawl up and cover her hair or her bare shoulder.

I drew the thick window curtain and went back to my desk. By the time I finished rewriting the composition it was evening. Tahereh was certainly waiting for me.

In the kitchen Mother was folding grape leaves for the dolmeh. I said, "I am going to see Tahereh."

She didn't raise her head, and I understood that she wasn't in a good mood.

I thought up an excuse. "I have to ask her about something."

This time she raised her head. "What?"

I looked at dolmehs, large ones, small ones, piled every which way in the pot. "The thing is . . . I want her to correct my Armenian composition."

My mother straightened up so fast the gold chain around her neck with its jeweled cross bounced up and caught on the button of her dress. "Your Armenian composition to be corrected by the daughter of the Muslim janitor! Shame on you!"

Mother was usually in a bad mood after a visit from Grandmother, but not this bad. Mother would never call Tahereh "daughter of the Muslim janitor." Perhaps Grandmother had gone too far this time, or maybe it was because Father had said that he was coming home late.

I ran my hand over my head. The skin on my head was full of goose bumps. The tiny hairs on the back of my neck were bothering me. I looked out of the window at the balcony and tried to think of a better excuse. The white paint on the balcony railing was peeling, and the leaves of the geraniums in the vases on the window sill were yellowish. I was sure Mother had forgotten to water them. I remembered last winter when we were invited to my paternal aunt's house.

Aunt had put the basket of vegetables she had planted herself in her greenhouse on the table, and when the guests praised Aunt's skill, my father said, "But nobody's as skillful as my wife! In a city where even the rocks blossom, my wife can wither a tree in two days!"

Grandmother and Aunt, who rarely smiled, had burst out laughing.

There was still a pile of grape leaves and dolmeh stuffing on the table. I felt it would be no use insisting. Just for something to say, I said, "Are we having dolmeh for dinner?"

Mother didn't answer. I was thinking of calling to Tahereh from the window and telling her I wasn't coming; suddenly one of the leaves came apart in Mother's hand and the stuffing spilled onto the table. Mother pounded the table with her two fists and said, "Ah!"

Quickly I said the first thought that crossed my mind: "Your dolmeh tastes so much better than Aunt Shakeh's dolmeh."

For a few moments Mother didn't move; then she said, "Go, but come back soon."

I closed the door of the house. I stood there and took a deep breath. A drop of rain fell on my head. The smell of fresh bread was coming from the bakery near the house. I thought of going and buying shirmal[5] bread. Tahereh loved shirmal. Then I thought, If it rains we won't be able to play. On the other side of the street the lights of the lemonade shop came on. Khanom Gregorian was standing behind the counter talking to a man and woman, each with a glass in their hands.

I didn't like the taste of any of the flavors of Khanom Gregorian's lemonades, sour cherry, orange, lemon, but loved her lemonade machine with its three tall narrow glass cylinders with delicate designs of flowers and leaves. On two of the cylinders stood two brass eagles with outspread wings, facing each other. On the wall, above the lemonade machine, was a big oil painting of the two high peaks of the Ararat mountain range: Big Massis and Small Massis. Khanom Gregorian had brought this painting from Armenia. My father, who was a member of the church and school association, said that Khanom Gregorian had written in her will that after her death the painting should be given to the school. Tahereh had asked me several times, "What about the lemonade machine?" and I had asked my father, "What about the lemonade machine?" and Father had shrugged his shoulders.

The man and woman came out of the shop and left. Khanom Gregorian's hand was making a circle on the counter. I knew that she was cleaning the counter with her white flowered handkerchief.

Khanom Gregorian's handkerchiefs were always white and flowered, big or small flowers, red, yellow, or blue. Knowing the names of those flowers was one of our secret games, Tahereh's and mine. When I was in the first grade, the evening of the day I learned the letter "L" in Persian and could write "Tulip Flower,"[6] my father and I went to the lemonade shop. My father and Khanom Gregorian were talking to each other and I was looking at the flowers on the crumpled handkerchief on the counter.

My father said, "He has been the school janitor for years. Now that it is time for his daughter to go to school, it would not be pleasing to God if we were to say that since he is not Armenian she should go to the school on the other side of town. The Association has agreed that the girl should study right here."

My father was speaking the way he did whenever he was practicing his speech for the school and church association at home, or whenever he talked to Grandmother.

Khanom Gregorian put a glass of sour-cherry lemonade in front of me.

I said, "I don't like lemonade. Are the flowers on your handkerchief tulips?"

I said "tulips" in Persian and Khanom Gregorian laughed. "'Tulip' in Armenian is *kakach*."

She turned to my father and got serious. "You are right. It would not be pleasing to God."

I passed through the open door of the school. I ran till I reached the priest's grave. I jumped onto the stone and sat dangling my legs; they didn't reach the ground. The wind was covering the skin on my head with goose bumps. I touched my head and prayed to God that Tahereh wouldn't make fun of me. My back was to the church. The lights in the second-floor classrooms turned off. There was only a yellow light through the open window of the first room on the right. The principal lived in this room. Along the row of the ground-floor classrooms, only the light in the middle room was on; the room belonging to Tahereh and her parents. I stared so much at the school building and the dark windows and those two lights that it seemed to me to be a big laughing mouth, with only two teeth. At first I laughed, but then when I turned my head involuntarily and saw the church, I was scared. The cold and damp of the tombstone were going into my body. Why wasn't Tahereh coming? I looked at the door of the janitor's room, then at the windows of our house. Nobody was at the window. I jumped down and ran.

Tahereh's mother opened the wooden door of their room. Her chador[7] was over her shoulders. She looked at me and smiled; then her hand went up and moved her long straight hair back from her face. Tahereh's mother was taller and thinner than all the women that I had ever seen. She spoke very little and I had never heard her laugh out loud. When she walked it was like gliding over the ground. Every time I saw her I remembered the small waves of the sea that came softly, closer and closer, tickled the shells on the sand and then pulled back slowly. To my twelve-year-old eyes, Tahereh's mother was the most beautiful woman I had ever seen.

As if she felt cold, she pulled her chador over her shoulders and said, "Have you come for Tahereh? Come in. She is saying her prayers."

She leaned against the door. The stones in her pendant earrings were like pomegranate seeds.

There was an acrid smell in the room. Tahereh was in the middle of the room. She had on a flowered chador that reached to the floor. I could only see the roundness of her face. She was looking at the ceiling with concentration. There were no chairs in the room. I sat on the floor and leaned against the wall. Tahereh was now looking in front of her feet.

I was paying so much attention to her praying that I didn't see her father at first. Thin, with a dark complexion, his arms around his knees, he was sitting on the other side of the room, smoking. I wanted to say hello but his eyes were closed.

Tahereh's mother was still leaning against the door, her back to the room.

I stole a peek to see if I could see the windows of our house. I couldn't. I kept looking at Tahereh and thought, What will Grandmother say if she finds out that Tahereh prays?

Tahereh was the only non-Armenian in town who didn't make Grandmother frown when people talked about her. Nobody was allowed to speak colloquial Armenian or use Persian words in Grandmother's presence. Tahereh spoke Armenian with Grandmother and Mr. Principal and the teachers as if she were reading from the Armenian literature book. She went to church with us every Sunday, and just like Grandmother she would close her eyes tight and kneel down and cross herself and read all the prayers and sing the hymns from memory.

In church, my attention would wander. Sometimes I played with drops of melted candle wax in my hand or stared at the light that, through the stained glass windows, shone on the painting of Jesus and Mary. I would feel sleepy because of the smell of the mastic and the hymns of the priest and the deacon, and when I woke up and saw Tahereh praying seriously or listening to the priest's sermon, I would be ashamed of myself and tell myself, "You are not a devout Christian." The same thing Grandmother told everyone, to their faces or behind their backs. Then I would take a deep breath and decide to pay attention and be a devout Christian; and exactly at that moment Tahereh, no matter where she was in that small church, would turn her head toward me and wink or make a face and I would start laughing and forget the priest and the church and faith and sin. For such out-of-place laughter I would get an elbow in my side from Mother or Grandmother, and when I looked at Tahereh, she would be looking at the sanctuary or be busy praying with closed eyes, as if nothing had happened.

Grandmother had often said, "What has become of you that you must learn faith and religion from the daughter of the Muslim janitor!" and the day when, coming out of the church, she saw that Tahereh had a small cross around her neck, her eyes filled with tears; she kissed Tahereh's forehead and never again did I hear her say "the daughter of the Muslim janitor."

Tahereh's mother was still looking outside. She was barefoot and the wind was waving her long black skirt. Without socks, her calves were pale. I thought, Like fog, if I put my finger on her calf it would go in.

At parties whenever the subject of the school janitor was brought up, my father or the other men would say, "What a pity this woman lives with this crazy opium addict." Mother and the other women would pretend they didn't hear such statements; their faces would go blank.

The day Tahereh's father beat her mother and we ran from the uproar to the school yard, my father wanted to interfere and Mother got angry: "What does that have to do with you? If the woman weren't beautiful, would you have defended her?"

Tahereh's father was still napping. I was thinking what an ugly man he was when Tahereh removed her chador, tossed it in a corner of the room, and said "Race you!" and ran.

Before I could stand up and leave the room, Tahereh had reached the priest's grave and was hopping around the stone. Tahereh's walking was never like "walking." She always either ran or hopped or jumped. No boy could compete with her when it came to hopping.

When I arrived at the tombstone I said, "Your prayer is missing!"

Tahereh burst out laughing. I thought, Why is she laughing?

On days when Effat Khanom came to do the laundry, at sunset she would always grumble that "I must go, I'll miss my prayer."

My mother would say, "Well, say your prayers here."

Effat Khanom would say, "That may not be, ma'am."

Once when I was playing cops and robbers by myself in the midst of the sheets and the towels and the clothes on the line, I asked Effat Khanom, "Why don't you say your prayers here?"

Effat Khanom tightened the knot of her scarf under her chin, looked around, and said softly, "That may not be, dear son, there are crosses in this house! My prayer wouldn't count!"

I told Tahereh, "It means your prayer doesn't count. One may not pray with a cross around one's neck."

She put her hands on her hips and said, "Who says I have a cross?"

I said, "You have! I saw it myself!"

She took the chain around her neck and pulled it forward. "Come and look!"

A small Allah hung from the chain.

I said, "Where is your cross?"

She tossed back her braids and laughed: "For school and church I put on the cross, and for prayer-time, Allah."

We both jumped onto the tombstone and sat there.

I asked, "Why do you have both a cross and Allah?"

She shrugged her shoulders and swung her legs. "Because both of them are beautiful." All at once she said, "By the way . . ."

I lowered my head and said, "It died."

She tilted her head to one side and said, "Poor thing."

For a few moments she didn't swing her legs. Then she put her hand in her pocket, took out a piece of shirmal bread, divided it in half, and stuck it in front of me.

I didn't want to think about the ladybug. I showed Tahereh the big toothless mouth. Now that I wasn't alone I wasn't afraid, either of the big mouth or the church, or the rear yard.

Tahereh swallowed the shirmal bread and burst out laughing.

Sometimes I thought Tahereh really was a sorcerer. Among the people I knew Tahereh was the only person who didn't need me to explain things that it seemed only I could see. Like the baby frogs that were hidden in the grass near the harbor, or sunflower seeds, which were like no other seed. When I showed the monsters and angels in the clouds to other people, they couldn't see them and they made fun of me. My mother didn't make fun of me, but I had to show her so she could see, and then I could feel that she didn't think they were interesting. For Tahereh, everything was interesting. The shapes in the clouds, baby frogs, even difficult Persian and Armenian words. Sometimes she would find stones on the shore that looked like human beings or animals and were much more beautiful than my stones. What was more important, Tahereh wasn't afraid of anything. I had learned from storybooks that only sorcerers aren't afraid of anything.

Tahereh pointed at the light in the window of Mr. Principal's room and said, "Like a loose tooth! Like him with his loose leg!" And she laughed again.

One side of the awning of Mr. Principal's window was moving to and fro in the wind.

I didn't laugh. Like all other kids at school, I didn't dare to laugh at Mr. Principal or the awning on his window, even in his absence. Tahereh was the only pupil who wasn't afraid of Mr. Principal. She would walk behind him and imitate his limp, and when she talked to him she wouldn't turn pale and stammer like us. Mr. Principal, too, treated Tahereh differently from the other kids. He would never forgive us for the slightest mistake and he always had to force himself to answer our hellos, but he was always nice to Tahereh. When he was talking to Tahereh, we would see his rare smiles. When he smiled his face would lose its seriousness and grimness, and he would even become likeable. Whenever he pushed back his straight dark hair from his forehead with his bony fingers, it would remind me of the fragile shells I found on the shore, which broke very soon.

Whenever the subject of Mr. Principal was raised, my mother and her friends would say, "It is a pity such a handsome man has a crippled leg." My father and his friends would become quiet, then they would cough; then the subject would change.

Tahereh looked at my head. I was waiting for her to laugh, but she didn't. "You did the right thing shaving your head. I am sure it is easier to wash."

She tossed back her braids and took a deep breath: "I wish I could shave my head like boys. My hair bothers me a lot when I wash my head." One could never predict what Tahereh would do or say.

She jumped down from the tombstone and said, "Let's play hide-and-seek."

I said, "Okay." Then I hesitated a bit. "But we can't go to the rear yard."

Her eyes shone. "You can hide wherever you want to, and so can I! You close your eyes first!"

I put my head on the tombstone, closed my eyes and counted up to one hundred. When I opened my eyes and stood up, it was darker and the lights from the two windows struck my eyes. The wooden door of the janitor's room was moving. I thought, Maybe Tahereh has gone to the room. When I went closer, I heard talking.

Tahereh's mother was saying, "Are you imagining things again? I've told you hundred times the poor fellow is not after me."

The voice of Tahereh's father was slurred and deep: "And you think I believe that! You are waiting for me to die. You are dead wrong! I have no intention of dying anytime soon, and he wouldn't marry you even if you were the last woman on Earth! I know that bunch! They eat the bread of this country, but they don't want to so much as set eyes on us!"

I heard the sound of Tahereh's mother crying; the door to their room was wide open. I felt as though I had done something wrong and I flattened myself against the wall. The chador of Tahereh's mother had fallen and the light illuminated one side of her face. It was like the picture of an angel I had received last Sunday as a gift from the priest.

With one hand she wiped away her tears, then she laid the same hand on my face and said, "Are you looking for Tahereh? She should be around here somewhere."

The wind wiped the wetness from my face. I moved a few steps away from the wall, then I turned and ran.

When I reached the first graves in the rear yard, I stopped and looked around. Tahereh wasn't there. The wind was moving the grass to and fro, and graves appeared and disappeared.

I told myself, "I mustn't be scared! Tahereh must be hiding behind one of the graves."

I shouted, "Tahereh!"

There was no answer. I wanted to go back, but I couldn't. It was exactly like the times I dreamed I wanted to run but I couldn't.

I looked at the statue of the merchant's wife sitting in the middle of the grass. Her head was bent over the book, which could not be seen in the dark.

A hand touched my shoulder. I thought it was Tahereh. I turned. It wasn't Tahereh. It was someone much taller than Tahereh and me. I looked up and saw a pair of frowning eyes and a bony hand pushing a hank of black hair away from a forehead.

A deep voice came out of my mouth, like a dog howling with its muzzle closed. I tried to escape. Grass stems were rustling against each other, and when my eyes fell on the statue of the merchant's wife I saw her with her head up gazing at me. Then her hand went up and pulled the stone shawl over her shoulder. My breath was stopping.

I turned, bumped into Mr. Principal, and ran.

I couldn't control my body. My feet were running, a low howl was coming out of my mouth, my eyes were seeing the raised head of the merchant's wife and the frowning face of the principal, and my hands were pounding on the door of the house. When my mother opened the door I fainted.

There was a bowl of water on the nightstand. Mother dunked a handkerchief in the water, wrung it and laid it on my forehead.

My father was walking around the room. "Didn't he say what happened?"

My mother's bracelets made a sound. "No. He has been very frightened. He has a fever."

"I can't understand why he is afraid of everything."

"Are you going to start that again? Well, he is a kid."

"A twelve-year-old boy is a kid? When I was twelve, I was a real fire-eater."

My mother's bracelets struck the bowl of water. "Oh yes, you ate plenty of fire, didn't you. You are still doing it! Thank God, Edmond is not like you, either in his manners or his appearance."

My father was a short, fat man who didn't at all like to hear that he was short and fat. He sat on the chair and put his feet on my desk. My mother hated that. Father pounded his feet on the table a few times. "That girl certainly scared him. Ha! A twelve-year-old boy unable to handle a girl! When I was twelve . . . It's all your fault! How many times have I said he shouldn't play with this girl! It is a good thing you have only this spoiled boy! He is either in the street or at people's homes."

The wet handkerchief tickled my forehead. My mother said, "God help us, he's started again."

My father still hadn't forgotten my mother's sarcasm about his appearance: "You should learn from Shakeh! She is raising four children instead of one. Her kids are always clean, and so is her house. Arsham is two years younger than Edmond and goes hunting with his father. If your spoiled boy saw a rabbit he would run away."

The bracelets didn't move. You couldn't hurt someone more than this. My mother didn't have any children after me, and even her sister sometimes said, "Instead of smoking all the time and staring at your coffee cup, take care of your household."

My father was still talking: "I am sure the janitor's daughter has done something. I don't want to see him going to her anymore!"

My forehead was hurting from the pressure of Mother's hand. I thought, If they think it is Tahereh's fault, they won't let me see her after school. I looked for a way to clear Tahereh without saying anything about my encounter with Mr. Principal.

I yelled, "Graves . . . !"

My mother jumped out of her seat. "Holy Mary!"

My father was silent for a few moments. Then he roared, "I've said it a thousand times; this is not a fit place to live! That damned graveyard has ruined the kid's spirits!"

Mother caressed my face. She pulled the blanket up under my chin and said, "Sleep, my little boy, sleep."

She stood up, picked up the bowl of water, and went to the door. As she was passing my father she said, "I've told you a thousand times I don't mind! Anytime you buy a house, I'll find a tenant for this place and we'll move out."

Through my half-open eyes I saw my father chewing his mustache and following Mother to the door with his eyes.

I put my head under the blanket. When I put my head out, the light was turned off and the door was closed. I was tired, but I couldn't sleep. I was thinking about Tahereh and where she might have hidden. About whether I had really been afraid of the graves or Mr. Principal. Why did it seem to me that the merchant's wife had her head up? I remembered my aunt saying Father wants to take my mother's house from her. But the merchant's wife was looking at me. She looked like someone. I remembered the wet face of Tahereh's mother and her father's words: "I know this bunch." What did he mean? Why was Tahereh's mother crying? Why didn't I like to go hunting like Arsham? Why didn't people see the shapes in the clouds? I was sure I had just imagined that the hand of the merchant's wife had risen. I went to sleep to the sound of my mother's bracelets.

Next day Mother didn't let me go to school. She brought my breakfast to my room: a soft-boiled egg and bread and butter and hot chocolate. The same things that I liked a lot and Mother rarely had the patience to make for me. She sat on the edge of the bed, facing me.

After every spoonful of egg and every sip of milk I said, "Thank you."

As if I was apologizing for a sin by repeated thanks. Every time Mother and my father fought over me I felt guilty. Mother touched my face a few times and straightened the blanket a few times.

Finally she said, "Stop it! Why are you thanking me so much?" And she turned her head toward the window.

I knew that from where she was sitting she could see the mossy tiles of the church roof and also part of the sky, which was cloudy that day. All of a sudden I felt sad and started to cry. Mother held me tight in her arms for a few moments. The she stood up, picked up the breakfast tray, and left the room. Her eyes were red.

As always, I became numb after crying. I pulled the blanket up under my chin and looked outside through the window. From where I was lying I could see the window of the principal's room; the shades were down. I thought, Is it possible that Mr. Principal might forgive me for what I did yesterday? My older aunt's son who was finishing the last year of high school had many stories about Mr. Principal's toughness. When she heard these stories, Grandmother would say, "That is right. Children should respect the rules."

Mr. Principal had come to our city a few months before my parents got married, and most of the Armenians in our town had first seen him at this ceremony.

Once I heard my mother telling my aunt, "When I came into the hotel lobby, I saw him sitting in front of the entrance, smoking. It was like a painting. He was like someone from another planet, somewhere very far away, or from the very distant past."

My aunt laughed: "Is that why, right at the door, you went into the bathroom and cried for half an hour?"

My mother said, "Don't talk nonsense," and laughed, and I felt she was forcing herself to laugh.

Mr. Principal didn't have a family or a close friend in our city. He rarely went to the places that he was invited to, and after school he spent most of his time in his room. Aside from Tahereh's mother, who went to his room to clean it, the priest was among the few people who dropped by and sometimes stayed in his room for hours. Grandmother said that before he came to our city, Mr. Principal had wanted to become a priest. Many times I had seen him through our windows entering the church at night or coming out of it.

Every time Mother saw that, she would smile softly and say, "What a godly man!"

My father would sneer: "What a silly man! There are better things to do at night." And he would pinch my mother's cheek and laugh.

Mother would push away my father's hand as if she were swatting away a cockroach, and Father would laugh louder.

I woke up with the school bell. I got up and went to the window and stood there. Children were playing in the courtyard. Anush, a hand on her hip, was fighting with one of the boys. Tahereh was there, too, but she didn't raise her head even once to look at my window. The bell rang and Mr. Principal said something to the students, who were in lines. Tahereh's mother went up and down the stairs a few times with a tea tray. School was over and the children left. The teachers left, too, and Tahereh's mother went upstairs with the broom and dustpan. I was sitting sadly on the bed thinking that I had no friends when Mother stuck her head inside the room and said, "Tahereh has come to see you."

Happily I jumped down from the bed.

Mother hesitated a bit. "Don't tell your father."

I turned myself around and thought, What should I show Tahereh first, my toys or my storybooks?

Tahereh came in. She looked around and went straight to the

window. She had her dark blue school uniform on. On the back of her skirt was a big circle in a color different from the rest of her uniform.

I wanted to say something: "The back of your skirt is dirty."

She drew a big X on the glass with her finger and said, "It is not dirty, it is getting worn out."

Then she came back and sat on the edge of the bed. "Every night we spread our bedding on the floor and put it back together in the morning."

She picked up the storybook on my bed and flipped through it.

I said, "You keep it! I have two of them."

She took the book and stood up, and said, "I must go," and left.

Next day I was waiting for Mr. Principal to question me but nothing happened. When I saw him in the hallway and fearfully said hello, he shook his head without looking at me and went on his way. He wasn't paying attention to anything. I said to myself, "If his absentmindedness lasts a few more days, I am saved."

A few days later the Easter vacation began.

My maternal aunt and her husband came from Abadan. With an armful of souvenirs, as usual. For me they brought small colored stickers that I stuck on the Easter eggs; for my father, an English hunting knife, and for Mother, an evening bag with glass beads on it and a big box of early sour cherries. At night, the whole family came to our house. Mother was happy to see her sister and was laughing all the time. After dinner she put a basket of sour cherries on the table and said, "What on earth am I supposed to do with a box of sour cherries?"

Aunt's husband pointed to us kids, who had attacked the basket: "With this army of grasshoppers it will be finished in two days."

Mother yelled at us, "Stop it! You'll get a stomachache!"

Grandmother pushed aside a burned cutlet on her plate with the tip of her fork, and said, "What large sour cherries! They are so good for jam."

Mother was in such a good mood that she agreed with Grandmother: "What a good idea! I will use all of them to make jam!"

Grandmother and my paternal aunt looked at each other and sneered. I saw that sneer. Mother lips tightened in a thin line. When she leaped from her seat and picked up the basket angrily and said, "I'll use all of them to make jam," I understood that she had seen it too.

The next day, Mother said, "Will you help me take out the sour-cherry pits?"

My maternal aunt had gone to see my paternal aunt. Mother said she had a headache and didn't go.

I said, "On condition that I play with the pits later."

She said, "On condition that you don't throw them all over the place."

I would stick the knitting needle in the sour cherry. The pit would come out and drop in the bowl under my hand. Red juice was dripping from my fingers. I was a brave general who was killing the enemy soldiers with one thrust of the spear and would toss their cut-up bodies aside.

In the book my father read sometimes whose pictures my mother had forbidden me to look at: I had seen a strange photograph: the photograph of a hill made of human skulls. I wasn't yet going to school.

Once I asked my father, "What is this picture?"

My father said, "The heads of the Armenians who were killed by the Ottomans."

Just then my mother came in and yelled at my father, "Stop it! He is a kid; he would be terrified."

My father, who was staring at the photograph, said, "There is no difference between kids and grownups; everyone must know what has happened to his people."

When I grew older I understood why, every year, the celebration for my birthday, which was on the twenty-fourth of April, took place a few days before or after. Every year, on the twenty-fourth of April, Grandmother and Khanom Gregorian fasted, went to the church and lit candles.

The smell of jam was all over the house and I was making a hill of the sour-cherry pits.

Late in the afternoon, Mother gave me a jar of jam: "Take this to Mr. Principal."

It was a few days since I had had any news of Tahereh. New toys and visits and return visits had kept me busy. I missed her. I jumped up to go.

Mother pointed at a corner of the room: "First, you pick up the pits!"

The jar of jam in my hand, I went inside the school. There was no one in the courtyard. I went to the janitor's room and peeked

inside. Tahereh's father was sitting in a corner, his head leaning
against the wall, his eyes closed. An acrid smell was coming from
the room. Tahereh wasn't there. Her mother wasn't there either. I
turned and looked at the principal's window. Suddenly I remembered
why I had come. Happy that I would see Tahereh, I had completely
forgotten my fear of facing Mr. Principal. I told myself, "There is
nothing to fear. I am a big boy. My second-trimester exams were
good. And I am almost done with my Easter homework."

I went up the wooden stairs. The second-floor hallway was half-
dark. How different it was from the times when with other kids we
went down the hall, shouting and yelling! It was as if I was seeing
the corridor itself for the first time. It had a high railing on one side,
facing the courtyard, with a few plaster columns full of mementos of
schoolchildren. On the other side were the classroom doors. The
wooden floor was creaking under my feet. How come I had never
heard this sound? The closer I got to the principal's room, the more I
felt the old fear.

I told myself: "I hope he is not there. But if he is? First I say
hello, then I say, 'Mother has sent you this jam.' I shall give him the
jar, say good-bye, and go home. But if he doesn't stretch his hand out
to take the jar? I shall put it on the table. Which table?" I realized
that even in my imagination I was talking to Mr. Principal very book-
ishly.

I remembered that I had never seen Mr. Principal's room. But
Tahereh had seen it. Tahereh said the room was full of books. There
were books on wooden shelves up to the ceiling. She said there was
also a large cross on the wall. I had asked Tahereh, "You mean Mr.
Principal has read all the books?" Tahereh said she was sure he had.
She said that in his room Mr. Principal either reads or writes, and
sometimes he kneels in front of the cross and prays.

As I went toward the room I saw the door was half open. I knew
that I had to knock, but the sound of crying coming from inside confused me. I forgot I was doing something wrong. I stuck my head in
and looked around the room. The first thing I saw was the big cross
on the wall, and then books, in the shelves all around, on the floor,
on the big table in the middle of the room. Mr. Principal was at the
table, his head in his hands.

Next to the table, a woman was seated. The evening light was
shining on her face and I could see her profile very clearly. I remembered the picture of the blessed Mary in the church sanctuary. She

was Tahereh's mother. She was playing with the corner of her chador and crying. She was talking as she cried. I couldn't hear what she was saying. Her voice was soft and tired. Like the times she was talking to Tahereh and me. I knew I shouldn't stay there, but I did.

Mr. Principal stood up and put his hands in his pockets. Then he took them out. With one hand he pushed his hair back from his forehead. With another hand he closed a book on the table. The he came toward Tahereh's mother.

I heard a sound behind me. The wooden floor of the corridor was creaking under someone's steps.

I turned.

It was Tahereh's father. I ducked behind one of the columns.

With his heavy tread Tahereh's father reached the principal's room. He pushed the door open with something shiny in his hand.

For a few moments there was only the sound of the wind twisting in the corridor. Then there were mixed sounds, wailing and crying and things being dropped on the floor.

I was frozen behind the column. I felt something terrible was happening. I thought I must go. I thought I was going. I was passing the school yard; then the house, stairs, balcony, and now I am in my room. It was like the nights when I was thirsty and half-asleep, half-awake, and I imagined that I had gotten up and gone to the kitchen and was drinking water but I was still in bed. I was thirsty.

I heard the sound of the breaking of a glass and then things were thrown in the school yard. Tahereh's mother was screaming, Mr. Principal was saying something in a low voice, and Tahereh's father was yelling, "I'll kill you!"

I moved back, sat on the floor, and gazed at the plaster column. At the bottom of the column something was written that had later been scratched out; then there was a plus sign, again crossed out, then the equal sign, and then a crooked heart with an arrow through it. I heard footsteps on the stairs. A few people passed in front of me, running. My father, Mother, my maternal aunt and her husband. I closed my eyes.

My father and my aunt's husband were shouting, "Stop it, you crazy fool!"

I heard my mother shouting, "It's all this miserable woman's fault!" Then I heard a slap, Tahereh's mother crying, my parents talking and the high voice of my aunt, who kept saying, "God save us!"

As I stared at the heart with the arrow at the bottom of the column, I thought, Whose names were hidden under those scratches? Who was in love with whom? Who didn't want people to understand who the lovers are? The door of the principal's room opened, and Father and my aunt's husband hauled out Tahereh's father, who was crying. Behind them, my aunt was pushing Tahereh's mother.

I peered out from behind the column and watched them till they went down the stairs. At the end of the corridor I saw a shadow. It was Tahereh. I stood up to go toward her, but she disappeared.

The wind was twisting in the corridor.

I went back and looked in the principal's room. He was sitting on the chair with his eyes closed. My mother was standing next to him.

Everywhere there was silence.

Mother wiped Mr. Principal's forehead with a white handkerchief and said, "You ought not to blame yourself. Everybody knows that it is not your fault." Mother never used such bookish language, even in front of Grandmother.

Mr. Principal didn't move. Then he opened his eyes and gazed at the cross on the wall.

Mother paused for a few moments. Then she crumpled the handkerchief in her hand and came to the door.

I went back. My foot struck something. I looked. The red sourcherry syrup had poured from the broken jar of jam onto the wooden floor of the corridor.

When I raised my head I was looking right in Mother's eyes. She seemed to grow nervous for a moment; then she stroked her hair. When she opened her mouth to say something I turned and ran.

Tahereh was not in the courtyard. I looked into their room through the window. Her father was huddled up in a corner of the room. He was whispering and shaking his hands. Her mother was sitting in another corner crying.

I left the window. I was feeling sick. I wanted to cry. I lowered my head and set out. I was scattering sands all around with the tip of my shoe. When I raised my head I saw that I was in the rear yard of the church. Tahereh was sitting beside one of the graves, on the grass. I went over and sat down next to her. She was cutting a long blade of grass to pieces.

Without looking at me she said, "Aren't you scared?"

I pulled a few blades of grass.

Tahereh said, "I don't understand why you are afraid of this place. These people are dead. Dead people are not scary. Could a dead person hit you or hurt you? But my dad hits me and my mother, he hurts us. I am afraid of my dad. No! I am not afraid of him; I hate him! I wish he was dead!" She stroked her cheek with her hand. I looked at her. She was crying. I had never seen her crying. I put my hand on her shoulder. She pulled away very fast, stood up and began walking. There was something strange about her walk. I sat there for a while and cut grass to pieces.

When I went home, Mother didn't look at me. She just told me to wash my hands, eat my dinner, and go to bed. From my bed I could hear the voices in the living room.

My maternal aunt said, "Really! You have to defend such a woman, don't you!"

My father said, "I am not defending her. I do know she is not that kind of woman."

My aunt laughed. "How do you know?"

My aunt's husband said, "So it is your honorable Mr. Principal who . . ."

I heard my mother's bracelets: "Does anyone want tea?"

My aunt said, "God save us! The things one sees!"

Just as I was going to sleep, I suddenly understood why I had thought Tahereh's walk was strange. For the first time she was walking slowly and without any rush. She was neither running nor jumping nor hopping, and for the first time I was alone in the graveyard behind the church.

NOTES

1. Miss. or Mrs.
2. The dialect used in the province of Gilan, in the north of Iran.
3. A Persian proverb meaning what's past is past and one should not think about "could have's" and "would have's."
4. A famous dish made of stuffed grape leaves.
5. A kind of bread made with milk and sugar.
6. The word for tulip in Persian is *laleh*.
7. A woman's outdoor—and on occasion indoor—wrap, covering her whole body.

The Pool

Banafsheh Hejazi

He was not hot anymore. As soon as he put his feet in the water he felt all the heat was flowing out of the tips of his toes. He both liked it and felt it was giving him goose bumps.

Slowly, he dipped his feet farther into the water; the hairs on his feet floated on the water. The hotness of the stones at the edge of the pool passed through his pants and gradually he felt the steam of the heat gathering in his body. The hot sun of the end of Khordad[1] was shining on his head and troubling his eyes. He poured handfuls of water on his thighs and soaked his pants and enjoyed it.

Every once in a while a breeze came and cooled him down and made him think about whether he should jump in the water or not. For a while he kept on pouring water on his chest and rubbing it. He poured a handful of water over his head; water came down along his spine and he felt something like the cool bill of a bird on his spine and felt as he did whenever Kazhal—his wife—caressed his back with her hand. He wanted to think about Kazhal but the weather was hotter than his imagination and the stones at the edge of the pool were burning.

He thought, "I wish Fereydun were here and we could play in the water," like the neighbors who tempted him every afternoon with their noise to go up and watch them from the balcony. "I wish Fereydun were here." Counting today, it was twenty days since Fereydun had gone and left him all alone in this big house. He had spent some of his time working. For a while he had gone to see the workers building upstairs, for a while he had gone to the co-op, and for a while he had watered the flowers, and the rest of the time he had lain down on a comfortable mattress they had found in the desert and slept on it at night, and had thought about Sanandaj, about their house and neighborhood, about unemployment and about Kazhal, and about Kazhal. . . . He had thought about Kazhal and her black eyes and her long hair that she used to braid like two thick ropes and would toss them over her shoulders and about that red headscarf with the flower design, so much so that he felt she was standing in front of him. He thought about Kazhal with her face that had a yellowish tinge and her two round red cheeks, so much so that he saw her sitting in front of him. How often he had touched those strong, skillful hands whose palms were calloused from carpet-weaving. How many times he had taken her hands, which were always sweaty and wet, in his hands. How many times he had taken her in his arms and she had looked down, shyly, with eyes whose lashes in profile seemed to be blond, and had said, "Don't do that Jalal, it is not good, someone might come!"

"Fine, let them come! We are husband and wife, aren't we?"

"Well, yes, but wait for the nighttime, when everybody's asleep. It is not good, people will say we are shameless!"

"Shameless? Fine, let them say so. There is no shame in a lawful act, and by the way, I haven't done anything." When their conversation reached this point, Kazhal would pull away and Jalal would try to fight back that feeling which had started all over his body and was gathering in one place and wait for the nighttime when everybody— his mom, his dad, his brother Fereydun, and his sister—was asleep. At night, Kazhal put their mattress on the roof. She would lay the mattress open behind the bramble bush in the evening so the heat of the sun would get out and the mattress would be cool at night, when they wanted to sleep.

He was really hot. The heat of the sun was truly burning his body. He poured another handful of water over his back and tried to remember Kazhal's fingertips once more. He poured a handful of water over his left shoulder, like the ablution at prayer-time. And ran his hand down his arm.

Then with his other hand he poured water over his right shoulder and let the water flow down. He was following the drops of water with his eyes, watching them penetrate the hairs on his hand and slow down. He felt that his feet were soaked in the water. He moved them and lifted them out and looked at his big toe and his other toes. He spread them and remembered the times his mother took him to the public bath. He remembered how hard his mother rubbed him and scrubbed the soles of his feet with pumice and it tickled, and as he laughed he would cry all the time and his tears and watery mucus from his nose would mix, and intimidated by other women who would yell at him because of his screaming, he wouldn't look up and would wipe his nose with the back of his hand and keep on sniffing. When they came out of the bath he would be like a bouquet of flowers, as his mother used to say. A bouquet of flowers, the palms of whose hands and the soles of whose feet were white and wrinkled, and whose skin was a bit puffy.

Now the skin on his feet had grown a little older.

A bee came buzzing to the pool to drink. Jalal's attention moved from his mother and the bath to the water and the bee. His head was hot. He thought, "I hope my nose doesn't bleed." He raised his head and looked up at the sun. What time was it? He turned toward the garden and the rosebush, where he had hung his watch. For a few moments he didn't see anything; shadowy spots appeared in front of his eyes. He closed his eyes completely and bent over and stretched out his hand to take his watch from the bush; his hand couldn't reach it. He pulled himself farther along the ground but the hot stones pricked his side like needles. He jumped. He brought his legs out of the water. He pulled himself closer. He reached a leaf, took it and pulled it. The leaf tore off. He tried again. He caught a thin stem near him. He pulled the bush toward him. He wanted to pick up his watch, but he changed his mind. He looked at his watch; it was four-thirty. In one or two hours the owner would come; he had only this couple of hours for swimming. They had painted the pool the day before yesterday—sky-blue. He had tried the paint yesterday to see if it had dried. It was dry.

He had washed away the dirt and turned on the water. It had taken them exactly twenty-four hours to fill the pool. The water was limpid like tears.

He put the palm of his hand in the water and scooped up the water and spread his fingers. The water spilled into the pool. He scooped up another handful and poured it over his head. The water came down through his hair, drop by drop. His hair was oily. It was one or two weeks since he had bathed. Maybe it was since before

Fereydun left. He couldn't remember. He had washed himself with just water, in the sun, but he didn't remember taking a bath. He scooped up another handful of water and rubbed it in his hair, like soap; then another handful. He cupped both his hands and took the water and poured it over his head and did it over and over until his hair was completely wet.

His eyes fell on the surface of the water; it was rippling and the sun was playing on it.

The reflection of the clouds had fallen on the water. The clouds were moving and waves had started off as well, and it seemed that the sky was completely cloudy, but the hot sun was still shining. He poured some water under his legs. He had cut off the legs of his old jeans to make it like a bathing suit. His pants felt heavy. His pants were steamy and his body was itching.

"I wish Fereydun were here so we could sprinkle water on each other and keep busy. But it doesn't matter; those days are over now. Tonight Fereydun will come and bring me some news from Sanandaj. I am sure he will come with good news." Fereydun had taken some money with him. The engineer had paid all their wages. The day before Fereydun's departure they had gone shopping and bought everyone a gift.

Last time Kazhal had asked him for two combs with diamonds. He and Fereydun searched high and low until they found them. All that night, Jalal had secretly held those combs in his hand and kissed them and had closed his eyes and imagined Kazhal sitting in the bed and setting them in her hair, one on each side, and laughing. Then he had seen her taking the combs out of her black hair and putting them down above her head and pulling the striped Shushtari sheet over them both. The scene was so vivid that, involuntarily, he had called out to Kazhal, and Fereydun had asked, "What is it? What do you want?"

Now Fereydun was coming back; and he would bring him news from them. Surely Kazhal has asked when he was coming back. In the two years they had been married he hadn't spent so much as three months with her.

Kazhal missed him a lot but she didn't say anything in front of others. Last time, two or three days before he came to Tehran, she was impatient, always crying, and she wanted to come with him. She was asking for all kinds of things; she wanted a child, and she wouldn't be satisfied with just a scarf anymore. He had sent Kazhal a gold picture frame for the photograph taken of them together last time.

He wished he was in Sanandaj. He wished he was in Sanandaj and looking at that photograph on the mantelpiece between those two vases full of plastic flowers. Certainly it would go well with the gold edging of the *cheminée*. He remembered the fans on the *cheminée* with their wool tassels.

The memory of the coolness of their one room saddened him. He was very hot. He jumped into the water.

The water reached to the middle of his chest. He felt cold. He jumped up and down. He enjoyed the touch of the cold water on his body, a kind of pleasure accompanied by pain. His legs, which had been dangling for a while, had gone to sleep and couldn't bear the weight of his body, and the agitation of the water was upsetting his equilibrium. His legs were emptying under his body. He tried to control his body by using his hands. Little by little he felt his legs; now he could stand in the water. He grabbed the metal railing around the pool and bent his legs a bit and the water reached his shoulders. A lazy pleasure began moving from his shoulders toward his waist.

He bent his knees more and while holding on tight to the railing went under the water. For two years he had been working in this building. The day he had come here with Fereydun, they had begun working on this pool and he had always thought about the time when this pool would be finished. Now after having waited for two years he was the first one to set foot in the water. The pool belonged to him; he had a right to it. For two full years he had thought about the time when this pool would be full of water. Especially when he could hear the sound of the neighbor's kids from their pool. Whenever the Colonel dived in the water and taught his son how to dive, this wish would clutch more strongly his heart. He wished the Colonel were there and would teach him how to swim. "How delightful it is to go into the water." He went down into the water again and opened his eyes. The water was so pure, so transparent, and he saw his legs, but they were kind of distorted, and very white. He had never seen his body so white. He saw the hair on his legs waving like river grass. The coldness of the water made his body stiff and the front of his pants was billowing out. The hair on his chest was floating in the water. He couldn't breathe. He stuck his head out. Water came out of his eyes. Water went through his nose and into his throat. He began coughing. He jumped up a little and spat. His spit fell on the brown slippers he had left near the pool. His slippers seemed to be looking at him. They seemed to be walking, toward the pool. His towel—his white towel—was farther away on the stones. He returned and pressed his back to the wall of the pool and opened his hands; his forearm and arm rested on the railing. The weeping willow, right on the other side of the pool, had bent its branches toward the pool and was waving slowly in the wind. The rosebushes seemed withered under the sun. Jalal's eye fell on his watch, and he remembered that the owner might arrive at any time. What time was it? He set out for the other side of the pool. He pushed the sole of his foot against the wall of the pool and threw himself onto the water. He went forward a little and moved his hands one at a time and tried to move his legs like a swimmer. Water was surging under his body. He was halfway across when he remembered he didn't know how to swim and he had reached the deep part of the pool. He stopped and all of a sudden the ground under his feet was not there. He went down under the water. He was afraid. He couldn't breathe. He went to the bottom. It seemed that the floor of the pool was going down. He tried to put his feet somewhere. He moved his shoulders. He moved his whole body. Water was going into his stomach. He closed his mouth and tried not to breathe. The pool had stretched and grown bigger now. He tried to reach the railing around the pool but the walls were moving away. He could see the walls but no matter how hard he tried, he couldn't reach them.

He thought, "Oh, darn, I am drowning. Am I dying?" No, how could he die, just from having gone to the pool? Just because he was bored and didn't know what to do? Because he was hot? Of course it wasn't really the heat; he was bored. The memory of Kazhal had penetrated his skin and his body has grown hot. In fact, he had not been feeling well since morning. Wherever he went he saw Kazhal. When he was having lunch, Kazhal was sitting on the other side of the newspaper they used for a tablecloth and looking at him. When he wanted to prepare tea, it was as if Kazhal had taken the kettle from him and had poured the tea for him. Kazhal had put the dishes away; Kazhal had picked up the newspaper and folded it and kept it for the night. Kazhal had brought him the sugar. Kazhal had come to his arms, Kazhal had hugged him and told him, "Jalal, I want to have a child." Kazhal had embraced him firmly. Kazhal's scent was still in his mouth. Kazhal's lips were firm and a little chopped, because she used to suck them. Kazhal herself sucked her lips all the time but wouldn't let Jalal do that. She said it hurt her. Now Jalal was in pain too. So much so that he had shut his lips tight. Water was coming into his head through his ears. In his head was the sound of the rushing of water. Little by little he felt sleepy and heavy. His stomach had become full of water. It was then that he saw the waves were growing calm and the water was not moving anymore. His eyes opened slowly. The water was quiet and motionless and there was no rushing in his head. His mouth was open but water was not going into his throat, but his rib cage was still hurting. He saw that he was coming to the surface. On the surface the sun was shining. The tips of the weeping willow branches touched his nose. Sparrows were flying in the sky and wisps of clouds were moving. Jalal was sleeping on the water. He remembered his mother who, whenever he got into mischief, would tell him, "I hope to God you sleep on the water!" What a nice mother! How much she had suffered for him and Fereydun, and always grumbling, "Don't go near the river, you will drown!" He and Fereydun, afraid of drowning, played on the beach and never went to the water like the others, so their clothes were always muddy. Mother washed the clothes and used to grumble, "I hope to God you sleep on the water!" Now Jalal was sleeping on the water. So, Mother was not really angry when she was washing the clothes. Sleeping on the water is not bad, it is fun.

He had gone to the pool just in time, before the return of the engineer and his wife. What time was it? Jalal rolled in the water and slept on the water, on his stomach. He didn't hear or understand anything anymore. He lay on the floor of the pool and put his hands under his head and drew his legs up to his heart. Exactly like those nights when, away from Kazhal, he had curled up and had tried to feel, even for one moment, the firmness of Kazhal's body and to take her in his arms. Now he had to sleep; he was not hot anymore.

NOTE

1. Third month of the Iranian calendar.

One Woman, One Love

❧ *Farkhondeh Aqai*

There were no empty seats available at the Golshan Shad-Kam pastry shop. A few customers were standing in a corner eating ice cream; and a few more were buying pastries. Mozhgan and Puran, excited and disheveled, entered the pastry shop. They had come a long way to see Aqa Gudarz. They were coming to this shop for the first time. They wandered around the shop. Only some dried-up cookies were left in the shop-windows. Squeezing Puran's hand, Mozhgan pointed at the man sitting behind the cash register and whispered, "That must be him, the murderer Aqa Gudarz." She went on, raising her voice, "They don't have any pastries left; let's have ice cream."

Their faces pale, they both stood in front of the cash register. Mozhgan ordered two ice creams and searched for the money in her bag. Aqa Gudarz was a short man with gray hair. He had a purple satin half-buttoned shirt on. A gold chain was shining on his gray chest hair. He had a protruding belly, and his face was red. He looked at the girls, took the money from Mozhgan and wrote down "Two fruit-flavored ice creams," and turned to the other customer, who was asking him, "When are you going to have cream puffs?" Aqa Gudarz replied, "They are all sold out. We won't have any more more until tomorrow."

The shop was located on a corner, and the customers used both entrance doors. The girls took their ice creams and waited in a corner

153

for empty seats. They were watching Aqa Gudarz. Puran said, "I can't believe this. How can someone kill a person and go on selling sweets and ice cream?"

"Not one person; two . . ."

During those few days after the murder of Golshan Khanom, nobody talked about this second person. Aqa Gudarz's presence attracted people's attention more than the murder of those two people.

Two seats became available; the girls rushed over and took them. Their mouths wide open and their ice cream spoons in their hands, the customers were watching Aqa Gudarz. They would turn their looks away from him and put their ice cream in their mouths every time he raised his head.

A young man sitting next to the girls turned to his friend and said, "He tells everyone he killed them with an axe and later turned it in, and was released. His business picked up the day after the crime. That's his eldest son selling pastries."

Every head turned toward the shop windows. The son was young with a round face and light hair. He had a shirt on with green and pink stripes. He was putting the cookies in a box. He weighed them, closed the box, and gave it to the customer. The customer was staring at the boy. Puran said, "He looks so much like Golshan Khanom." A young man turned to his wife and said, "Aqa Gudarz has forbidden the boy to close the shop even for an hour. He himself came to the shop to sit behind the counter the day after the crime."

Mozhgan and Puran were two high school students who attended Golshan Khanom's hair-dressing class twice a week. The beauty salon didn't have a signboard and Golshan Khanom never charged for her services. The neighborhood girls would come to her in the afternoon and the woman would teach them all she knew. This was the first time the girls had come to the Golshan Shad-Kam pastry shop. Aqa Gudarz had put his wife's name on the shop. That might not appear so strange these days, but twenty years ago when they first came to this town it took people by surprise. In the old days it was not customary for people to put their wife's or daughter's name on their shops. But Aqa Gudarz, disregarding people's gossip, put Golshan's name on his shop and added "Shad-Kam," "prosperous," to it as well. That was what he always wished for her to be: a prosperous Golshan. Later, however, he was suspected of putting this name on his shop to lure Parviz down there to kill them both.

Two years after he bought the pastry shop, he bought the haberdashery next door, knocked down the divider wall, and enlarged the pastry shop. Although he continued to bring ice cream and some pastries from outside, he built a kitchen underneath the shop and bought a few ovens and refrigerators.

In the beginning, every once in a while, Golshan Khanom liked to come to the shop and sit next to her husband and crack seeds. She would wear her white floral chador[1] and cover her bleached golden hair under it. She would sit next to the cash register and crack handfuls of watermelon seeds while watching the street. Sometimes she brought along her children as well. She would bundle up her two sons and bring them to the shop to sit there and watch the street, the cars, and the people while cracking seeds.

She never paid much attention to the people around her, not even to her kids or Aqa Gudarz, who loved her so much that he had put the shop in her name. He had bought her a piece of land next to the Water Supply Company as well as an orchard at the end of the dirt road by the river. Golshan was his whole life, but the woman always ignored him. She was in a world of her own, somewhere far away. Sometimes she even talked to herself, but nobody suspected she was crazy. She was always well-dressed and nicely made up. It was as if she was always waiting for a guest; a dear guest. The woman was tall and fair-skinned, with high cheekbones and almond-shaped brown eyes. She liked to display her white neck by wearing low-cut blouses. Every day, she would spend hours in front of the mirror trying different hairstyles, wearing her hair down or up, putting in a pin or curling it. She covered her high forehead with a big piece of curled hair to make it look nicer. When she wanted to look modest she would gather her hair up behind her head, leaving two curls on each side to make her look more beautiful. She would wear her lipstick, put on big round earrings, and wear a shiny nail polish with a colorful dress. She would, however, always wear her chador; a white floral chador.

Later, when the boys were grown up, she signed up for a swimming class, then a cooking class, a baking class, and after that, classes for embroidery, beadwork, and lacework. Later she took a beauty class. She liked this class more than the rest. She worked for her own pleasure. The neighborhood girls would come to her beauty salon. She would put on sad music and hum along with the song. She wasn't talkative; she listened most of the time. But whenever she talked, she liked to end her sentences with, "I swear on the life of my three kids." The girls would laugh and say, "But Golshan Khanom, don't you just have two boys?" She would then laugh and say, "I don't know, I was just talking." She would grow quiet, stand in front of the mirror, and check her makeup. Mozgan and Puran always came to her place together and left together. One day Mozgan had asked Golshan Khanom, "Do you know Atefeh, Akbar Aqa's daughter? She has run away from home." Raising her eyebrows, Golshan Khanom asked, "Who is Atefeh?"

"The same girl who once came here with us and you gave her a haircut."

"Oh, yes. I see."

"She got married secretly. Now they have arrested the boy. Akbar Aqa would not give his consent to release him. And Atefeh beats herself up and cries."

Puran had said, "Is that fellow worth all this trouble and ruined reputations?"

Mozgan had said, "All this happened because of love; something you find in poems."

Golshan Khanom had laughed and said, "Should one be a poet to feel all that? I didn't understand what it meant when I was young. But to be honest, now I envy whoever is in love. I enjoy listening to people talk of love. I feel happy whenever I hear people are in love. I laugh with joy. I seldom laugh. But at moments like this I go on laughing. I enjoy talking and thinking of love. To me love is like two souls in one body."

Mozgan had said, "It would sound very convincing if it was Atefeh saying all these things. But it is different when someone older talks about love with such passion."

Golshan Khanom had sulked and replied, as if talking to herself, "It has nothing to do with age. My heart will never get old, because it has never been fulfilled. Believe me, I swear on the life of my three kids." The girls and Golshan Khanom had laughed.

But if Gudarz had heard this, he would have said, "Did you mention that again? When are you going to forget it? When?"

And Golshan Khanom would have answered, "Only when I die. I will forget it when I die."

In the boys' absence, Aqa Gudarz would ask, "Aren't these two your sons?"

Golshan would answer, "They are my sons; but what about my other child who has never seen a mother?"

Gudarz would burst out angrily, "You don't know if that child is still alive or not."

"I know he is alive. He will come one day. He will come and take me away."

Perhaps it was because of what she had said that afternoon when Gudarz entered the shop and his son said, "A stranger has come several times since this morning asking for you," that his body temperature increased and then suddenly dropped. He shivered and asked with a frown, "Who was he? What did he want?"

The son said carelessly, "He didn't introduce himself. He said he is an old friend of yours. He also knew Mother. He asked about her. He said he knows you from Tehran, from Shahpur Avenue."

It seemed like yesterday. The house on Shahpur Avenue with a big green yard and a pool filled with water and surrounded by moss. There were two verandas on each side of the yard with rooms occupied by different families. Parviz's room was in the basement next to the lavatory. He was a schoolboy from the provinces. He was tall and innocent. Every Friday, he brought his clothes to the yard and sat by the pool and washed them unskillfully and hung them on the trees to dry.

In those days, Gudarz was broad-shouldered and of medium height. He had a thick black mustache. He did traditional wrestling and had trained muscles. In winter he would wear a navy-blue woolen coat with eight buttons in front. He used to put on a hat with a brim. In summer he would wear a short-sleeved shirt with a tie or a floral scarf around his neck. His wife, Golshan Khanom, was very young, with two kids. They had the best room in the house. Gudarz was hot-tempered and liked to intimidate the people around him. He would also get into physical fights with his wife. He had divorced her twice and both times had made up with her after a week. Golshan Khanom had grown used to the man's character. She would wear her white chador every day and sit by the pool to wash the dishes or the clothes. In the evening she used to sweep the veranda, spread a carpet on the floor, and put her children there.

Parviz would come back from his classes in the afternoons and go to the faucet by the pool. He would wash the teapot and his tea glasses, and then he would bring his tray of tea to sit under the apple tree and drink it. He would open his book and study. Back then, he didn't know that he would marry Golshan and end up raising her child all by himself.

Tall and strong-looking, with a youthful face, Parviz was now standing at the door to the shop. He had a blue shirt on with a sky-blue jacket and a pair of white pants. His shiny combed hair looked attractive with a few strands of gray hair on his temples. He looked calm. Gudarz was sitting behind the cash register with a wide-open, slackened mouth. The last time he saw Parviz was twenty years ago at the local police station. He had hired people to beat him up. Dried blood had covered Parviz's face. He had made the boy give a commitment to divorce Golshan Khanom. But the boy wanted to keep the child. The police officer had threatened him: "You are a child yourself, what do you want a child for? Do you want me to notify the authorities at your school to expel you?"

Then Parviz had sat on the chair next to the police officer and started to cry. The officer had come out of the room and had said to Gudarz, "He has agreed to divorce the woman, but he wants the child. We can't force him to do more than this." And Gudarz had responded, "The hell with him. I don't want to see him and his child anymore."

Later, everything changed for Gudarz. He married Golshan Khanom again. He quit wrestling and shaved off his mustache. He sold his shop in Tehran and wandered off to different cities without leaving any trace behind. Finally after many years he returned to his hometown and started the Golshan Shad-Kam pastry shop.

He spent every single day of the twenty years in a state of apprehension about Parviz's possible return to them. And now, that moment had arrived. Parviz was standing in front of him. As if he had rehearsed this moment before, Parviz said in a voice louder than usual, "Hello, don't you know me?" And stretched out his hand toward Gudarz. Gudarz got up, looked at his son quickly, and shook hands with Parviz. Their hands were hot and feverish. "Yes, yes. We haven't seen you in a long time." Parviz sat behind a table and the boy brought him ice cream. He had recognized the boy from his resemblance to Golshan Khanom. From the long silence, the boy realized he had to leave them alone. Parviz said, "I wanted to talk with Golshan."

"What talk after twenty years?"

"I have to tell her about her child."

Gudarz didn't say anything. He opened his account book and pretended to be busy. When the boy returned he felt the heavy and suffocating silence in the room was making his heart stop. He didn't know that in a few months he would have to stick an axe in this strange man's chest. He had begged his father, "Not Mother, I can't, I can't kill Mother." And Father had said, "You just help me, I will do the rest." The boy had asked with pale lips, "What will happen to my brother? What is he going to do?" The man had thought of everything: "I will explain everything to him when he comes back from his military service." During the interrogation and at the court he had repeated several times, "I killed them both. With an axe, while they were in bed."

The night of the crime, the three of them were at the orchard by the river. A light was glimmering from far away. It was foggy and dreamy. The mountains and the trees were hidden behind the fog. The sound of the river close by could be heard. The thick autumn trees looked lonely and scattered despite their being next to each other. The black and white hunting dog was staring at them and waggling his tail. "We'd better stay at the orchard tonight." And they had stayed. The boy knew about the plan and the axe had been sharpened.

Gudarz didn't even spend one day in prison. The next day he went to his shop to sell sweets and ice cream. People came in groups to watch him.

Parviz had said to Gudarz, "If it wasn't for the name of the shop, 'Golshan Shad-Kam,' I would never have been able to find you." And then he had added with laughter, "Maybe you never minded my coming back." The first night of Parviz's return, father and son turned off the lights of the shop and pulled down the shutters, while Parviz was standing next to them waiting to go and visit Golshan. Gudarz had told him with a frown, "It's late." And Parviz had answered firmly, "I won't stay for long. Just a few minutes."

Their house was not close, but the three of them walked to the house. They were silent on the way. At the door, the boy knocked. Golshan opened the door. Gudarz entered first and announced, "We have a guest." After him his son entered, then Parviz. Golshan was dumbfounded. She couldn't believe her eyes. She said, "Is that you, Parviz? Where is my son?" And she sat down right at the door, shocked, with a lump in her throat. All these years the man had undertaken the raising of their son with the hope of one day finding the woman. Parviz said, "He is a university student now, second year medical school in the USA."

He took a look at the woman, who was now middle aged but well made up. There was no trace of youth left in her, but she was all the man had imagined, and all that he had imagined of love during the years he had searched for her. She looked more like a mother than a lover. But beyond her looks he could find the essence of love and that which the man had remembered of her. She was his first and last love. The woman spread all the photos of his son that were taken during the different stages of his life out on the table. Parviz said, "I didn't think I would be able to find you this year; otherwise I would have brought him with me."

The woman looked at the photos passionately. The son resembled the Parviz of those years. Parviz was a provincial student who was supported by his father. He was the same age as Golshan. He didn't have any jobs and was not of an age to get married. Gudarz had asked Parviz to marry Golshan so that he could remarry her after the third time he had divorced her.[2] Gudarz had even paid for all the expenses of this marriage of convenience. All this had happened because Gudarz had one day given the documents for the third-time divorce of the woman along with two hundred tomans as her dowry to the landlord to hand them to Golshan. That day, the children's crying had made Parviz come out of his basement door to stand and watch. The other neighbors had all gathered around Golshan. After that day, Parviz had dared to bring fruit and watermelon seeds for the woman and leave the homemade cookies and jams his mother had sent him behind her door. The woman would watch the boy through her window and would come out to sit by the pool to crack seeds.

It was agreed that the marriage would last only one day, but Golshan refused to get a divorce. Parviz never set foot in Golshan and her kids' room. The woman would come down to the basement, and clean and cook for Parviz. Unlike Gudarz, Parviz was not macho and rough. He used to listen to the woman. He always talked to her with passion and excitement. He had an olive complexion, with disheveled hair, a small, elongated nose, and narrow lips. He used to talk with all his heart and soul. He used to look at the woman with admiration. He would encourage her to go to school. He used to bring her books. The woman was exposed to another world and a different kind of man.

Gudarz would come to see his children in the afternoon.

Whenever he brought up the subject of divorce from Parviz, the woman would remain silent; until one day she said, "Don't even talk about divorce; I am pregnant."

That day Parviz got his first beating. Gudarz was waiting for him to come back from school and they ended up at the police station. But they had to wait for the woman to deliver her child. The day the woman came home from the hospital, Parviz was forced to give a commitment at the police station to divorce the woman. But he wanted to keep the child to remember their time together.

Golshan put all the photos together. The last one was of the boy among his friends. She asked Parviz, "Where are you staying tonight?"

"I have a room at the hotel. I am not planning to stay more than a few days."

"Let's go to the orchard with Gudarz tomorrow."

The next day the three of them went to the orchard. Later they did that every day. They would sit on the veranda in the orchard and listen to the roar of the river flowing beneath. They would listen to the cawing of the crows. They would watch the fog that would grow dense and thin as it danced. They would smell the freshly baked bread. Parviz would stir the wood in the stove to relight the fire. His joyful face would look feverish from the heat of the fire. The bubbling noise of the teapot on the woodstove and its steam was a reminder of life, of love and kindness; what the three of them had been denied all these years.

Parviz had said he had not come to stay long, but he did. Golshan had said that she only longed for her child, but that was not all she longed for. Gudarz had promised his son to assume all the responsibilities after the murder, a few weeks later, at the same orchard, in the same room.

NOTES

1. A woman's outdoor—and on occasion indoor—wrap, covering her whole body.

2. According to Islamic divorce law, if a woman is repudiated three times, she has to marry another man and have sex with him and get divorced before she remarries her first husband.

That Day

❧ *Nushin Ahmadi Khorasani*

S he puts on her blue jacket and white pants. She seems anxious. The man is worried for her. An hour has passed after noon. In haste she finishes dressing up and putting her makeup on. She has to get to the meeting place before the others, because she wants to take part in organizing and setting up. The man walks worriedly around the room with a false smile on his face to hide his anxiety and says, "It's a long time since you put on makeup, isn't it?"

The woman, however, can detect the transparent anxiety on the man's face. Blowing him a kiss, she searches in her handbag. She takes all the addresses and phone numbers of friends and acquaintances out of her handbag; all clear!

"Must you go now?" the man asks repeatedly, and adds, "I'll get dressed right now and give you a ride." The woman refuses. "No, Ramin, thanks, better not take the car out; they are watching the traffic; they might get suspicious and ruin the day for us. I'd better take the bus; don't worry about me."

"At least I can come and hang out around that area. If something happens, God forbid, I can at least be there to ..."

Before he finishes his sentence, the woman reminds him to take care of the child: "Don't forget to turn the TV on for Golku; she likes the children's programs a lot. Don't forget, dear. There is no need to worry."

During the meeting last week, I noticed all my friends looked worried. "Try not to give the address over the phone; be sure to notify people by going to their houses."

I must admit, I wasn't at all apprehensive until Friday. Akram is too cautious; this is not such a complicated case; besides, the enforcers of the laws are preoccupied today. On Friday, though, when I walked out of the house, as I was putting my black overcoat on over my suit and my navy-blue headscarf on my head, the strange silence on the street made me panic. Even our neighbor, Amir Khan, who always sat on a stool in front of his house to tease the kids, was not there. I thought, "Well, today is Friday; maybe Amir Khan never comes out on Fridays." I wanted to calm myself with this thought. The cold, sneaky wind blowing through the buildings in the street penetrated my bones. Hearing the roar of the wind in my head, I started walking in haste. The cold of the month of Esfand,[1] the sight of the dry trees, and the thick clouds in the sky had given a gloomier look to the city, as though the dust of sorrow had been sprinkled over the crooked, smoke-covered brick buildings of the city.

"Stop crying, hurry up, quick, move quickly, get in the patrol cars. Stop crying. This is no time for sobbing."

"Who's crying, mister? I just want to know if you have permission to enter the house. How can you just enter people's houses? This is not right. Do you think you can do as you wish? Go on, get lost! You can't enter this house without an official permit; put your gun away."

The cawing of a crow distracted me; I thought, "What childish thoughts; why should they raid the house? I must be paranoid; Golbarin is right, though, we are the ones responsible for this."

The wind was blowing hard and pulling up the hem of my overcoat. Wastepaper and garbage were dancing in the air. Two patrol cars were moving in opposite directions. I was cold. It felt as if dozens of inquisitive eyes behind the windows were watching me. As soon as I saw the bus in the station, I started running, holding the hem of my long overcoat in order to move freely. When I got on the bus, I collapsed onto an empty seat. There were only four people on the bus. An old, dark man and a relatively young man with a child were in the men's section in the front, and two women were sitting comfortably in the women's section. As I sat on my seat, one of the women started complaining: "It's about forty-five minutes that this heap of junk hasn't moved. He says he doesn't have enough passengers. Nonsense! What should we do if there aren't enough passengers? Wait forty days and forty nights?"

The driver, who was sitting comfortably on his seat smoking a cigarette, shouted, "Oh, man, they have sent the women to the back of the bus so we can't hear their grumbling, but God preserve their voice, it's as if they have swallowed a loudspeaker. . . . Okay, lady, we are taking off, she's been grumbling nonstop . . . God be praised . . . and this is my weekend."

The soldier in charge of the tickets looked at the complaining woman and me. I was about to say something when the bus started to move.

I was sitting next to the window looking at the big yellow posters on the walls around the square. "Participation in the election is a religious duty, obeying the leader, supporting . . . the Society of Combatant Clergy. . . ." The walls were covered with election campaign posters and different pictures. The posters with lifeless colors were pasted on the wall every which way. Among the green and purple posters, one could also see announcements about women candidates, whose black veils had covered the entire surface of the posters, allowing only their downcast eyes to be visible.

I said to myself, "Why should these two days coincide? It was our bad luck!"

The bus was moving, and it seemed as if the pictures were moving as well. The heads on the pictures were separating from the bodies, moving, and colliding with other posters of hairy faces, who were insolently staring at the viewer. The pictures looked alike: round black beards, serious-looking oval faces with a piece of cloth tied around the head. It looked as if they were all pictures of the same person.

I was probably keeping my mind occupied with these images to avoid seeing the armed Revolutionary Guards, the *Pasdars,* who were standing at the intersection in their dark green uniforms. The usually crowded city looked like a military graveyard with cohorts attending a funeral.

Two elderly women got off at a stop on the way. A few stops before Revolution Square, a petite woman in her thirties got on the bus. As soon as she entered the bus, her perfume filled the air. I glanced at her; she was wearing heavy makeup, but one could easily see the anxiety on her face. A familiar, mutual, and heartfelt feeling awakened in me. I wanted to initiate a conversation with her. The truth was, I wanted to read her inner thoughts. I was curious to find out if she had a destination similar to mine on this day. Yes, she definitely has a plan for today. One can see it on her face. I realized this as soon as she got on the bus.

I was immersed in these thoughts when she got off the bus on Vesal Avenue. I looked around; there was no one left on the bus except me, and I got scared: "If the Revolutionary Guards approach me, I had better act calmly or else it might lead to a harsh confrontation; no, a catastrophe must be prevented. I would tell them that I have invited all the people. 'If you want to arrest anyone, I am the one. Nobody here had any idea why they were invited; honestly, they did not know.'"

When the bus reached the last stop, at Revolution Square, the woman got off in haste.

It was still a long way to Guisha; she had to take another bus. She crossed Revolution Square. The asphalt seemed darker to her, and the statue in the middle of the square looked sulky and upset. The nipping cold made her tie her scarf tightly. She picked up speed in order to reach the bus station faster. There was no sign of the usual hustle and bustle of traffic and pedestrians in the square. The sound of the radio coming through the loudspeakers installed at the four corners of the square repeatedly reporting the vast participation of the people in the election was annoying to her ears. A military march in the background was spicing up the report. The woman kept on walking without paying any attention to the state radio.

The thick clouds looked so dark, as if the air had been sprayed with gray color. It seemed as though the night was near. I looked at my watch; it wasn't three o'clock yet. It felt like the distance was stretching. The wind kept on blowing, making my eyes and nose watery; I had to keep wiping my tears away with a tissue. I still had to walk about five minutes to get to the side street next to the square. As I was struggling against the wind to hold my overcoat and scarf in place, I noticed three women in black veils approaching me along the empty street. The strong wind was blowing on my face, slowing my movements. My anxiety increased: "Have they found out? Why are these women coming toward me?" Holding my head up, I continued on my path with firm steps. It's been quite a few years now since I have learned to present a calm and dignified appearance, despite an inner turmoil. The three women finally got closer to me. I was trying to stop my tears, but since the wind was blowing right on my face, it was impossible. One of the women looked at me with surprise; she probably thought I was crying. The three of them had their backs to the wind and could not feel it. Two other women passed by me with reluctance. They were staring at me from head to toe. I tried to look at them in the eye. They finally passed me and I was relieved.

When the woman arrived at the station, she noticed an old, bent woman sitting on the sidewalk, waiting for the bus. She waited for about twenty minutes. But there was no sign of the bus. The old woman got up with difficulty and came closer to the woman: "It's about an hour and half that I've been waiting here, but the bus hasn't showed up yet; I don't know what is wrong. What is the time, dear girl?"

The woman looked at the old lady in surprise: "Well, Mother, why didn't you say so earlier? Perhaps the bus won't show up at all . . . what? Time? Yes, it's past three."

"If I had told you earlier, dear, you wouldn't have believed me. I go to my daughter's house every Friday to visit my grandchildren. I always go this way; I don't know any other way; I am afraid I might get lost . . ."

"Mother, don't you know today is Election Day? If the bus hasn't showed up yet, it probably won't come at all. Take a cab or go back home. Do you want to take a cab with me?"

Slowly, walking back to her spot, the old woman said, "What? Go back home? Do you know how many buses I have to take to get home? No, dear, the bus will definitely come. How could it not come?"

I really wanted to accompany the old woman; perhaps it made me feel safe. But it was too late, and it was no use insisting. I crossed the street. At the intersection, a few cabs passed by me. I waited for about a quarter of an hour until finally an orange-colored taxi stopped in front of me: "I won't go all the way to the end of Guisha; get in if you want. . . ." I got in immediately. I wanted to get there before everyone else. It was now past three o'clock, and I wasn't there yet. The car heater was on; it warmed me up, and I felt relaxed. My muscles felt relaxed, I felt better. I wanted the taxi ride to take longer so I could enjoy the warmth inside the car more. In my mind,

I reviewed the plans for the day: "It's great, I hope everything goes well and nothing happens."

I looked at both sides of the street through the car windows. I noticed the driver was watching me in the mirror. That look, as always, was oppressive and offensive. This time, though, one could sense, in the depths of this look, astonishment at the presence of a woman alone, out in the streets on such a day, with some makeup on—and of course a worried look. For a moment, I thought of going back home. I remembered what Ramin had told me earlier. My apprehension had increased, and I felt something bad was about to happen. At this point the driver's question brought me back to myself. "If you like, I can—" Interrupting him immediately, I frowned and very firmly, without looking at him, said, "Thank you, sir, a bit faster, please, I am late; I have to get to the hospital," even though I didn't know if there was any hospital in Guisha at all. The sentence came out of my mouth spontaneously. I think I said this to give the driver a kind of a warning. Or perhaps I was justifying my being out alone on such a quiet day.

He dropped me off somewhere in the middle of Guisha Avenue. I now had to walk up the hill to get to Sepideh's house. I looked around to see if I could find a familiar face. A big dog suddenly appeared in front of me and started to bark. I got scared, and I couldn't breathe for a moment. Instead of moving to the side, I spontaneously leaped forward. The dog had gone away. As I was trying to control myself, I saw two young armed Revolutionary Guards standing in front of the mosque. I was trying to breathe normally. Seeing the Revolutionary Guards, I immediately pulled down my scarf to cover my forehead. I took the appearance of the dog as a bad omen. I passed by the officers as the blowing wind, together with the barking of the dog and the loud sound of the military march coming from the mosque's loadspeakers was banging in my head. I took a peek inside the mosque. Aside from a few election officials in civil outfits, the veiled women whom I had seen before and a few old men, there was no one else there. As the patrol car passed by me, I noticed Paghah's husband, Khosrow, driving his car in the distance. Afshin was sitting next to him. Seeing them made me feel confident. But I crossed the street, showing no reaction as though I didn't know them. When I reached the alley, I saw Fargol's tired and determined face. She was in her black overcoat and carrying a black bag. A smile came to my face as I saw her. Fargol made a turn toward the alley where

Sepideh's house was; maybe she hadn't seen me. I slowed down intentionally for Fargol to enter the house before me. We shouldn't enter at the same time, I thought; it's not safe. Finally I rang the third-floor bell of Sepideh's house in total panic. The door opened at once. I was in the middle of the stairway when I saw Mahnaz coming toward me from upstairs. "Where in the world have you been, Shadi? You are very late; everyone is here; we got very worried. . . ."

Seeing Mahnaz and hearing her warm voice, I took a deep breath of relief, kissed her and said, "I saw Khosrow and Afshin." "Yes; they are driving around the house to let us know as soon as they see anything suspicious. This certainly wasn't part of our plan." "The patrol cars are driving around also," I said. "They might notice them; this is not safe; it might make them suspicious." "Don't worry now, let's go in the salon; they are all here, about a hundred and ten people, can you believe it, Shadi? A hundred and ten. . . . What should we do if they suddenly raid the place?"

Sara opened the apartment door. As the door opened, a pleasant warmth caressed the skin of my frozen face. Sara looked cheerful in her orange outfit; handing me a small bouquet of flowers, she said with a kind smile, "Hello, Shadi, congratulations. Here, put it on your shirt. Why are you so late?" We kissed each other. Her smiling face and perspiring palms revealed the conflicting moods she was in. She always had sweaty palms whenever she was anxious. I held her wet hands in my cold hands and thought, "I do hope nothing happens. No, nothing will happen. These worries are all caused by the cold weather." The salon was crowded with women in their colorful dresses, sitting next to each other. A small bouquet of flowers was visible over the dresses of red, blue, white. . . . The pleasant fragrance of different perfumes had filled the air. Several baskets of flowers in the middle of the room were adding to the splendor of the mixture of cheerful colors. I took off my overcoat.

Before anything else, I went to the ladies' bathroom and quickly tidied up my disheveled hair and refreshed my makeup. The worry would not let go of me. Sepideh and Sahar were standing in the middle of the room. Sahar's golden dress next to Sepideh's sky-blue skirt and blouse brought back for me the memory of eighteen years ago at the seaside. I had just met Ramin then. After that year, I never saw the sky and the sea that color.

Sahar's voice inviting everyone to silence brought me back to myself. The crowd quieted down. All eyes were looking at her.

Sahar's usually innocent face and voice had a firm and serious tone today. After inviting everyone to be quiet, in a loud, strident voice she said, "On this eighth day of March, International Women's Day, I congratulate you all, my dears."

She hadn't yet finished her sentence when a roar of joy and clapping arose from the crowd. The roar was so loud, it gave Shadi goose bumps. Everyone except her was clapping so hard that the room was vibrating. Her frozen hands moved spontaneously. A smile came to her lips and along with the others, slowly and then with all her strength, she started clapping; with all her strength, so that all the muscles in her body started shaking. The vibration and the pleasant warmth caused by this were melting her frozen body. She then held Sara's hand, on which the sweat had dried by now, and said to herself, "No matter what happens today, it is worth it!"

NOTE

1. Third month of winter in the Iranian calendar.

Butterflies

Mansureh Sharifzadeh

"Where are you off to in such a hurry?"

Hosseini turned and saw Ms. Mahmudian; she was holding her wet hands away from her body. "I was at the library," she answered.

Ms. Mahmudian shook her head. "You are either at the library or busy reading books." Then, pointing at her glasses, "Look at you with these glasses; they are as thick as the bottom of a glass." She rubbed her nose with her fingertip. "Why don't you have surgery to get rid of your glasses?"

"After two Caesarian sections, the thought of surgery sends shivers up and down my spine."

"Then wear contact lenses; otherwise you will end up with a deformed nose."

"I never thought of that."

"I know a doctor; I'll give you his number; make an appointment to see him this week."

"I'll think about it."

"Don't 'I'll think about it' me; when I tell you to wear contact lenses, just say okay."

Hosseini smiled. Pointing to the end of the hall, Ms. Mahmudian continued, "Let's go to our office for a while; there is no one there."

"Some other time."

"Come on! Let's go."

Followed by Hosseini, Ms. Mahmudian crossed the corridor. A man coming from the front passed by and greeted them. Hosseini greeted him back. He was a tall man who always wore well-tailored suits. Hosseini always responded to this man's greetings, although she didn't know him that well. When he was far away from them, Ms. Mahmudian turned to Hosseini and asked, "Why did you say hello to him?"

"Shouldn't I have?"

"No; didn't you see I ignored him?"

"I didn't notice."

"He looks as though he wants to eat a woman with those eyes." Her white complexion was turning dark blue. "You know Tavaniha? All you have to do is say hello back to him, then he will have thousands of other requests. . . ."

"But I have always said hello back to him and he has never—"

"Listen to my advice. In this place you just turn and look at the walls whenever you pass by someone; just pretend you don't see them."

They reached Ms. Mahmudian's office. She opened the door and stood aside. "Please, come in."

In the room, Ms. Mahmudian took a tissue from the box and dried her hands. She then pointed at the desk next to the door: "You see, they have put a new desk there again."

"A newcomer?"

"No, an old-timer. There is not enough air here for three people, let alone four."

"Who is she?"

"You don't know her. She took a leave of absence after having a child. She is back now. She has a two-year-old son." Frowning, she continued, "All day long she talks about her son's diarrhea or his constipation. I don't understand. Looks like women with kids don't have anything else to talk about." Ms. Mahmudian went to her desk. Her desk was covered with lots of papers and receipts. She turned her desk lamp on and held her hands under it. "My hands are allergic to cold water." She showed her hands to Hosseini. "See how red they are. God knows when they will start the hot water in the pipes." She then said, "Why aren't you sitting down?" She picked up a chair against the wall and put it next to her desk. "If I am not mistaken, all seems to be going well with you. Perhaps that's why you don't call."

Hosseini sat down. Ms. Mahmudian tucked a lock of her bleached hair under her scarf. She then sat on her revolving chair with her legs crossed. "You must be feeling relaxed these days to have checked out so many books from the library."

Hosseini put the books on Ms. Mahmudian's desk. Ms. Mahmudian opened her drawer and took out a round tin box decorated with pictures of chocolates wrapped in colorful shiny paper. She opened the box and held it in front of Hosseini. "My brother has just sent them with a perfume and two lipsticks." She continued with a smile, "Too bad you are not into putting on makeup; otherwise I would give you one of the lipsticks." Hosseini took a chocolate and thanked her. "Take more, for your children. I won't even touch them; I am on a diet," Ms. Mahmudian said. She then put a few more chocolates in Hosseini's lap. "Are you afraid you might gain weight?"

Hosseini put the chocolates in her pocket.

"Would you like some tea?" Ms. Mahmudian asked.

"No, thanks," Hosseini answered.

Ms. Mahmudian lay back in her chair and went on, "I was in your room a while ago, but there was no one there."

"They went to the bank."

"Why didn't you go?"

"I had to go to the library. I asked them to cash my paycheck for me."

"Saidi and the others?"

"Yes, they insisted."

"So you have become very chummy with them."

"They're nice kids; last week we went to a play together."

"So why didn't you invite me along?"

"Rostamkhani said you don't like the theater."

"She is wrong. On the contrary, I love theater." Holding her head up, she frowned: "How would she know?"

"She said you told her once that people who sit for hours staring at the stage must have nothing better to do."

"I meant to be sarcastic because she is in the office all day and spends all her evenings at the movies and theaters."

"Her husband is a director."

"I know, but what does that have to do with it? The husband of my office mate, Mrs. Azimi, is an artist, but the poor woman runs around and works like a dog." Shaking her head, she continued, "If you see her hands, they look like the hands of a common laborer, all because of hard work. And the way she looks . . . like a maid."

Hosseini said, "She gets guest complimentary tickets. She took us with those tickets."

"Nonsense; she is afraid to leave that man of hers alone." Shaking her head again, she went on: "She covers her face with thick layers of foundation and pretends it's her own natural complexion." She put her hands around her neck and continued, "These men, they all like coquettish women; if they end up with a modest woman like you, they don't even want to glance at her." She tugged the end of Hosseini's scarf. "Well, girl, pay some attention to your appearance. Wear a smaller scarf. What is this overcoat you are wearing? It looks like a priest's robe."

Hosseini sat up straight. Ms. Mahmudian continued, "A man's love for a woman lasts for two years at most; then he starts whining."

"As a matter of fact, my husband does like modest women."

"He is pretending, my dear. He was flirting with that Ms. Rostamkhani when he came to pick you up yesterday. He was in seventh heaven; he was all smiles."

"My husband?"

"Yes, my dear. According to a friend of mine, no man can resist that Rostamkhani."

"That's very strange!"

"Not at all. That woman is a witch. She has bewitched everyone with her sweet words. Though she is a newcomer, she has pushed all the old-timers aside. I would just have to teach her a lesson."

"But Ms. Rostamkhani was saying nice things about you."

"Nonsense. She doesn't realize that I know she has been talking behind my back. Ms. Najafi, my office mate"—she pointed at Ms. Najafi's desk next to the window, a big brown desk with books neatly arranged on it; she then continued—"she is related to Rostamkhani's husband. She told me Rostamkhani keeps asking her how I manage to live all by myself." Holding the edge of the desk with her fingers, she came closer to Hosseini and said, "I would not have gotten a divorce if I had given in to men's power so easily, like you. There are a lot of men who have their eyes on me. The man we just saw in the corridor, Mr. Bozorgmehr, is crazy about me. . . . "

Hosseini looked at the wrinkles on her forehead visible under a thick layer of foundation. Ms. Mahmudian got up and went toward the window. She looked outside for a moment and said, "They are on their way back."

She then frowned, cut a leaf from the twining plant behind the window, and returned. She sat behind her desk again and crushed the leaf in her hand. Her fingers turned red. Pointing to her fingers, Hosseini said, "They are red."

Ms. Mahmudian opened her fist. "You see its juice is red. Like blood." She tossed the crushed leaf in the wastebasket, took a tissue, and cleaned her hands. "I'll grow you a cutting."

"Thank you."

Hosseini reached out to pick up her books. Ms. Mahmudian said, "Stay a few more minutes." She then took out a plastic bag from her big leather purse and put it on the desk, took a plate out of her drawer and emptied the contents of the bag onto the plate, and held four tangerines out to Hosseini. "The easiest fruit to eat."

Hosseini took one. Ms. Mahmudian continued, "I liked you from the first day I saw you. You were in such a rush, do you remember? I was starting my car. I don't know why, but all of a sudden you ran back toward my car."

"I had left my books."

"As soon as I stopped, you fell on the hood of my car. When I got out of the car, I noticed your face was pale; you were scared, but you kept saying 'It's okay.'"

"I didn't want to bother you."

"I really liked you. When I heard you were a new employee in our office, I decided to protect you. You see, here people don't get friendly so easily."

She looked into Hosseini's eyes: "There is something in your eyes that makes people like you. Remember? I laughed, you laughed too. Then I gave a you ride. . . ."

She sighed and said, "Those were the days. . . . We'll try to have days like that again, if you want, we'll try again . . ."

She shook her head: "Ever since you committed yourself to this damned project, you don't even come to say hello, let alone—"

"I'm very busy."

"What is this project, after all?"

"The influence of Persian literature on the West."

Ms. Mahmudian sneered: "Talking about the influence of the West on the East is something, but God only knows what will come of this stuff."

"It may surprise you, but Goethe wrote his *West-Eastern Divan* influenced by Hafez. Fitzgerald wrote so many poems inspired by Khayam, and . . ."

"Whatever, why are you killing yourself for it? Is this your first job?"

"I used to teach before. But then I got laryngitis. I was told teaching is not good for my throat, and I came here."

"So you are very inexperienced."

She got up and stood behind Hosseini. She put her hands on Hosseini's shoulders. "Why didn't you go to the theater with me?"

She then leaned against the metal bookcase by the wall. "What play did you say it was?"

"*Uncle Vania.*"

"Oh yes, by Brecht. It has a very interesting plot. Especially—"

"It's by Chekov."

"What are you talking about? It's by Brecht. I am sure."

"But . . ."

"How was it anyway?"

"It's too bad you weren't there."

"No, I mean, how was the performance?"

"Except for a couple of actors, they were very bad. They had put a swing in the corner of the stage. The professor's wife kept throwing herself onto the swing and uttering aphorisms to her lovers. Think of it, a swing in the guest room."

"How tasteless!"

"These Iranian directors have no talent. They ruin the plays with their stupidity."

"But films are getting much better."

"It's all the same. All they think about is the box office. That's all."

Ms. Mahmudian sat on her chair and asked, "Are you going again this week?"

"We have made plans to go to the mountains this week."

"Just the three of you?"

"No, with our families."

"How do you dare to take your children . . .?"

"We always take them mountain climbing."

Ms. Mahmudian lowered her voice: "That's not what I meant." She then looked around and leaned closer: "Don't be fooled by her pretending to be so nice; she is full of complexes." She shook her finger and said, "See, she hates all children because she is childless." Lying back on her chair, she continued, "I saw Mrs. Afkhami in the corridor a few days ago. You know, she gave birth to twins."

"I don't know her that well."

"How can you not know her? She is the receptionist. She has just highlighted her hair. She has burnt her hair just because she has been too stingy to have it done at a hair salon."

"Oh yes, now I know who you are talking about."

Ms. Mahmudian shook her head: "Well, anyway, I saw her in the corridor, I congratulated her, then Saidi passed by and asked why I was congratulating her; for her hair? No, for her newborn babies, I told her. She then told me that trouble doesn't require congratulations. She couldn't hold her tongue; she was bursting with jealousy." She took one of the tangerines and told Hosseini to peel hers. She then continued, "Well, I don't have any children either, but I love them. I recently went to the orphanage to adopt a child. But they told me they don't give any children to single people."

She sighed and peeled her tangerine. Hosseini said, "But she has waited in line so many times to get milk for my children."

"She probably did that to make a good impression."

"In any case, she has included me in her circle of friends."

"You are so naïve. You probably have forgotten by now, you thought your former office mates were friends with you as well. But they were pretending."

"Well, I was wrong."

"These women are pretending as well. Especially that Saidi . . . I know her well. She doesn't get friendly with anyone easily. Don't you know the story of that girl, Tabibzadeh?"

Hosseini nodded. Ms. Mahmudian went on: "When she came to this office, nobody knew her. Her desk was in the same place where yours is now. Saidi started to make friends with her, and she won the girl's trust."

She bent over to throw her tangerine peels in the wastebasket. "The poor girl had nobody. She had just come back from England. It was during Ramadan. She had an ulcer and couldn't keep the fast. Saidi made her a cup of coffee and put it on her desk. She then called the authorities upstairs to tell on her."

Hosseini swallowed her saliva with difficulty. Ms. Mahmudian put a few slices of tangerine in her mouth and gestured to Hosseini to peel her tangerine. She swallowed the tangerine and continued, "She gave the poor girl hell until she quit her job."

"You mean Ms. Saidi did that to her?"

"Yes, who else?"

Ms. Mahmudian laughed and said, "It's not a big deal; you shouldn't worry while you have me for a friend. I have lots of connections. I'll ask them to put you in another room if things don't work out where you are. . . ."

She then moved close and said quietly: "I have never mentioned this to you, but remember when your former office mates were bothering you?"

"I'll never forget it."

"By the way, what did they do to you that made you not want to stay in the same room with them?"

"They would knock the vase over on my desk, the water would spill on my papers and . . ."

"Well, how do you know they did that?"

"Ms. Moradi said so."

"What a sneak that Moradi woman is. She has been in this office for four years and we still don't know a thing about her."

"After what her ex-colleagues did to her, she doesn't trust anyone."

"No wonder she keeps to herself so."

"She used to tell me that it is impossible to find a real friend in the workplace."

"Nonsense, I have friends in this office who are closer than sisters to me."

"She used to say that all her troubles are because of her beauty. Just like butterflies who are dried and put in a frame because of their beauty."

"How vain of her! Who said she is beautiful?"

"I think she looks like a goddess. Especially her gray eyes . . ."

"If someone ugly had said that, I could understand. But you, why are you such a weak character? What is wrong with you? Look in the mirror. True, your eyes are not blue, but these black eyes of yours are a thousand times more beautiful than her blue eyes."

Toying with the telephone wire, Ms. Mahmudian went on: "Anyhow, that day when I took you to their room and asked them to put your desk there, she didn't seem to be happy about it at all."

"She didn't talk to me for a few days after that."

"Each time she saw me she said she is afraid of newcomers. That now they have to watch for what they say and do."

"Well, she told me about it later and apologized a great deal."

"How sneaky; it was only a few days ago she told me they are so afraid of you that they have to go into another room to make their private phone calls."

"Saidi said that?"

"Don't ever believe them; they say one thing to your face and another behind your back."

Ms. Mahmudian looked at the window. She was putting the tangerine slices in her mouth and eating them.

Hosseini also leaned forward and looked at the window. Two pigeons were quickly eating the bread crumbs in the flower box on the windowsill.

Ms. Mahmudian said, "Ms. Najafi throws them bread crumbs when she eats her breakfast."

"The janitor also throws bread crumbs to the pigeons every day."

"Do you know why?"

"Well, after all, in this cold weather the pigeons . . ."

"Think of it, at the end of the week, she takes two of the fat ones home." She then pointed at her neck with her finger, and laughed.

Hosseini sat up straight. "You mean, those pigeons . . .?"

"Yes, ma'am."

"My God . . . how cruel . . ."

"Well, she has to feed her children somehow in this inflation. You know how many kids she has?"

Hosseini looked at her watch. "Well, excuse me, I have to—"

"Not until you have finished eating your tangerine." Ms. Mahmudian opened a folder and looked through it. "Why are you in such a rush?"

Taking a pile of papers out of the folder, she continued, "It's a year since this was translated, but they don't have enough paper to publish it."

The sound of the telephone ringing filled the room. Ms. Mahmudian picked up the phone. "Hello. . . . Yes. . . . No, she is not here, she is out of the office."

She put the receiver down. "She has gone to see Madam."

"Madam?"

"Yes, she is the best in reading coffee cups. Najafi is one of her steady customers."

"Ms. Najafi? But she strikes me as a woman of high morals."

"Oh, please! Her being so obsessive has caused her husband to leave her. Think of it, she puts all her clothes and her children's clothes in the washing machine as soon as she gets home from work. She also has to take a bath when she gets home. She must have forced the man to do the same thing and that's why he has left her."

"I feel so sorry for her. She has to walk up the hill with her child in her arms every day. I always ask my husband to stop and give her a ride every time we see her on our way."

Ms. Mahmudian was tidying the receipts and other papers on her desk. She suddenly turned to Hosseini and as she was shaking her finger, she said, "No offense, but why do you offer rides to everyone? Is your husband the people's chauffeur?"

"But in this cold weather?"

"You are acting like those lower-class people who offer rides to friends and neighbors as soon as they buy a car. Does anyone give you a ride, even if you freeze in this cold?"

Looking into her eyes, Ms. Mahmudian continued, "I am at least ten or twelve years older than you are. You should listen to my advice. It's for your own good."

Hosseini bent over to throw the tangerine peels in the wastebasket. Ms. Mahmudian said to her, "We'll go there together one day."

"Where?"

"The Madam I was telling you about. My treat."

"But I don't believe in things like that."

"You'll get hooked if you come once."

Hosseini got up.

"How is this Wednesday? I'll buy the coffee," Ms. Mahmudian said.

"I'm very busy."

Ms. Mahmudian frowned, "Oh, come on, you are so stubborn." She got up; her face had turned red. Hosseini opened the door. Giving her a hug, Ms. Mahmudian said to her, "Let me know if you change your mind; we'll go together and have a good time."

"But I'm not into that at all."

Ms. Mahmudian closed the door. Breathing a sigh of relief, Hosseini quickly went along the corridor. She was close to the stairway when she remembered she had left her books back there. She returned. Once she was at the door, she heard Ms. Mahmudian's voice. She was talking to someone: "Tell Rostamkhani that Hosseini is spreading gossip behind her back. . . . No, no, just say it. . . . No, don't knock her vase over. Do something else; take her glasses and hide them . . . I don't know, do something."

Lida's Cat, the Bakery, and the Streetlight Pole

Azardokht Bahrami

Not that you should think there is no affection between us, no.
We still love each other. That's why there is a lot of gossip
behind our backs. His brother, for example. As soon as the blank
check was returned, he came, over-night, all the way from Shiraz, to
tell me, "Sister-in-law, divorce is the only solution; I know my brother well. There is no hope for him and he's no good to you." His sister, too, kept insisting for six months. She talked and talked until
they arrested Said. When I went to her house, she told me, "You see
now; didn't I tell you? One day you will finally realize the truth
behind my words." I would let Said know about my decision as soon
as I saw him, I thought. But when I saw him, I smiled and talked
about everything but divorce. I talked of Lida's cat, which slept on
the sofa in Said's absence; of the neighborhood baker who changed
his bakery into a butcher shop after they killed his son; and of the
new streetlight pole they have installed in our alley that is so close to
our kitchen window that I put my pickle jars in its hole. I can easily
reach it when I stretch my hand out of the kitchen window.

None of them were of any help. For that sister and brother, one
million was not a lot of money. The matter didn't concern them at all.
Mehri pretended to be putting in some effort. She would call every
day, giving me hope. At night, though, she would call to say it didn't
work. True, they each have a few kids, and expenses, but if they dug
into their pockets, they could each come up with a couple of hundred

183

thousand tomans. I could arrange the rest myself. All they could do was gossip behind Shirin Khanom's back. I mean our landlady. She had just come back from the United States with her twelve-year-old daughter. She had also lived in Canada for four years. She is strong like a man. Well, she has been free for a long time; she has lived a free life. Said likes to socialize, and we didn't have any friends. They would come up to our place. We used to watch films and crack seeds. She would perhaps wear short skirts and sleeveless blouses, but Said is a chaste man. I trust him. Whenever Mehri was there, she would get mad. "You are too naïve," she would tell me. Well, maybe she still didn't know her brother. Said has always been charming.

Everyone likes him. His charm has fooled my mother. Whenever he complains about me, she always defends him. Mother likes him very much. Don't you think so? Everyone likes him, and so does Shirin Khanom. She always gave her car keys to Said and didn't even ask for them back. Whenever Said refused to take the car she would say, "Said, dear, the car needs a tune-up; take it to the shop; only you can take care of it." And then she would disappear for a week so that Said could use the car and drive to the factory. Mehri would call early in the morning saying, "Simin, do you know where Shirin Khanom is right now?" I would say, "She is at home." She would say, "No, for my sake, go check." I would reply, "Do you want me go and call her?" She would tell me, "I swear by your life, Haji just told me he has seen Said and Shirin Khanom together in her car; please go see where they are." And I would not. I would only turn the radio on, put the receiver next to it, and busy myself with throwing the leftover roasted seeds off the plates and washing them. He never minded my not being able to have kids.

Let's assume Mehri was right. His brother once swore he had seen Shirin Khanom's car in front of the factory. I said to him, "Of course, Said often drives her car." He said, "No, this time it was different." He said that day he was stopped when he wanted to enter Said's office. But he had recognized two shadows behind the office window. I told him it could have been anyone. At times, Said took me with him to his office. He had to stay in the office night and day one month before the New Year. A couple of times he took me to stay with him in his office. On those occasions if we didn't take Shirin Khanom's car, she would drive to Ab-Ali the next day, buying a Sangak[1] bread fresh out of the oven on her way. After breakfast, she would leave the car there and go back home in a cab.

She was the only one who took me to a doctor. She referred me to lots of doctors. She would make appointments and would give me their address or would take me with her; she would also arrange for the tests and the X-rays to be done on her insurance. The last resort was the herbal medicine. She once went to Mahalat and got the instructions from Naneh Aqa. You would mix beeswax with egg yolk and boil it. Then you had to thread a cotton ball. Dip the cotton ball in the mixture, put it inside overnight, and pull the thread out in the morning and discard it. Then at night you would use another cotton ball. She would make sure I followed through. Well, I couldn't do it every night. Once when Mehri was at our house she saw the threaded cotton balls in the refrigerator. Well, I got pregnant only once. True, it was out of the uterus. But I carried it for three months. If I had been more careful, and if Said had not been in prison, maybe we could have kept it in the incubator.

The news of Said's imprisonment caused the misfortune. She was the one who paid the hospital bill. But none of our relatives liked her. Wherever I went they would pull me aside asking me if Said has taken another wife. Just like you? What should I do? I just smiled and acted as if nothing had happened.

No, dear auntie, it is not your fault. I know Mama has given you this commission. Mama was always against my marriage. She never knew why. I left my home for Mama's house only once. I didn't tell them I had left Said. I told them Said was away on a business trip. I told them he would come and get me when he came back. Those few days, Mama was very hard on me. As soon as I said anything, she would raise the question of divorce. I think she had suspected. It was always like that; she only liked Said when he was around her. But when he was out of sight, nothing could convince Mama that he was not as bad as she thought.

This is not true with Papa, though. He was always fond of him. He never believed me. He would always blame me. On the third day, he started asking me why I wasn't going back to my home. He thought perhaps I was not paying enough attention to my husband, or that maybe I was not paying attention to my appearance; maybe I smelled of fried onions. He would say, "Said is a complete man, and he deserves a complete woman." I don't know, maybe he was referring to my inability to have kids. Perhaps Papa was right. After that, I decided to never let them get involved in my private life.

But it wasn't just them; there was Mehri, his brother, and Haji as

well. Each member of the family would start giving me words of
advice as soon as they saw me. And whenever they came over to our
house, Shirin Khanom would come to say hello. We were used to
each other; every night we were down with them or they would come
up to be with us. Whenever they saw her, the aunts would start
rolling their eyes. Whenever his mother came to stay with us, it was
awful. She was a sharp woman. She was in a wheelchair, but she had
her wits about her.

One night it was around three o'clock when she called me. I
went to see if she needed something. She didn't say anything. She
turned over and put her hand under her head. I asked if she wanted
me to change her. She couldn't control her bladder. We used to put
diapers on her. She said no. She closed her eyes and asked me to be
quiet. I went closer. She asked if Said was back. I said no. She said
he was. I told her he had called to say he would not come home that
night. She said, "He is back; go check Shirin Khanom's place." I
said, "Mother, do you want me to go to people's houses at this time
of night asking for my husband?" She told me, "Simin, I'm telling
you, your husband is in that house. I am his mother, and no one has
ever been able to fool me." If you tell her that, say, you have to be
somewhere two years from now at a quarter past four, she would
wake up that very day at the same time to remind you of your
appointment! The morning of that night Said came home early with a
dish of halim[2] and two loaves of fresh bread. His mother just gave
me a meaningful look.

Said had a good relationship with Shirin Khanom's daughter.
They would play around, wrestle at times, while Shirin Khanom and
I cracked seeds and watched a film over and over. And sometimes we
would laugh at them. Said loves kids. Once, Mehri had to come with
her kids to stay with us for a few days. They were having their house
renovated, and Haji had asked the construction workers to go there.
It was Chahar Shanbeh Suri[3] and Said was making fireworks; they
had an argument with Lida. Lida had taken a firecracker and would
not give it back. She wanted to set it off herself. Said tied up her
hands and feet and snatched it back from her. And Lida got on his
back and started kicking him. Mehri couldn't believe her eyes. She
kept talking to me until morning.

Let's assume whatever they say is true. Was it anyone other than
Shirin Khanom who got Said out of prison? She mortgaged her car,
borrowed half a million, and got Said out. Above all, she was the one

who took me to the doctor when Said was in prison. Did any one of them come to visit me at the hospital? She took a trip to Dubai. When she came back, she brought me two nightgowns and a table-cloth.

We went to the factory for Sizdeh-be-dar[4] this year. There is a nice meadow there. I went to wash the dishes by the river after lunch. Lida joined me after a while. She was upset. She insisted on washing the dishes quickly and rejoining them. I wasn't in a hurry, though. We talked a great deal and washed the dishes well. She told me I was very naïve. That I had my eyes closed and was not seeing the things that were happening around me. I took my shoes and socks off and put my feet in the water. Lida refused to put her feet in the water, despite my insistence. She constantly turned to look at them. She couldn't see anything from that far. On our way back we could hear Shirin Khanom's laughter from far away. Stupefied, Lida was staring at me. So what, I thought, let them laugh together. Is laughing a crime? I intentionally called them—I didn't want to catch them at that moment in Lida's presence—and they called back to me. When we got back, Said was still lying down holding his hands under his head. Shirin Khanom was sitting down hugging her knees. Suppose she buttoned her blouse immediately. Suppose she quickly gathered her hair with a pin. Maybe he was massaging her feet. What is wrong with it? As a matter of fact, if it wasn't for Shirin Khanom's sugges-tion, or for her car, we wouldn't go to celebrate the Sizdah-be-Dar. If Said was coming home three nights a week it was because of them.

His brother came over the other night to search for Said's check stubs; he searched all his belongings. I told him it was not a nice thing to do. He didn't pay any attention to me. He also found a letter that he read several times. He wanted to read it to me. I wouldn't let him. He gave me the letter to read. I didn't. I folded the letter, put it in his drawer, and locked it up. When Said was released, Shirin Khanom, Lida, and I went in a taxi to get him. Shirin Khanom's car was mortgaged. We hugged each other in front of the prison door after four months. Shirin Khanom just shook hands with him. So did Lida. On our way back, Shirin Khanom bought kababs. We ate right there in the street. As soon as his brother came and saw everyone gathered there, he slapped him on the face, took him to the room, and showed him the letter. Said came to the kitchen and helped me pour tea.

That night when the guests left, we stayed up all night and

talked. Said kept apologizing. He told me he loved me a lot and would not give a strand of my hair for any other woman. He showed me another letter. I didn't read it. He read some parts of it to me. In the letter he had said how much he loved me. I knew Said loved me. He himself wrote it in his letter. He also read Shirin Khanom's letter to me; I didn't listen. I only remember she had written that she wanted him to marry her for a few months for the kid's sake. Then he could come back to me. I didn't pay much attention to what he was saying. But Said read the entire letter. They had corresponded a few times when Said was in prison. I knew Said loved me. I love him too. I knew Said was sincere in his apology. When he asked not to talk about it anymore, we didn't; I mean, we don't. I knew Said well; seven years is a long time.

In the morning, Shirin Khanom knocked at our door. Said opened the door. Shirin Khanom shoved fresh-baked bread, the jar of jam, and the dish of butter through the door and left. She said, "Have fun!" loudly. Said came to me. He sat on the pillow and said, "What do you say, Simin? Do you agree?"

NOTES

1. A kind of flat bread.
2. Puree of wheat and meat.
3. The last Wednesday before the Persian New Year festival.
4. The thirteenth day of the New Year festival on which people picnic.

Part Three
Aware of the Image

The Lark

Nahid Tabatabai

They told her I was Hossein's Aunt, Hossein's Aunt Gohar. As soon as she came in, before anyone else I jumped up and hugged her. I hugged her tight, and kissed her, her face, her eyes, her hair. The poor thing was startled. Hossein came closer and said, "She is my maternal aunt." And then made a sign to her as if he wanted to say, "She is not all there." If it had been any other time I would have been hurt, but this time, I didn't care. I just wanted her in my arms. Thank God, thank God, she is a real lady now. Tall and slim, like her father. White and blonde, like myself back then. Her eyes that, may God preserve them, were the same as in her childhood. Why didn't Hossein tell her that I was his mother? At least she would have thought that I was her brother's mother. Well, perhaps she would have thought I was a rival wife of her mother's and she wouldn't like me. I was hugging her, crying. I should go and fulfill my vow. I had vowed to light forty long candles in the Emamzadeh.[1]

I hadn't slept all night. In the morning I got up before everybody else. I had ground the meat and washed the rice five times before the others woke up. I was cleaning the chickens when the bride came and took the knife. Then they sat me down on the big wooden seat next to the pool and didn't let me lift a finger. We made sweet rice and chicken and dolmeh[2] and sholleh zard.[3] What a sholleh zard! I knew she liked it but I didn't know how I knew. She ate and said, "Oh, this is good!" Hossein said, "Aunt Gohar made it." He was talking about me; and then she looked at me and laughed, laughed and said, "You've gone to a lot of trouble." Mahmud Khan, God bless his soul, also liked sholleh zard very much. Although he did me wrong, may God forgive him. What is past is past, and I hope to Fatemeh Zahra[4] that the future will be better than the past. They told her I was Hossein's aunt. Then everybody gathered around her. I wanted to yell, "Leave her alone, let me have a good look at her." But they were not leaving her alone. The children had surrounded her and kept calling her auntie, auntie. Her uncle was sitting next to her and laughing. At first, when they came, he stared at me a little, but then, I think, he thought that the resemblance between Hossein's mother and me was because we are sisters. He hadn't seen me for a long time. The last time I saw him he was running after a bicycle wheel and rolling it with a piece of wire.

I have no complaints about Mahmud Khan, God bless his soul. What is past is past. I hope to Fatemeh Zahra that his children are in good health. In the late afternoon I brought her baqlava.[5] I had made it myself. She ate it and said, "This tastes so familiar." Because when Mahmud Khan dropped by every once in a while, I used to give him two boxes of baqlava to take home. The taste was familiar to her. That's why she knew the taste. Thank God, thank God, what a lady, what a beautiful lady. May God preserve her eyes.

I was seventeen when the Master came to our room and told my father, "Mashhadi,[6] tomorrow we will marry Gohar to Mahmud Khan." My dad, God bless his soul, didn't utter a sound. I ran to the room in the back and collapsed right there. What did it mean? They wanted to marry me, the gardener's daughter, to the Master's son. I stayed in the room in the back until my father went to the garden. When I came out my mother was crying. I went ahead. When she saw me she wiped away her tears. I sat next to her and said, "Mama, did you hear?"

She didn't answer. I asked, "Why do they want to do that?"

"Your dad says it's because the Master doesn't want his son to go into military service."

"Well . . .?"

"Nothing; he will marry you to the Master's son, which will mean he has a wife."

"You mean I won't be his wife?"

"Yes, but after a while he's sure to divorce you and go about his business, like all the masters."

"Then what about me?"

"Nothing; what can I say? I wish we had married you to Mashhahdi Jafar's son sooner."

"I don't want to."

"It's not up to you. It is not up to us either. When the Master makes a decision, Shemr[7] himself couldn't stop him."

The following day Mahmud Khan, God bless his soul, came from Tehran. They sacrificed a sheep in front of him. I went to the room in the back again. Since childhood, whenever my father wanted to hit me I would go to the room in the back, and he would not come after me. But this time they took me by the wrist and hauled me out of there. Karbalai[8] Hassan, the village *mollah,* was sitting in a room. They sat me in the room and threw a white scarf over my head and forced the "I do" out of me. There was no one else in the room. Nobody whooped for joy; nobody clapped.

At night he, God bless his soul, came into the room. I had gone to the room in the back again. He sat next to the door and said, "Come out; I don't want to harm you. I didn't want to marry you, but now that I have, I am not going to divorce you. Now, why have you gone and hidden yourself over there? You are afraid of me, and you are hiding between the bedding and the jars of pickles and jam? Calm down, I am not going to hurt you."

God bless his soul, he did hurt me. I forgave him. What is past is past. In fact, he wasn't that bad a man. Whenever he came to the village he would drop by. The first year, I gave birth to Hossein. He bought me a gold bracelet, the one I have on. From that day on I didn't take it off, but I will, one of these days. I will take it off and put it on Soheila's wrist. My Soheila, not their Shirin Khanom. When I was a kid I used to ask my mother, "Mama, what is a wedding?"

God bless her soul, she would say, "It means that they put a bridal gown on you, and a lace veil on your head, and you can wear powder and rouge, and you will be beautiful and lovely."

I would say, "I don't want to."

Then when it came time for Mahmud Khan to arrive, my mama said, "Don't make any trouble. Be calm and patient. You will be a bride; you will have children."

I said, "Did you see how Akbar Aqa's daughter screamed when she was having a baby?"

She said, "For as long as the world has existed, women have screamed and have given birth. And no woman has ever died from giving birth."

God bless him, he was very wise. The first time that I was alone with Mahmud Khan he told me stories; the story of the White Horse, the story of Narenj-o Toranj. He told me stories until I fell asleep. When I woke up in the morning, there was a blanket on top of me, and Mahmud Khan was standing at the window. I coughed. He turned and laughed, and said, "Now you can go, and if anybody asks you something, just laugh and say, 'I don't know.'" When I came out of the women's quarters, I saw my mother asleep on the ground in the hall near the stairs. I kissed her face. She woke up and put her arms around me and cried. Then we went to our own room. She sat me next to her and said, "Are you well?" I said "I don't know," and laughed. Now I was different from the rest. Servants treated me with respect, even the Mistress sent me a length of cloth. I didn't see Mahmud Khan for two or three weeks. I think he had gone to Tehran. They said he finished school and wanted to go to work. God forgive him, at least I wasn't a servant anymore.

In less than a year, Hossein was born. Mahmud Khan was very happy. He brought a suitcase full of clothes and toys for him. Until Hossein was one year old, every time he came he dropped by to see us. But after that, little by little it got so that he would come and I wouldn't see him. They would only call Hossein to see his father. The first couple of times when he came and didn't ask for me I cried, but then I accepted God's will. I had to thank God that at least he wanted his son. I kept myself busy with the child and didn't say a word. My father and mother were content. Mama didn't work in the kitchen anymore. I didn't work at all. Mashhadi Akbar's daughter, although she was her Master's sigheh,[9] was working all day long, and she would be beaten at night. Her Master used to get drunk and hit her with a whip. In comparison to these Masters, Mahmud Khan was an angel. When Hossein grew older, the Master ordered a room to be built for Hossein and me next to my father's room. Some days he, God bless his soul, would come to the garden and call Hossein. May his spirit rest in peace now, then he liked Hossein very much. He even sat him on his lap a couple of times. When Hossein was about two, Mahmud Khan came from Tehran a few times and saw

Hossein only once. This really hurt me because Hossein was old enough to understand, and he would see him coming and going and he was crying for him. After a few times when Mahmud Khan came and went, they told me that he was going to marry. Someone from a high-class family, like himself. I cried for two days and didn't eat anything. The second night, my mother was really upset with me. She hit me on the head and said, "Hmph! What did you think? You thought Mahmud Khan would settle for a gardener's daughter? Get up, pull yourself together; get up and take care of your kid." God bless her soul, she was right. I got up and ate, but the food tasted like poison. I didn't dare cry in front of anyone anymore, but I was cut into pieces inside.

A couple of months later, Mahmud Khan came to see the Master. This time there was a city woman with curly black hair and a sleeveless white dress sitting next to him in the car. When they stepped out of the car I saw her shoes. The heels were so thin, as if she was walking on nails. I was waiting for her to fall down. But she didn't. It was I who had fallen down, because of Mahmud Khan. Now, just seeing his shadow made my heart tremble. After all, he was my son's father, wasn't he? A couple of times I wanted to go to him, but my mother warned me, "Don't go to him; you might say something, and he might get mad and divorce you." She was right. I didn't go to him. I hid Hossein from him. Every time he came I put on my chador[10] and went to my aunt's house. I didn't want him to divorce me; I didn't need that. After Mahmud Khan, I couldn't look at anyone's face. When I was saying my prayers, I prayed that he wouldn't remember Hossein and me. God forgive him, I was satisfied that Hossein bore his name.

After Mahmud Khan was married, every month his driver, Hassan Aqa, would come and bring our monthly expenses and one toy for Hossein. Hossein loved Mahmud Khan. I didn't see him for a couple of years, other than the occasional times he came to the village. Then they would take Hossein to the women's quarters and I could only see him here and there in the garden walking on the pavement. Every time he came and left, I cried for a week. My mother, God bless her soul, would get angry and say, "Go thank God he has not divorced you. It was clear from the beginning that this was going to happen."

My mother liked him because after I was married to him she was exempt from doing any heavy work. In the spring of the third year, Mahmud Khan came to the village. As soon as he arrived he came to our room and said, "I have bought you a house. Mashhadi doesn't need to work anymore." He put us in the car and took us there. The house was much more than what we needed. There were three rooms around a big yard and a blue-tiled pool. This is the house that Hossein, when he grew up, tore down and built a two-story house instead. But he didn't change the pool and the small gardens. I mean, I didn't let him; they reminded me of my dad. The pool remained, and the tall trees around it and Hossein and I. We were happy. Along with Mama and Dad, we went to the new house. My dad planted roses all around the pool, hoping that Mahmud Khan would come and see and enjoy himself. But Mahmud Khan came to that house only twice, and I wished he had never come.

We were just beginning to settle down in the new house when one afternoon someone knocked at the door. I opened the door; it was Hassan Aqa the driver. I thought, Well, for sure he has brought the money, but Hassan Aqa said Mahmud Khan had gone to his father's house and he would be here, meaning to our house, after that. I was happy and worried at the same time. After his marriage in Tehran he hadn't come to see us anymore. With my mama, God bless her soul, I quickly prepared some food. I changed Hossein's clothes. I put some makeup on and waited. I was really upset, and felt as though my heart was being wrung out.

Mahmud Khan came after sunset. I remember well. It was summer. Mahmud Khan said he would sit in the yard. My dad, God bless his soul, sprinkled the yard with water. My mama brought a small rug and spread it out next to the pool. She brought fruit, candy and watermelon, and my father prepared a water pipe, and then they put on their going-out clothes and left. They said they were going to a relative's house. I was completely confused. Hossein was three years old. He was in the room playing with his toys. It was only Mahmud Khan and I. I was very worried. I hurried up and laid the cloth for dinner. I thought for sure he would go to the Master's house after dinner. He had never stayed with me overnight. But even after I cleared the table he didn't leave. I was puzzled. I got the water pipe ready and set it in front of him. He took a puff and said "Gohar, my wife, Mahlaqa, cannot have children. She thought it was my fault. Somehow I managed to tell her that it wasn't my doing. At first she didn't believe me, but then she went to the doctor and got tested and found out that it was her."

Then he began talking about everything. In my heart I thought, Maybe he is tired of his new wife and has come to us; and—it is not hidden from God and I won't hide it from you—I was happy. But I was wrong. Mahmud Khan loved his new wife very much, even if she couldn't have children. One should tell the truth; he really loved her. Good for her, she was lucky. She wasn't like me, unlucky and sad. God be merciful to my mother, she used to say that a woman is born to suffer.

When Hossein was four, Soheila was born. As soon as I saw her I fell in love with her. She had big eyes and curly hair. Mahmud Khan really loved her, but Soheila's birth brought me pain and torment. Her arrival brought me bad luck. I never knew whether Mahmud Khan wanted to have another child with me so that he could take her, or if he decided to when he saw her. God bless his soul, he was a real clever man. It wasn't for nothing that his grandfather had been a member of Parliament for a while.

When the child was about seven or eight months old, he came to the door with Hassan Aqa the driver. He had bought me earrings and a necklace and a bracelet and he thought these things could take the place of my child. May God . . . no, God bless his soul. Thank God I didn't die and lived to see this day. He is dead; I am alive. My daughter is back home. He took the child from my bosom by force and laid her in the arms of that . . . May God forgive me. He said, "I will take her to Arak[11] and take care of her. You will have less to worry about and the light of my house will be lit as well." May God not bless his soul, he took away the light of my house. Of course that is not fair; Hossein was the light of my house too, but my breasts were still full of milk when they took the child. For a week I had a fever and I didn't touch food. My child Hossein used to sit next to me and cry. In a week my milk had dried up. My mama, God bless her soul, was hovering around me like a butterfly, giving me advice. She would say, "Well, honey, Hossein belongs to you, and Soheila belongs to him. In fact you should thank God that he didn't take both of them." Or she would say, "Your child is with her dad, she hasn't gone away with a stranger. For sure they will treat her wonderfully, like a flower. Besides, she will be raised up differently with them; she will be a lady. Don't be sad." My mama was talking and I was crying, as if my milk had changed into tears and was pouring from my eyes.

From that time on Hossein and I didn't let a day go by without news of Soheila. Wherever they went, we would find a friend, a worker or something, who could go to their house and bring us some news. They had changed her name to Shirin. Whenever I really missed her I went around to their house to have a glimpse of her. Once I even went to Arak. On the way to her school, I was going to jump out and hug her. God preserve her, she was in first grade. Mahlaqa Khanom was holding her hand, taking her to school. I could see how she was taking care of her and how much she loved her. What beautiful clothes she had put on her. I was not worried about that, but I was dying to kiss her face.

When they returned to Tehran I sent Hossein to their house on the pretext of taking them flowers. Wherever they went Hossein would find them. Sometimes I sent some baqlava, hoping that she might eat one. I would find out when she was sick, when she had an exam, when she bought a car. I was even at her wedding. We went there with the Master's servants to do the cooking. Away from Mahmud Khan's eyes, I would take a peek inside the yard to see her. I was dying to go and put my bracelet on her wrist. Why didn't I do it? I don't know. Maybe because I was afraid, and maybe because Hossein had promised his father not to make any problem for him for as long as he was alive. Mahmud Khan had told Hossein, "I have a warm family life. Give me your word you won't destroy it." As if we were not human beings. One must just be lucky. Of course, God knows he took care of Hossein pretty good. When he received his high school diploma, he gave him some capital and Hossein went into business building and selling houses. Many of the houses in Karaj[12] have been built by Hossein. When his business picked up, everybody called him "engineer." Then at the age of thirty he got married, to the granddaughter of my dad's aunt, and a hundred thousand thanks to God, he brought up good kids. My daughter-in-law is very kind. A hundred thousand thanks to God, she doesn't let me lift a finger. She respects me. All and all, my only grief in life has been separation from Soheila, and it seems that this is also being taken care of.

I tell Hossein, "Honey, now when are we going to tell her that I am her mother?" He says, "Wait, it is too soon." It's unfair. When he wanted to tell her he was her brother he couldn't wait, but now that I want to tell her who her mother is, he keeps talking about sooner or later. He says, "Mahlaqa Khanom doesn't know." I say, "Allright, so she doesn't know. Isn't it better for her to know that Shirin is Mahmud Khan's daughter than the daughter of two complete strangers?" He says, "How about Soheila? Soheila thinks that Mahlaqa is her mother." I say, "Well, what is the difference? When she finds out I am her real mother she will love me too." He says, "I have to think."

You can think so much that . . . may God forgive me, I have no patience anymore. I want so much to sit next to her and take her hands in mine and tell her how much I suffered from being separated from her. She is now a mother and understands these things very well. I want to tell her how many times I have walked behind her, how many times I have touched the door of her house, and how much I have dreamed about her. I want to tell her that I know she is a lady and I am a village woman, but blood is a whole different thing. Blood draws. I have had enough. I should sit in front of Mahlaqa Khanom and say it is true that Mahmud Khan was yours, it is true that you both came from the same class, I have no problem with that, but my daughter is mine, mine too. How I have waited. It is enough. I want to hug Bahareh,[13] tell her stories, buy her a bracelet, if she would permit me. I'll tell, I'll tell everything. Next time when Soheila comes here I'll tell her everything. Next time when Soheila comes with her arms full of gifts and clothes, next time when she comes and sits in this room, I'll sit next to her and tell her I am not Hossein's Aunt Gohar. I am Hossein's mother, your mother. Then we will go to Mahlaqa Khanom. I'll take her some baqlava. She will certainly be happy to know that Shirin is Mahmud Khan's real daughter. Although I am sure she doesn't want to see me. It doesn't matter, I'll take her baqlava. We'll make up gradually and if she wants, every now and then I will go there and wait on her; if she wants. I hope to Fatemeh Zahra that everything will be fine; oh, God, I vow to light forty long candles in your Emamzadeh so that . . .

NOTES

1. Literally, "born to an Emam." Emamzadeh is a mausoleum where it is believed a descendant of an Emam is buried.
2. A kind of Iranian dish made by stuffing grape leaves.
3. Sweet rice pudding flavored with saffron.
4. The youngest daughter of Muhammad, the prophet of Islam.

5. A very sweet pastry.

6. A title used to refer to those who have made a pilgrimage to Mashhad, a Shi'i Muslim holy city in Iran.

7. Leader of the Caliph Yazid's army. In the battle of Karbala (680 A.D.) he killed Hossein, the third Emam of the Shi'is. For Shi'is, Shemr symbolizes unstoppable, merciless power.

8. A title used to refer to those who have made the pilgrimage to Karbala, a Muslim holy city in Iraq.

9. According to Shi'i Islam, a man and a woman can marry each other for a limited period of time. Sigheh refers to the temporary bride.

10. A woman's outdoor—and on occasion indoor—wrap, covering her whole body.

11. A city in Iran.

12. A small city near Tehran.

13. Soheila/Shirin's daughter.

My Mother, Behind the Glass

Fariba Vafi

I told my sister Ashraf I was going home to get my books. I lied to her. If I had told her that I wanted to take my mom's photograph from the album, she wouldn't have let me go. She would have made a face and said something mean to me. See, my mom is her father's wife. Since mom has been inside, she doesn't want to set eyes on her. She doesn't know how much she has changed. How could you expect her to know? You'd have to go and see her to believe it. When they arrested Mom, Ashraf came to our house. She grabbed my hand and took me to their house. She didn't say a word.

I said, "How about my mom?"

Her eyes narrowed, the way they did whenever she felt sorry for me. "You are a big girl now. You don't need your mom."

Then her husband came in, and Ashraf didn't say another word. I really hated her husband. The way he looked at you made you feel ashamed of yourself. . . . If it weren't for those little imps of sister Ashraf's, Majid and Mahin, I wouldn't have stayed there. Of course, I didn't have anywhere else to go. And my brother Reza had gone to Tehran. I say it was because of that woman. I don't know what she told Reza that made him so angry that if you stuck him with a knife he wouldn't bleed.

That day my brother was not speaking at all. But his face was as red as could be. His wife's neck was straight; it was disgusting the way she was looking at us. Mom was crouching in a corner and

watching Reza out of the corner of her eye. Sister Ashraf kept going
over to brother Reza and begging him not to leave. But my brother
was looking at her with his bloodshot eyes; finally he said, "Get out
of my way."

To tell the truth, I was afraid of brother Reza, and in my heart I
wanted him to leave us alone. I didn't like his wife at all. She always
picked on Mom. Whenever I came back from school I would see
them fighting over something. Brother Reza always took his wife's
side. If his own mom were alive he wouldn't let his wife be so bold.
When he left, my brother didn't even look at Mom. They took all
their things and left. And then Ashraf left. Then I realized how bad
things were. The house was different; it was sad.

Mom lifted her head and said, "To hell with them; let them go."

Then she stood up and tidied the house. She was trying to act
normal. But she was unhappy. I knew it. I went to the yard. When I
returned I saw Mom's eyes were red. Mom used to cry in hiding as if
she was ashamed if others saw her tears. But I saw her tears. From
behind that damn glass. Yes . . . there. . . . When I looked up I saw
Mom's face was full of tears and full of wrinkles and lines under her
eyes.

When Mom wanted to leave the house she would spend one
hour, yes . . . a whole hour in front of the mirror and rub her face as
if she were going to a wedding. Sometimes she put cucumber skin on
her face and when I looked at her I laughed. When she was done with
the skin she would get busy with her eyes and eyebrows. Mom's eyes
are very big and they are always somewhat moist. Her eyelashes are
long. When she put eyeliner on her eyes, she was very beautiful.
Then she would take the tweezers and attack the hairs on her face.
Then she would put a very red lipstick on her lips and look at herself
in the mirror, smiling. And then she would change and put on a very
nice perfume. I used to run to her then, and she would put a little perfume on my clothes, too. Then she would go out.

Since Dad had died, Mom was spending a lot of time by herself.
She went to parties, one after another, as if she were making up for
those days Dad didn't let her go anywhere. When Dad was alive,
Mom was not allowed to go anywhere. I don't know why. But once,
Dad had seen Mom talking and laughing with Yousef, the owner of
the convenience store. I still remember what Dad did to Mom that
day. He took his belt and kept hitting her. Mom was screaming.

You see, Dad was very old, and so when Mom cursed at him he would get angry and hit her more. Then Dad got sick and died. Oh, God, what a bad time that was. Mom was crying like the rest. But I knew she didn't really feel that bad. Well, she never liked Dad. She always said so herself. Mom used to curse her parents, who had made her life so miserable. But I knew that she didn't curse them from the bottom of her heart. I had seen her taking them many things from the house secretly; cooking oil, rice. . . . Every New Year she sent them money so that they could buy me gifts or send her presents. I had learned all of these things.

Once, Dad's first wife found out and made such a fuss that you wouldn't believe it. Then they cursed each other and pulled each other's hair; a big fight. Dad's wife and Mom fought a lot. Then Dad's wife got cancer and died. Mom thought things would change and Dad would stop picking on her and wouldn't beat her anymore. But Dad's behavior got even worse. He always wanted to know where Mom was going and with whom. Reza and Ashraf also ignored Mom after the death of Dad's wife. And then Dad would beat Mom for every little thing. Mom always said, "I will finally kill myself and be free from this damned life."

Once she really wanted to do something. That day she had been beaten really bad by Dad. She kept screaming and swearing she would kill herself. At night she brought two bottles of pills from the back room, and she was about to take them when I rolled around in my bed and whispered, "Mom!" as if I was talking to her in my sleep. Mom looked at me for a minute. Of course my eyes were closed, but I knew she was looking at me. Then, all of a sudden, she hugged me and began crying. Then I was in her arms, and my hair was wet from my tears. I wish Dad weren't so mean. I wish I could sleep in Mom's arms forever. I wish I had stayed small, like that night, so Mom wouldn't leave me alone at home and go out. . . . Oh, God, I wish she were home now and I hadn't come to Ashraf's house. I wish she would take me there with her. What would have happened?

Once, when she was going out, I said to her, "Mom, take me with you."

"You sit here and study. I'll be back soon."

She always said she would be back soon and she never came back soon. I followed her into the alley. I saw that she covered her face and rushed to the street and got into a cherry-red Peykan.[1] The driver was a young man and had a red shirt on and was staring at Mom. I didn't like him at all. And then the Peykan took off. I came back alone. At night, when Mom came home, she had bought me a beautiful barrette.

I said, "I don't want it."

I was being stubborn. I didn't want to talk to her, but Mom was very happy. She took the barrette and put it in her own hair. She had recently dyed her hair blonde. It suited her well. She was younger and more beautiful. She stood in front of the mirror and laughed. As if someone else in the mirror were looking at her; maybe that same young guy. I had never seen Mom that happy. But I don't know why I didn't want to talk to her. Her laughter was kind of strange. You wouldn't like it. I'd say it was that guy's fault they arrested Mom.

I used to go to the back room of Ashraf's house and sit and cry. I missed Mom a lot. Once Ashraf came into the back room. I wiped away my tears but I think she understood.

"What is wrong?"

"Nothing."

Then she sat next to me. "Do you miss her?"

I didn't say anything and kept my head down. My tears ran down my face. Sister Ashraf stroked my hair. "You shouldn't miss her. If she had a little bit of affection for you, she wouldn't leave you at home while she is going out with strange men. She has ruined our reputation."

My tears were pouring down. I think sister Ashraf took pity on me. "All right, I'll take you to see her. Stop crying."

Then she took me there and said she would stay outside the door and wouldn't come in. If her husband found out he would skin her alive. Then she said, "I hope she has learned her lesson and won't do things like that anymore."

That day I went and sat behind the glass. Sister Ashraf was outside and didn't come in with me. I was afraid, very afraid. It was so crowded. My heart was racing. Then suddenly a voice came from the other side, and a woman came behind the glass. I say "a woman" because I didn't recognize her at first, but it was her, Mom. Oh, God, she had changed a lot. Her face was full of lines and wrinkles, and her eyes were sunken. She was really old. I felt so sorry for her. I got a lump in my throat and burst into tears and began crying, "Mom!"

Mom's face was covered with tears. She had a worn-out chador

on and was sitting behind that thick glass, like a strange woman, crying.

I told her, "Mom, do something so they will let you out. I don't
want to go to Ashraf's house anymore."

Mom was just crying behind the glass.

NOTE

1. A brand name of a car made in Iran.

Downfall

Nosrat Masuri

S he covered her belly with the sheet. The nurse said, "We'll put
you to sleep soon, then you won't feel anything."

She moved her feet on the bed. "How long should it take?"

"Fifteen minutes at the most. It's small; it will be over soon."

"Yes, it's small. Very small."

She saw the doctor in his white uniform with his gloves on entering the room. On his face, only two eyes with green pupils were visible. A white mask covered his face. He held the needle in his hand.
Her stomach muscles constricted.

"Are you afraid?"

"It's only twenty-one days old."

"This makes it easier. It would complicate the procedure if it
were older."

She felt the burning caused by the needlepoint inside her. She
shivered. Her fingers were clenched. Her nails were digging into the
flesh of her hands.

She felt the weight of the man's hand on her shoulder. "It's nothing, dear. Have some patience."

The man's bluish green pupils were wandering in his eyes. The
heavy air in the doctor's office was suffocating her. Through the
opening in the door, she saw the doctor, who had gone out to the
veranda and was standing next to the jasmine bush.

She looked at the man and put her hand on her belly. The man said, "I told you not to think about it. I know it's hard for you."

She turned her face. The doctor smelled the jasmines. The room was stuffy. The bluish green pupils were moving fast in his eyes. The nurse dried the sweat on her forehead.

"Sir, please, you have to leave the room."

She saw the doctor picking some tools up from the tray and putting them in her. She didn't feel any pain. The light at the end of her bed was bothering her eyes. The rest of the room was dark. She could hear the wind outside. The tree branches were colliding. Two green eyes were carving her inside. The white gloves were red. It felt as if a heavy weight was hanging from her. Through the opening in the door she saw the trees bending. She could hear their roar. A drop of sweat rolled down her face. Her eyelids got heavy.

The nurse asked, "Are you hot?"

She shook her head. She felt she was being stretched. Being stretched, until she was suddenly released. She shrank again. She turned into a black ring. She felt dizzy. She was about to fall into a well. She was clawing the air. She was falling down.

"We are almost done. Hang on a little bit more."

She opened her eyes. Two green lights bothered her eyes. She saw the doctor's hand penetrating inside her. He pulled something out of her with red strings dropping from it. The doctor was holding it between his fingers, looking at it.

She could hear the man's voice in her ears. "The doctor says it's just a clot of blood . . . a clot of blood."

The doctor was speaking with the nurse. He was laughing. The sound of his laughter filled her ears. She was climbing a mountain. The sounds were echoing on the mountain. She stood and looked around. The sounds were banging in her head. She was detached from herself. She was someone else. She could hear a moaning sound. She opened her eyes. The nurse was bending over her. Red forks were digging inside her. She was climbing the mountain again. She was cold. The snow was being crushed under her feet. The wind was blowing drops of snow on her face. She slipped. She clawed the air. She grabbed a piece of ice. She shivered.

She heard her own moaning sound. "I'm freezing. I'm freezing."

A hand touched her forehead. A voice said, "Not much left. Almost done."

Her eyes closed again. She was cold. There was no one on the mountain. Drops of snow were hitting her face. A deep canyon had opened up under her feet. The voice said, "Calm down. Calm down."

She saw the doctor's hands moving. The white mask dropped from his face. He was laughing. She slipped. She was falling into the canyon. She stretched out her hand. She saw the man. He was laughing. "We had no other choice, dear. No other choice."

He was smiling. She felt the heaviness of something on her chest. She saw the nurse moving the stethoscope on her heart. She put her hands on her chest. Her chest was shaking. Something was growing under her chest. It was growing bigger and bigger. All her body was shaking. Her entire body had turned into a big heart. The heart was growing, bigger and bigger until it burst. Her hand was clawing the air. She slipped and fell down the canyon.

A voice from far away said, "It is finished. Finished."

War Letters

✒ *Marjan Riahi*

To write these new letters, she had spent more than what the retirement income would have allowed her. The letter she wrote to the UN Secretary-General was typed with black ink. The letter she wrote to the head of the Commission for POWs and MIAs was also typed with black ink, and the letter to UNESCO with blue ink. She didn't know why she wrote to UNESCO, but she did it anyway. She didn't know English, and when she received the translated texts, she looked doubtfully at those unfamiliar letters and wondered whether these were her own words.

From this point on she wrote letters everywhere, regardless of whether it was relevant or not, and kept a copy for herself. When she looked at the copies from ten years back, she sometimes laughed. All her sentences were quite official, and although she had cried while writing them, it seemed as if those letters had been written by someone quite in control. At the beginning of one of her letters she had written, "In accordance with . . ." And then at the end of all her letters she had written, "And again peace, I wish you success." But now her phrases were completely different.

To the foreign minister she wrote: "When Habib was a child, he used to sit, for hours, on a branch of the plane tree and wait for a long time to capture a starling. Then he would paint one of its wings, and then he would let the bird fly so that he could happily claim that one of the starlings in the sky was his." She wrote to the president:

211

"Until the age of seven he always said nalwut instead of walnut, and he always broke the closed pistachios with his teeth. He always had problems with his teeth." To the office of the leader, she wrote: "When he was eighteen, he searched three cities to find a book," and she thought it must have been during that time that he thought he had grown up. She wished he could have kept calling a walnut a nalwut, and that he had not made any decision at the age of twenty-one, and that he had not gone anywhere or at least that he had asked for her permission. At the end of all these letters she wrote, "These are a mother's words."

The lastest news from those who came back was that some people had been hidden from the UN forces. Others had seen them from far away. According to them, there had been someone who was tall with blond hair and who could capture birds with his bare hands. They called him Habib. Iraq had said that all those who had to go back to Iran had already done so, and Iran was saying no, they had not. And she kept writing letters. She even wrote a letter to Iraq, to the President's Palace. She wrote that she missed Habib. She wrote that she knew Habib was there; people had seen him there. She wrote, "What use is he to you; send him back." At the beginning of the letter she begged, but at the end, she cursed them.

One morning, after a sudden thought, she made a strange decision. She wrote a letter to every single parliament representative, to every single cabinet member, and to whoever she thought was important. To each one of them she sent also a photograph of Habib. To the representative of Yazd[1] she sent a picture of Habib at age five, with his mouth full of qottab;[2] to the representative of Esfahan she sent Habib's picture at the age of seven, in his New Year suit, standing in the middle of the veranda of Ali Qapu.[3] To the representative of Qom she sent a picture of Habib at the age of ten, taking part in the mourning ceremony of Tasu'a.[4] To the defense minister she sent his picture at the age of twelve, standing next to his father's grave, in a black shirt and pants with muddy legs. To the interior minister an official two-by-three picture that he had taken when he had just passed the university admission exam; to the education minister a picture of the first few days at the university. And for herself, she saved a picture that showed Habib in the dirt, with walkie-talkie and helmet, ammunition belt, canteen, and a smile. When all the letters and pictures were mailed, she bought a few big organizers so that she could file the responses properly. Six months later in one of the organizers she had only two letters, whose sentences were much the same. She picked up a napkin and dusted the organizers.

Following the advice of those who wrote a lot, she bought a ballpoint pen. But the very same evening she realized that not a word was left. She placed a blank sheet of paper in an envelope, without any address on it, and pressed the pen between her fingers. Something caught between her lungs. The pen leaked ink. Everything was completely black.

The mailman came. He brought a registered letter. He rang the bell; nobody answered. It was obvious that the letter was from somewhere important. He came the following day, and the days after. But no one answered. He signed in his book in place of the recipient, and tried to push the letter underneath the door, but the envelope was not going in. It seemed that something behind the door was stopping it from getting in. He looked underneath the door. The yard was covered with autumn leaves.

NOTES

1. Name of a city in Iran.
2. A kind of very sweet pastry, very famous in Yazd.
3. Name of a very famous historical monument built during the Safavid period in Esfahan.
4. The mourning ceremony is for Emam Hossein—the third Shi'i Emam—and many members of his family who lost their lives in their war against the caliph Yazid. The main battle took place during the ninth and tenth (*Tasu' a* and *Ashura*) days of the month of Moharram of 680 C.E.

Refugee

Farzaneh Karampur

O nce they crossed the border, he reached her and gave her a
piece of bread. He had been walking by her side all day,
watching her. Inside the truck, he was now staring at her from the
corner.

The strong smell of urine and dung was coming from the floor of
the truck. A cool breeze was passing through the openings on the
sides and the big hole on top of the truck. It was very cold; she
wrapped her skirt around her feet. She was scared. There was a spark
in the man's eyes. Waiting for the right moment, he quickly caught
her attention. She felt warmer. A strange sensation passed through
her joints. She felt as if a hand had grabbed her unripe breasts. She
felt a twinge in her breast.

She pulled her blue headband forward. She hid her head between
her hands and hugged her knees. She closed her eyes and wished she
could sleep like the others. . . . The soldiers were running with their
helmets pulled down. Their boots were landing simultaneously on
the asphalt. The sound of sirens had filled the area. . . . The points of
the bayonets were shining in the sun. The blows of the gun-butts
were painful and knocked one's breath out. They were forcing
women and children out of their homes. . . . The instant a house was
set on fire, it was burning.

Like huge scary mouths, the army trucks were standing at the
entrance of every alley swallowing the men. They took Father, drag-

ging him on the ground. . . . He yelled, trying to say something, but his voice was lost in the uproar.

Grandma said, "Set the house on fire, leave only ashes for them!" Mother looked at the freshly washed curtains, at the hand-made rug that was her trousseau, and the canaries' cage. . . . Her eyes were filled with tears.

With her shaking legs, Grandma could hardly walk; she was unable to run. Mother was squeezing her hand with her fingers. The frightened, sobbing crowd was carrying her along like a wave.

She could see the stars through the hole in the top of the cab. In the darkness of the night the mountains an the bend of the road looked like the giant creatures in the stories. She was knocked against the woman next to her, who was asleep. She felt the weight of that look on her face. With every turn of the man's look, it felt as if a bowl of fire was rolling on her face. He touched his thick mustache and smiled. "Everyone is asleep; can't you sleep?" he asked her in a calm voice.

She shook her head and hid her face in her hands. With a sudden move of the car, the woman sitting in front of her woke up. She held the baby in her arms tight and mumbled something. A baby sucked the milkless breast of the mother and smiled, dreaming of milk. The weather was treacherously cold. No one had gotten a chance to bring an overcoat. Some even had not had time to put on shoes. She looked at the swollen ankle of the woman that was visible through her skirt. There were cracks on her heel; blood and dust had dried around the wound.

The driver stopped on the side of the road and got out. Everyone looked at him with sleepy eyes. He told them in Kurdish that he had to turn left and they could walk the rest of the way to the army camp by themselves.

With difficulty, they got up on their tired feet and got off the truck one by one without saying a word. When it was her turn to jump down, the man held her by her waist. He put her down with a smooth twist of his hands. His breath smelled of tobacco. He was warm and sweaty. The girl shivered and huddled in her clothes. The sound of a waterfall could be heard. They crossed the road. The creek and the poplar trees were hidden in the dark. A sleepy old man suggested they stay there until morning. The blister on her foot was burning. She took off her shoes and put her feet in the water despite the cold. Her toes froze. She felt the cold running quickly up inside her legs. Hunger was making her stomach churn, making her feel dizzy. She put her shoes under her arm and wrapped her clothing tighter around her body.

The children who had awakened were whining, thinking of food and warmth. . . . The wind was blowing through the grass and leaves. . . . It had the sound of the murmur of a frightened group of people. She looked at the silver-colored road shining under the moonlight through the trees. She felt someone breathing behind her neck and felt warmer.

Early in the morning the refugees started walking toward the army camp. Staring ahead, they were walking in the heavy silence. The pebbles on the road were hurting their feet. The cold wind had made an old man start coughing. The smaller kids were still asleep. Their heads were dangling over their mothers' shoulders. At the bend of the road a young man turned and looked behind him for the last time. Behind the trees and beyond the fields of wheat a blue piece of cloth could be seen on the thorns of a bush dancing in the wind. The redness of the girl's skirt was still visible from a distance in the middle of the field.

The Bitter Life of Shirin

Parvin Fadavi

A gusty wind started. The black clouds, weary of the nonstop downpour, were slowly disappearing from the sky. The city, washed by the rain, looked cleaner. Beyond the clouds, the sunshine was slowly covering the city. Clean trees were lined up along the sidewalk. The creek was flowing with the rainwater.

Holding her little girl Parisa's hand, Shirin[1] bought two bus tickets from the ticket booth and went to the bus stop. The wooden bench in the station, connected to a long metal shade by two poles, attracted her attention. Shirin was so tired that she simply collapsed on the bench. Her small black eyes looked worried and tired. Her face with its full lips looked pale. She had a small bump on her nose. A few strands of her straight hair had come out of her black scarf. Nervously, Shirin tried several times to tuck her hair under her scarf. She pulled her scarf down and touched her hair and forehead; the strands of hair were still showing. She touched her left cheek with her white handkerchief. As she touched her cheek, her face contracted with pain. She took a small mirror out of her bag. The mirror reminded her of the day she got it as a gift. A memory she could recall in fragments after the passage of six years: Behruz's warm hands at the time of their walk at the Qeytariyeh Park; Setareh Pizza shop with its red furniture; Behruz's especially easygoing manner at emotional moments, as if he was hiding his feelings behind his carelessness; Behruz's eyes smiling at Shirin, and his behavior that was mixed at

219

times with a colorless and intimate harshness. A kind of harshness that would make Shirin's heart tremble and cluster around her feelings in the beginning of their relationship.

Behruz had taken the mirror, which was wrapped around with a colorful gift wrap paper, out his pocket and said to Shirin, "A gift from a penniless man with a heart . . . a heart . . ." Putting his right hand on his heart, half closing his eyes, he had continued jokingly, "A heart full of emptiness," and laughed loudly.

The mirror had a leather cover and could be opened like a book. On the cover was painted the picture of a young woman with dreamy eyes and flowing hair. Shirin unfolded the mirror and examined her left cheek. Her cheek was black and swollen. There was a black ring around the swollen part. "Wouldn't it be better for me to go back?" she said to herself. But she looked at her cheek in the mirror again and mumbled to herself, "But this time it is different; very different." With a sudden recollection of the bitter memory, her eyes filled with tears. She blinked a few times and tried to suppress the lump in her throat. With tearful eyes, she looked at Parisa sitting by her side. With an insatiable curiosity, Parisa was looking around, holding her raggedy doll in her arms. Made of cheap fabric, the doll had dangling hands, and woolen threads hanging on each side of its face as its hair. Its eyes were made of two buttons. One of the buttons was broken. Its mouth was a black stitched line with two red circles at each end. The tear on the doll's head had been mended carelessly with a dirty white thread.

The bus station was filling up with people. At the end of the street, an empty bus became visible. It stopped with a moaning sound at the station. Its tires rubbed against the cold asphalt. Shirin's face contorted with the screeching sound of the bus. Accompanied by a young man, the chubby, joyful bus driver got off the bus. He had thick curly black hair. His eyes were small and smiling. Talking loudly and jokingly with the young man, he walked to the ticket booth. The young man was short and skinny. He had a worn-out green shirt on and was dragging his wide boots on the ground as he walked. A short line had formed next to the crowded bench. Shirin looked at her watch and mumbled, "There are still three hours left until Father gets home."

A good-looking plump woman with a navy blue scarf and overcoat moved closer to Shirin and asked her the time.

"Ten minutes past three."

With a faint smile and a thick Turkish accent, the woman asked, "Is this the end of the line?"

"No, it's the beginning of the line," Shirin answered.

The Turkish woman put down her basket full of fruit. An old woman sitting next to Shirin said protestingly, "But this is the beginning of the line."

The Turkish woman responded calmly, "No problem; I'll go back as soon as the bus comes."

The old woman raised her thick eyebrows, gathered up her worn-out chador,[2] and said out of the corner of her mouth, "She has no respect for others."

The Turkish woman looked across the street, ignoring her.

The old woman started grumbling, and some unclear words came out of her colorless thin lips. She crossed her hands over her knees, pressed the ticket hard in her calloused hands, turned to Shirin and said, "We ourselves are to be blamed for all our sufferings." She then gave a dirty, meaningful look at the Turkish woman.

All attention was now turned to the ticket booth. But the driver was patiently taking a sip of his tea, saying something to the ticket seller through his half-open door, then pulling his head out and releasing his laughter into the street.

The old woman grumbled again, "Must he drink tea now?" The passengers had started complaining. Throwing a sugar cube in his mouth, the driver approached the bus. With repressed embarrassment, the young man yelled at the passengers, "Men in the back, ladies in the front." With this simple sentence a commotion started among the passengers. Although a few days had passed since the new regulation—segregation of men and women in the public buses—most of the passengers threw a confused look at the driver's aide and the open doors of the bus. Grumbling and cursing, those who had lost their place in line rushed to the doors of the bus. As soon as she entered the enclosed space of the bus, Shirin's anxiety increased. She sat by the closed dirty window of the bus and held Parisa on her lap. The bus was full. The bus driver gave a glance behind him, looked at himself in the mirror, and started the moaning of the bus.

A gusty wind was blowing. Shirin was looking out the window. Parisa was putting her doll to sleep. The bus turned onto Jomhuri Square. Memories rushed to Shirin's mind again; memories so clear and vivid that they stirred her feelings up like the first day. Shirin's mind flew to a sweet, distant memory. . . .

It was the twenty-third of the month of Safar.[3] A huge pot was boiling on top of the big gas stove in their small yard. Hashem Aqa, the home-born servant of Khanom Bozorgh, her mother and the aunts had all gathered around the pot. Hashem Aqa was stirring the sholleh zard[4] with a long stick with a metal disk attached to it. Aunt Farkhondeh tasted the shole zard with a spoon, narrowed her eyes and said, "Looks like it is still not sweet enough."

Cunningly, Behruz got close to the pot; he dipped a spoon into the pot. He took the spoon out and with a funny gesture blew on it, put it in his mouth, and said, "Mmmm . . . delicious, very delicious." He added with a smile, "Just like my life." They all laughed. Aunt Farkhondeh asked, "Look, dear, see if it needs anything." Behruz dipped the spoon in again and instantly put the sholleh zard in his mouth; his tongue burned, but he didn't mind it. His eyes filled with tears, he said, "Yes, it only needs sugar [shirin]." They all burst out laughing again. Shirin blushed but didn't say anything. Of course Shirin felt pleased, just like any girl whose love had found a place in a man's heart. This love would lessen the vulnerability and insecurity from which she had always suffered at home. However, this love was not going to satisfy her fantasies. She always regarded love as a sacred event; she didn't believe in love gradually settling in one's heart. Shirin always pictured the birth of love to be unexpected and sudden, a simple event, an effective glance or a brief encounter. Love at first sight, a passionate love, deep and overwhelming. Naturally, Shirin couldn't expect an ordinary man to initiate the spark of this love. And Behruz with his medium height, thin mustache, big nose, big black eyes, thick eyebrows, and thin hair was so ordinary that he couldn't fit Shirin's expectations.

The realities of her environment, however, negated her fantasies. Her tough father drew the first line. Shirin reminisced again. . . .

It was a winter night and the yard was covered with a heavy snow. A nipping cold coming in through the cracks in the door was disrupting the warmth of the room. After dinner, instead of going to his room, Father stayed with them. He glanced at Shirin several times. It was clear that he had something to say.

Mother brought the after-dinner tea and humbly kneeled to sit on the floor. Finally, Father turned to Shirin and unexpectedly asked, "How old are you, Shirin?"

"Why do you ask?" Shirin replied.

"When I ask something, I want the answer. How old are you, I asked?" Father said impatiently.

"Twenty-one," Shirin mumbled.

Threateningly, Father shook his head and said, "Twenty-one years is enough. You have to settle your situation with us."

Confused and intimidated, Shirin asked, "What situation?"

"Looks like Miss is asleep," her father said. Turning to her mother, he continued, "People have started talking behind our backs and your daughter is asking 'What situation.'" Mother was listening carefully with wide eyes, showing that she would not disregard any of her husband's words. Father took a sip of his tea and said firmly, "A girl has to start her own life as soon as possible."

With a voice that could hardly be heard, Shirin said, "My home is right here."

With an impatient manner, Father nodded; he closed his eyes, pressed his lips together, and sighed. This gesture was always the beginning of a storm that, if not taken care of, could turn very violent. Mother let out a guilty smile, a smile that never covered her whole face. In a polite, calm voice she said, "That's true, dear, this is your home, but for how long? A girl should think of getting married early, as soon as possible."

With a growl, Father said, "Have you been talking nonsense again? What do you mean, early? Your daughter is twenty-one years old." He took another sip of the tea and continued sarcastically, "You are right, the twenty-one-year-olds of today don't know any more than the twelve-year-olds of the old days."

Shirin got angry; she wanted to say something but was stopped by the gestures of her mother, who was raising her eyebrows at her. In a rough tone, Father continued, "This is my last word on the matter. As soon as a suitor knocks at our door, you will get married, is that clear?" He got up and left the room immediately.

Shirin's dreams of a sacred, deep, and passionate love were suddenly shattered. Then, her attention was directed toward a man, Behruz, a serious presence in her life. Reasoning that at least Behruz loved her, she fell in love, in the way she didn't like: slowly and gradually. But once she settled down in her life with him, all her dreams fell apart.

This love lasted only the first year of their married life. Shirin never wanted her relationship with Behruz to be reduced to the level of her parents' relationship. That was why she always resisted him during quarrels, she always talked back when he made cold and bitter remarks, and she would ignore some of his requests.

But the night he came home late, everything suddenly fell apart for her. With a bitter despair she reviewed all her memories of life with Behruz. Strangely, her resistance against him seemed stupid and ugly. Unarmed, she sat waiting for him.

Behruz came home finally at one in the morning, and when Shirin asked, "Where were you?" he pretended he hadn't heard her and kept up a humiliating silence. Shirin tried to calm herself by thinking, "Well, things happen in a man's life." But when she noticed Behruz's cloyed and cold look at her body, and when he started answering her with indifference in their bedroom, something broke in her heart and a strange feeling of loneliness gripped her.

Remembering this misery, Shirin pressed her feverish head against the cold window of the bus and let out a sigh. Her sigh was louder than she thought, since she noticed the curious looks of a few passengers at her. Even the driver raised his eyebrows and stared at her.

The old woman sitting next to her said, "It is still too early for you to sigh like that, dear." Shirin forced a smile. "This sigh of yours, if it had come from a wretched woman like me, would make sense, but you, you are too young for this."

An elegantly dressed woman standing and holding onto a strap said, "What difference does it make, Mother; everyone's heart is bleeding these days."

The driver added jokingly, "No, sister, everyone is filled with rationed chicken and frozen meat these days," and laughed.

"Looks like you are in good standing," the old woman said in response to the driver's remark.

Shirin pressed her cheek and tried to turn her tearful eyes outside. Curious, the old woman asked, "What has happened to your face, my dear?"

Shirin opened her dry and feverish mouth with a forced smile. "It's nothing."

The old woman narrowed her eyes and in a hushed and secretive voice asked, "Did you have a fight?"

Shirin couldn't say any more; her eyes were filled with tears; she blinked a few times. Then she heard the old woman's firm and confident voice: "Have you had a fight with your husband?" There was no room for resistance. Shirin's tears rolled down her face and she nodded. Apprehensively, Parisa moved in Shirin's arms and clung to her.

The old woman shook her head. "Don't be sad, these men are all the same."

The driver raised one eyebrow and said, "You are being unfair, Mother."

The old woman responded, "Fair? Look at what fairness has done to this poor girl."

"People are not the same."

"On the contrary, all men are the same; first they beat you up and then they go after another woman." She turned to Shirin and asked quietly, "Let me see, have you reached the second stage yet?"

Wiping away her tears, Shirin said, "I don't know what to say."

The woman turned to the elegant woman and said in a self-assured voice, "See, didn't I tell you? Years of experience have turned my hair gray."

The elegant woman looked at Shirin with sympathy and said, "Men go after other women whenever they feel a lack in their lives."

The voice of the Turkish woman who was sitting in the backseat came from behind: "What are you going to do now?" The elegant woman said, "What do you think she wants to do? She is all packed up to go back to her mother's house." The old woman said in a warning tone, "No, no, don't you do that. Going back to your mother's house is not going to solve anything; that will worsen the situation."

The Turkish woman's voice was heard again: "Poor women, they are put down when they are kids; when they grow up they have to take care of their husbands and give birth to kids; then instead of enjoying their children they have to listen to their complaints and suffer."

With a smile that was showing her dentures, the old woman replied, "Very well said; thanks." She then turned to Shirin and continued, "Yes, my dear, don't make the mistake of going back to your parents' house."

With a smile that resembled her mother's guilty smile, Shirin said, "What should I do, then?"

"Go back," said a middle-aged woman who was sitting in the front seat staring with her sharp eyes at Shirin's tearful face.

"Go back where?" asked Shirin.

"To your husband," the middle-aged woman answered.

A young woman sitting next to the elegant woman burst out angrily, "Why should she go back to her husband? Has she done anything wrong?"

The middle-aged woman responded in a calm voice, "You are still young, my daughter. A woman who lets her husband leave her must be doing something wrong." Offended by this, Shirin tried to divert her attention by looking outside. The middle-aged woman put her left hand on Shirin's knee. "Don't be hurt at what I said; I mean you well. You are still inexperienced; you don't know men well yet. My dear, men are like children; you have to treat your husband the same way you treat your children. You shouldn't pay too much attention to him, spoiling him; at the same time, you shouldn't ignore him to the point that he gives up everything." She lowered her voice and continued, "Look, a woman should slip out of her husband's hands like a fish. To be and not be with him at the same time."

The old woman said, "Yes, she is right, go back to your home."

The elegant woman was heard: "What home?" Tying the knot of her floral-patterned scarf, she looked around curiously and continued, "How can a woman sleep in the arms of a man whose body has the smell of another woman's body?"

Nodding her head in agreement, Shirin said, "Yes, I think you haven't faced this disaster to give me advice like this." The old woman responded, "What disaster? Do you call this a disaster?"

The young woman turned her face away from them in annoyance and said, "You are a disgrace to all women."

Raising her voice in anger, Shirin went on: "Tell me, if a polygamous man is not a disaster, then earthquakes, flood, cancer, and smallpox are all God-given gifts."

The driver, who was beginning to realize the extent of the problem, stared at Shirin's pale, anxious face in the mirror. He felt sorry for her and felt the urge to rise in her support. He wanted to put his jacket around her shoulders, display his hairy chest through his half-buttoned shirt, chew on his mustache, wet it with the tip of his tongue, curl the tip of his mustache, and teach a lesson to this half-a-man who had hurt this woman. But when he heard Shirin's broken, sobbing voice through the women's chatter saying, "Why should I go back? I'll take him to court and get my entire alimony from him," the driver felt a kind of satisfaction about what the man had done to

Shirin and said to himself, "It serves you women right; having an eye on a poor man's money . . ."

The middle-aged woman pressed her lips together, shrugged her shoulders, and said, "We gave you our advice; the decision is up to you."

The bus reached the station. A weak voice came from the men's section: "Stop."

Shirin got up. The elegant woman, who was pressing her fingers together to fix her lace gloves on her hands, raised her finger in front of Shirin's face and said, "Don't you give in."

The young woman added, "This is not a man you are dealing with, he is a coward, a half-man. You should teach him a lesson."

Pulling Parisa behind her, Shirin passed through the crowd and got off. A few steps before the station, she stopped hesitantly. Everything she had heard on the bus crossed her mind in a flash. The middle-aged woman's words: "If you get a divorce, people will start talking behind your back. And besides, how are you going to support yourself financially? You don't have a supportive father, as you say. What would you do if, God forbid, your child becomes ill? Where would you get the money for the medical expenses? Besides, think of your daughter; this little girl might not mind spending a few days without her father, but how long can she take it?" The Turkish woman's voice: "If you get a divorce you will be isolated. You won't be able to find another man in your life, and there will be no future for your child. You will have to work like a dog to support her with this back-breaking inflation."

Feeling angry and confused, Shirin went back to the station and sat on the wooden bench, holding Parisa close to her. She looked at her daughter with worry, remembering the conversation: "Well, tell me, how old is your daughter?"

"She is five." And the old woman had responded victoriously, "Well, that's it. If you get a divorce, you will be able to have custody of your child for only two more years. You should forget about her after that."

Disappointed and cold, she felt the warmth of Parisa's body. A strange feeling was making her see this little being as the only light in her dark life. Shirin felt a kind of fulfillment, thinking of the fact that Parisa needed her, and that she would be willing to rise to her needs without any hesitation. She hugged her daughter tight. Parisa, who was astonished by her mother's sudden and deep expression of love, looked curiously at her face. Her mother's tired, beseeching eyes with dark circles around them, and her face that was trembling with anxiety, frightened her. She held tight to her mother and hugged her raggedy doll, each finding in the other's arms the peace that was being denied them. Shirin took a quick look at the end of the avenue. A bus showed up, and with a moaning sound stopped at the station.

NOTES

1. The word in Persian means sweet.
2. A woman's outdoor—and on occasion indoor—wrap, covering her whole body.
3. Second Islamic lunar month.
4. Rice pudding flavored with saffron.

✣ The Contributors

Nushin Ahmadi Khorasani was born in Tehran in 1969. She completed her education in health and environmental studies at Tehran University. She started her publishing career in 1992. Her articles deal mostly with women's issues, but she has also translated several books for children and young adults. She has published *Jens-e Dovom* [*Second Sex*] since 1998, a journal that includes articles on literature, history, as well as social and legal matters related to women. In 1998 she published a collection of short stories, *Zanan-e bi Gozashteh* [*Women Without Past*], and *Iranian Women's Yearbook*.

Tahereh Alavi was born in Tehran in 1959. After finishing high school she began working on children's literature. In 1986 she moved to France and studied there for six years. During this period she translated many books for children and youngsters. After returning to Iran she began writing for an older audience. Two collections of her short stories have been published: *Zan dar Bad* [*A Woman in the Wind*] and *Man va Heidegger* [*Heidegger and I*].

Farkhondeh Aqai was born in Tehran in 1957. She holds an M.A. in sociology from Tehran University and a B.A. in management from Alzahra University. She has published three collections of short stories and one novel, *Jensiyat-e Gomshodeh* [*The Lost Gender,* forthcoming]. Aqai's collection of short stories, *Raz-e Kuchak* [*The Little*

Secret] won the Golden Pen prize of *Gardun* in 1983, and in 1999 was selected as one of the best books of the past twenty years.

Shiva Arastuyi was born in Tehran in 1961. She completed her education in translation studies. She has written literary and film criticism articles for several journals in Iran. She has also worked as a social worker in the war front, as well as teaching creative writing in the College of Arts in Tehran. She is the author of several works including a novella, *U Ra Keh Didam Ziba Shodam* [*I Became Beautiful When I Saw Him*]; a collection of poems, *Gom* [*Lost*]; a collection of short stories, *Amadeh Budam Ba Dokhtaram Chay Bekhoram* [*I Came to Have Tea With My Daughter*]; and a novel, *Noskheh-ye Aval* [*First Draft*].

Azardokht Bahrami was born in Tehran in 1966. She is a graduate of the School of Seda va Sima in puppet theater (1987) and playwright from Farhangsara-ye Niavaran (1989). She has published most of her stories in literary journals. She has also worked as a screenplay writer and computer graphics specialist.

Mihan Bahrami published her first short story at the age of fifteen in *Ferdosi* magazine. After receiving her M.A. in sociology, she attended UCLA to study psychology. Shortly after her return to Iran, she pursued her literary and artistic activities in many different fields including cinema, theater, painting, literary criticism, and fiction. Among her collections of short stories are, *Heyvan* [*Animal*] and *Haft Shakh-e Sorkh* [*The Seven Red Branches*].

Parvin Fadavi was born in 1961 in Esfahan. She currently studies music and painting. She began writing at the age of twenty-six and has since written a number of short stories, plays, screenplays, and articles in literary criticism. Her most recent works include two collections of short stories: *Khorshid-e Tanha* [*The Lonely Sun*] and *Budan ya Nabudan* [*To Be or Not to Be*].

Farzaneh Karampur was born in 1954 and completed her education at the University of Elm-o San'at in construction engineering. Since 1996, she has been writing professionally. She has published many short stories including the two collections, *Koshtargah-e San'ati* [*The Industrial Slaughterhouse*] and *Ziafat-e Shabaneh* [*The Nightly*

Feast]. Her story, *Kamp-e Khareji* [*The Foreign Camp*] won the prize of the Association of the Literature of Expansion.

Farideh Kheradmand was born in 1957 in Tehran. She completed her education in drama and dramatic literature. Her writing career began in radio. From 1988–1990 she worked as a playwright, director, and actor in the Gulf area. In 1992 she left her work in radio to devote her time to writing. She has written several plays and has published several works in children's literature. Her collections of stories include *Parandeh-yi Hast* [*A Bird Exists*] and *Aramesh-e Shabaneh* [*The Nightly Tranquility*].

Mohammad Mehdi Khorrami was born in Iran in 1960. In 1982 he left Iran and continued his education in France and the United States. During his graduate studies he specialized in Persian and French literature. Currently he is teaching Persian language and literature at New York University. He is the author of *Sayeha-ye Zendegi* [*Shadows of Life*] and *Ketab-e Afarinesh* [*Book of Genesis*], as well as numerous articles on contemporary Persian literature.

Farkhondeh Hajizadeh was born in the village of Bazanjan in 1953. She later moved to Azarbaijan, where she continued her education, completed her degree in Persian literature, and began working as a librarian. During the past ten years she has published three collections of short stories: *Khaleh-ye Sagardan-e Cheshmha* [*The Wondering Aunt of Eyes*], *Khalaf-e Demokrasi* [*Against Democracy*], and *Az Cheshmha-ye Shoma Mitarsam* [*I am Afraid of Your Eyes*]. Currently, she is managing editor of the literary journal *Baya*.

Banafsheh Hejazi was born in 1954 in Borujerd and received a B.A. from Tehran University. She has been active in different academic and literary fields and her works cover a wide range of topics, including children's literature, architecture, painting, and women's issues. Among her recent publications are a collection of poems, *Napors Chera Sokut Mikonam* [*Do not Ask Why I Am Silent*], and a chidren's story, *Tara va Mah* [*Tara and the Moon*].

Khatereh Hejazi was born in Esfahan in 1961. In 1979 she moved to Tehran, and in 1985 she published her first book. Since then she has continued to write professionally. She attended university at the age of twenty-eight and completed her B.A. in philosophy. Hejazi has published a number of collections of poems and short stories, and two novels titled *Dar Shab-e Iliati-ye Eshq* [*In the Tribal Night of Love*] and *Asar-e Parvaneh* [*The Time of Butterfly*].

Sofia Mahmudi was born in 1956. She has studied sociology and Russian language, and has translated several works from Russian and English into Persian. She is the author of *Zan va Kudak* [*Woman And Child*] and *Yek Fekr-e Bekr* [*A Perfect Thought*]. She currently teaches English, works as a librarian, and writes articles on folk literature.

Nosrat Masuri was born in Tehran in 1940. She grew up in Azarbaijan and then completed her undergraduate degree in English language in Khoramabad. She began writing fiction professionally in 1984 and since then has published many short stories. In 1999, her short story "Entezar" [Wait] won the first prize of Lorestan Province.

Marjan Riahi was born in 1970. She is a graduate of Tehran University in business management. She also holds degrees in screenwriting and acting. She has published several short stories in different literary and women's journals in Iran. Her collection of short stories, *Eshareh-ha* [*Points*], was published in 1999.

Zoya Pirzad is the author of a number of collections of short stories including *Yek Ruz Mandeh beh Eyd-e Pak* [*One Day Before Easter*],—winner of the Seventeenth "Book of the Year Award" in Iran—*Mesl-e Hameh-ye Asrha* [*Like All Evenings*], and *Ta'm-e Gas-e Khormalu* [*The Astringent Taste of Persimmon*].

Fereshteh Sari was born in 1957 in Tehran. She received B.A.s in computer science and Russian language and literature from Tehran University. During her literary career she has received a number of prizes and scholarships including the Lillian Hellmann-Dashiell Hammett from Human Rights Watch (1998) and a one-year scholarship from the International Parliament of Writers (1999). During the past fifteen years Sari has written and translated many books, including her two recent novels, *Mitra* and *Atr-e Razianeh* [*The Aroma of Fennel*].

Mansureh Sharifzadeh was born in 1953 in Tehran. She holds a

B.A. in English literature and an M.A. in comparative literature from Tehran University. Since 1987 she has been a member of the research faculty at Tehran University. She also teaches literature at the College of Film and Theater. In 1999 she received a prize for her article on the poet Parvin E'tesami. Her literary works include *Molud-e Sheshom* [*The Sixth Born*] and *Atr-e Neskafe* [*The Aroma of Nescafe*].

Nahid Tabatabai was born in 1958. She holds a B.A. in dramatic literature and playwrighting. She is the author of *Banu va Javani-ye Khish* [*The Lady and Her Youth*], *Hozur-e Abi-ye Mina* [*The Blue Presence of Mina*], and *Jameh Daran* [*Tearing Garb*].

Fariba Vafi was born in Tabriz in 1962. Her first collection of stories, *Omgh-e Sahneh* [*Depth of the Stage*], was published in 1996. Her second collection of short stories, *Hatta Vaqti Mikhandam* [*Even When I Laugh*], was published in the fall of 1999.

Shouleh Vatanabadi was born in Tehran in 1955. In 1978 she left Iran to continue her education in the United States. During her graduate studies in comparative literature, she specialized in Middle Eastern literature. Currently she is teaching Middle Eastern culture and civilization at New York University. She is the author of several articles on Iranian and Azerbaijani literature. Most of her writings focus on women's issues.

Chista Yasrebi was born in 1968 in Tehran. She holds a B.A. in clinical psychology and an M.A. in educational psychology. She has also studied journalism at Tabatabai University in a program affiliated with UNICEF. She started her writing career by publishing articles in literary and art criticism. As a playwright/director she won first prize at the Festival of Women's Theater in Iran. She has published several collection of poems, translations, plays, and collections of short stories. Among her works are *Salam be Na-Momken* [*Greeting the Impossible*], *Rahil*, and *Abi-ye Kuchak-e Eshgh* [*The Little Blue of Love*].

❧ About the Book

In the present golden era of Iranian fiction, women writers—contrary to what many in the West perceive—are making a powerful contribution to the literary scene. Reflecting this, *A Feast in the Mirror* captures the diverse voices of contemporary Iranian women, offering glimpses into their lives and into the labyrinths of Iranian society today.

Moving from the framework of their own ideas, opinions, and experiences, the authors of the stories collected here explore new literary styles and structures. Khorrami and Vatanabadi provide a contextual introduction to the collection, a brief overview of each story, and biographical notes on the writers.

Mohammad Mehdi Khorrami teaches Persian language and literature at New York University. He is coeditor of *A World Between: Poems and Short Stories by Iranian-Americans*. **Shouleh Vatanabadi** teaches Near Eastern culture and civilization at New York University.